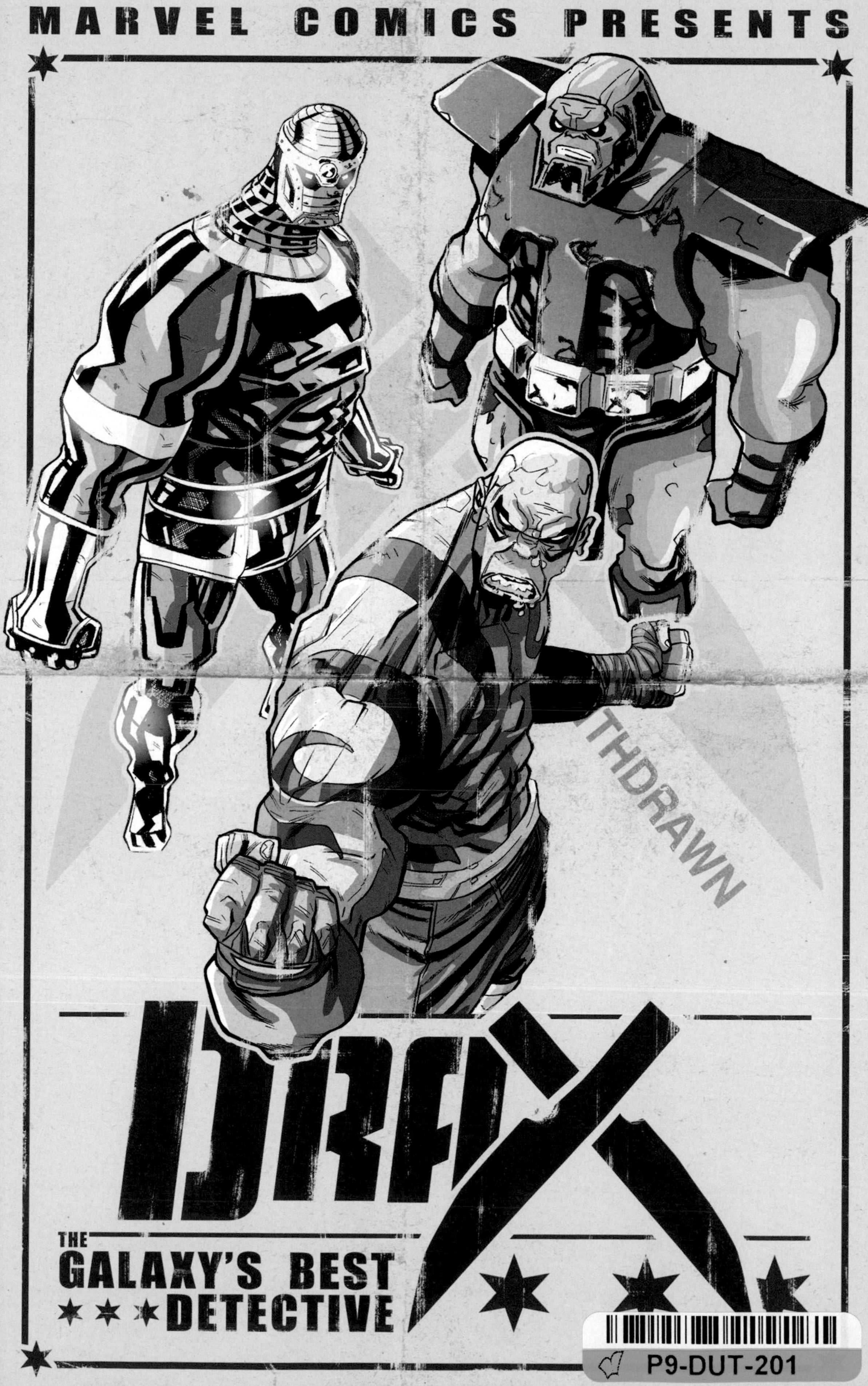
MARVEL COMICS PRESENTS
DRAX
THE GALAXY'S BEST DETECTIVE

"THE DESTROYER"
FIN FANG

DRAX vs FOOM

COLLECTION EDITOR
SARAH BRUNSTAD

ASSOCIATE MANAGING EDITOR
ALEX STARBUCK

EDITORS, SPECIAL PROJECTS
JENNIFER GRÜNWALD & MARK D. BEAZLEY

VP, PRODUCTION & SPECIAL PROJECTS
JEFF YOUNGQUIST

SVP PRINT, SALES & MARKETING
DAVID GABRIEL

BOOK DESIGNER
ADAM DEL RE

EDITOR IN CHIEF
AXEL ALONSO

CHIEF CREATIVE OFFICER
JOE QUESADA

PUBLISHER
DAN BUCKLEY

EXECUTIVE PRODUCER
ALAN FINE

DRAX VOL. 1: THE GALAXY'S BEST DETECTIVE. Contains material originally published in magazine form as DRAX #1-5. First printing 2016. ISBN# 978-0-7851-9662-4. Published by MARVEL WORLDWIDE, INC., a subsidiary of MARVEL ENTERTAINMENT, LLC. OFFICE OF PUBLICATION: 135 West 50th Street, New York, NY 10020. Copyright © 2016 MARVEL No similarity between any of the names, characters, persons, and/or institutions in this magazine with those of any living or dead person or institution is intended, and any such similarity which may exist is purely coincidental. **Printed in Canada.** ALAN FINE, President, Marvel Entertainment; DAN BUCKLEY, President, TV, Publishing & Brand Management; JOE QUESADA, Chief Creative Officer; TOM BREVOORT, SVP of Publishing; DAVID BOGART, SVP of Business Affairs & Operations, Publishing & Partnership; C.B. CEBULSKI, VP of Brand Management & Development, Asia; DAVID GABRIEL, SVP of Sales & Marketing, Publishing; JEFF YOUNGQUIST, VP of Production & Special Projects; DAN CARR, Executive Director of Publishing Technology; ALEX MORALES, Director of Publishing Operations; SUSAN CRESPI, Production Manager; STAN LEE, Chairman Emeritus. For information regarding advertising in Marvel Comics or on Marvel.com, please contact Vit DeBellis, Integrated Sales Manager, at vdebellis@marvel.com. For Marvel subscription inquiries, please call 888-511-5480. **Manufactured between 4/1/2016 and 5/9/2016 by SOLISCO PRINTERS, SCOTT, QC, CANADA.**

10 9 8 7 6 5 4 3 2 1

DRAX

★ ★ ★   ★ ★ ★

★ WRITERS ★

CM
PUNK & CULLEN
BUNN

★ ARTIST ★

SCOTT
HEPBURN

★ COLORISTS ★

MATT
MILLA WITH
RUTH
REDMOND (No. 4)

★ LETTERER ★

VC's CLAYTON
COWLES

★ COVER ART ★

SCOTT
HEPBURN &
MATT
MILLA

★ ASSISTANT EDITOR ★

KATHLEEN
WISNESKI

★ EDITORS ★

JON
MOISAN &
JAKE
THOMAS

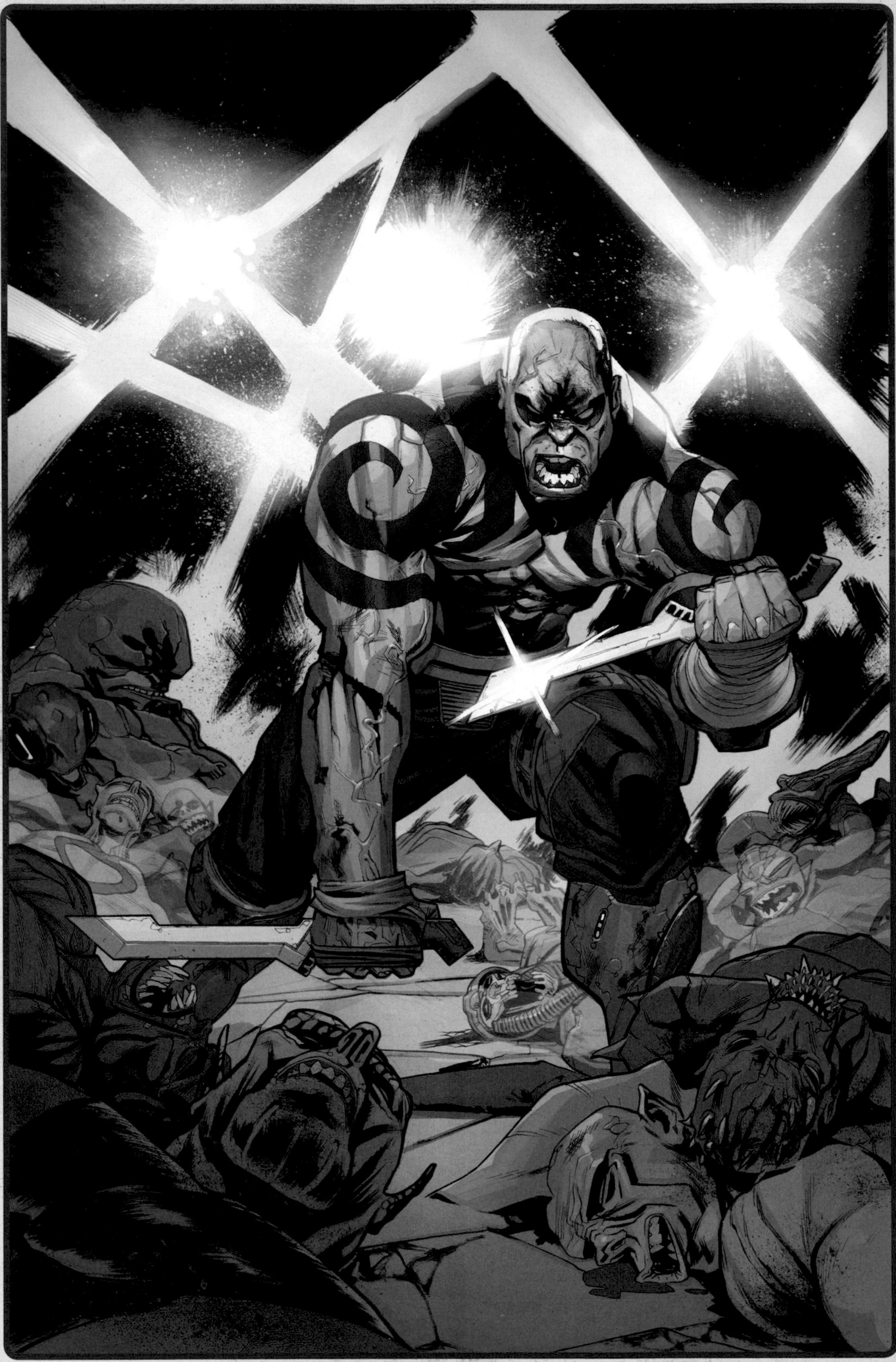

1

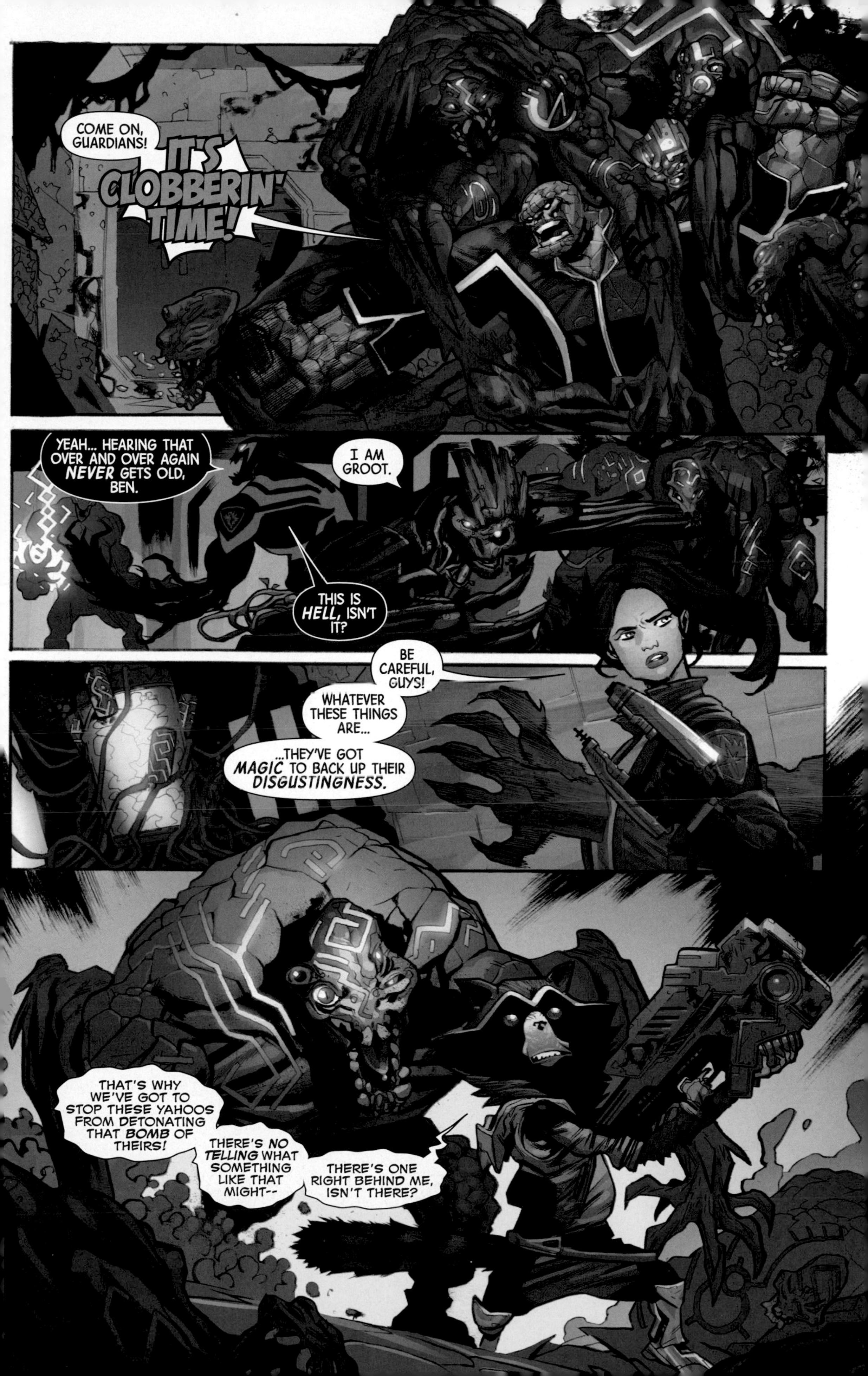
COME ON, GUARDIANS!
IT'S CLOBBERIN' TIME!
YEAH... HEARING THAT OVER AND OVER AGAIN NEVER GETS OLD, BEN.
I AM GROOT.
THIS IS HELL, ISN'T IT?
BE CAREFUL, GUYS!
WHATEVER THESE THINGS ARE...
...THEY'VE GOT MAGIC TO BACK UP THEIR DISGUSTINGNESS.
THAT'S WHY WE'VE GOT TO STOP THESE YAHOOS FROM DETONATING THAT BOMB OF THEIRS!
THERE'S NO TELLING WHAT SOMETHING LIKE THAT MIGHT--
THERE'S ONE RIGHT BEHIND ME, ISN'T THERE?

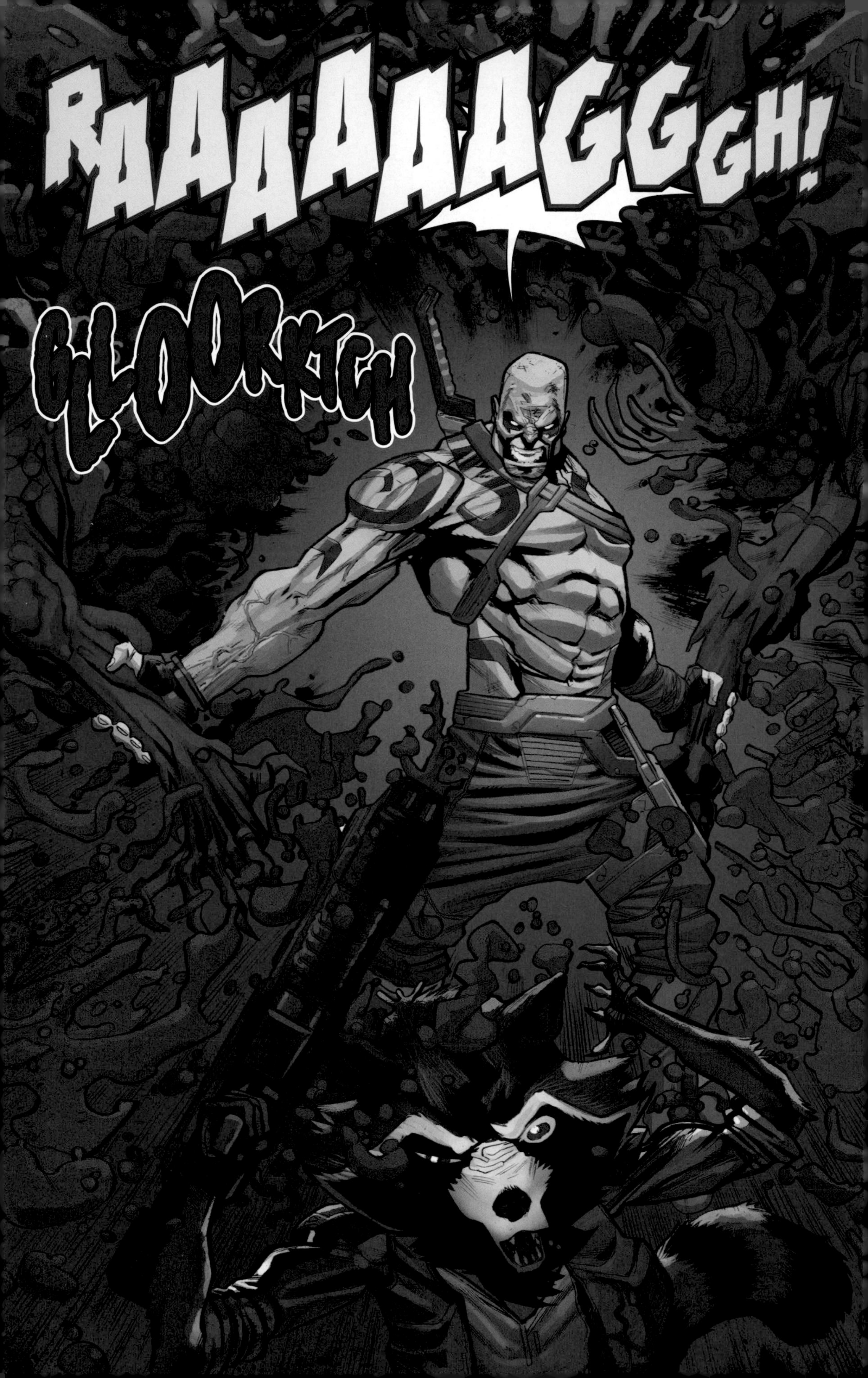
RAAAAAAGGGGH!
GLLOORKTCH

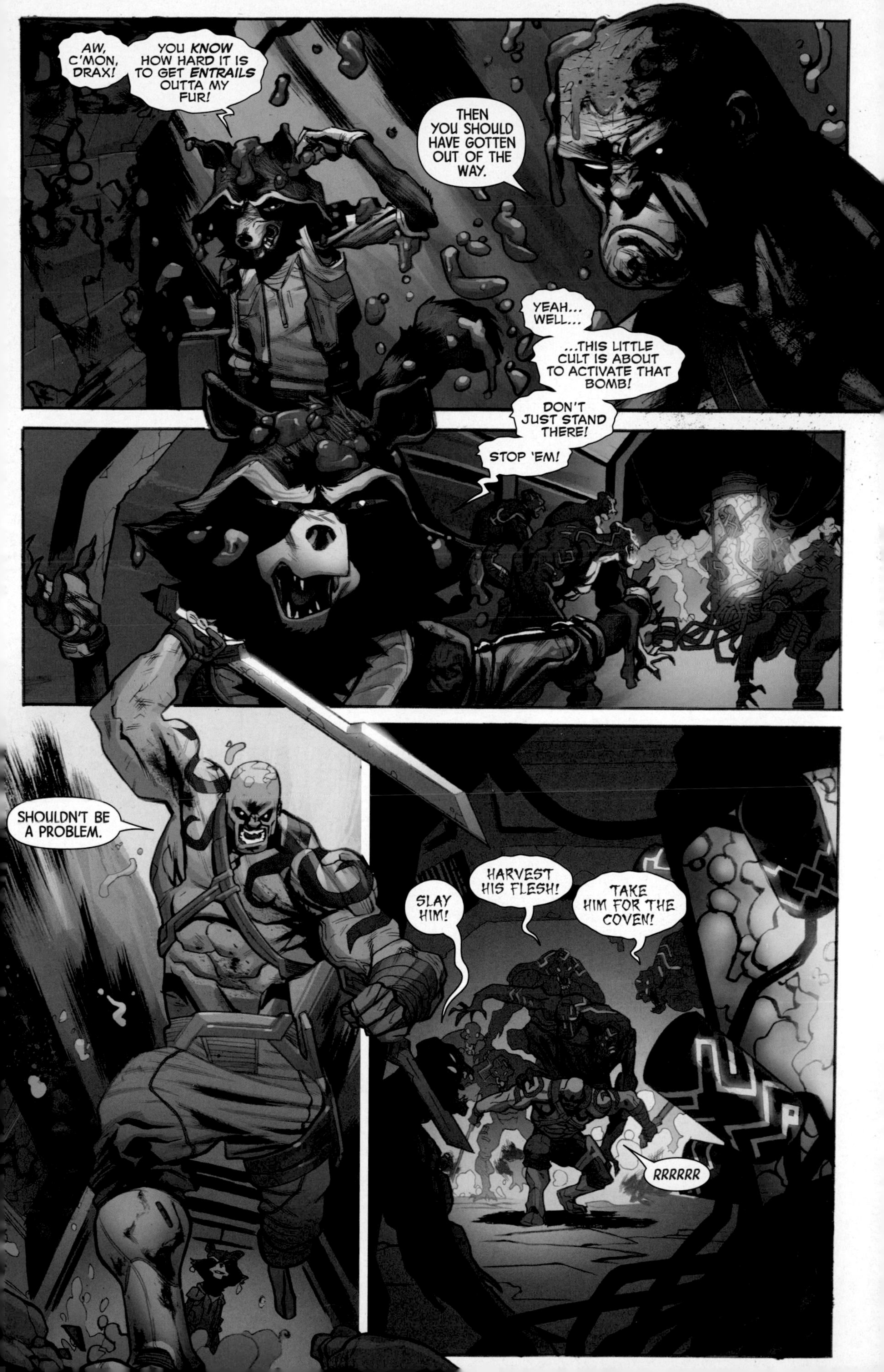
AW, C'MON, DRAX!
YOU KNOW HOW HARD IT IS TO GET ENTRAILS OUTTA MY FUR!
THEN YOU SHOULD HAVE GOTTEN OUT OF THE WAY.
YEAH... WELL...
...THIS LITTLE CULT IS ABOUT TO ACTIVATE THAT BOMB!
DON'T JUST STAND THERE!
STOP 'EM!
SHOULDN'T BE A PROBLEM.
SLAY HIM!
HARVEST HIS FLESH!
TAKE HIM FOR THE COVEN!
RRRRRR

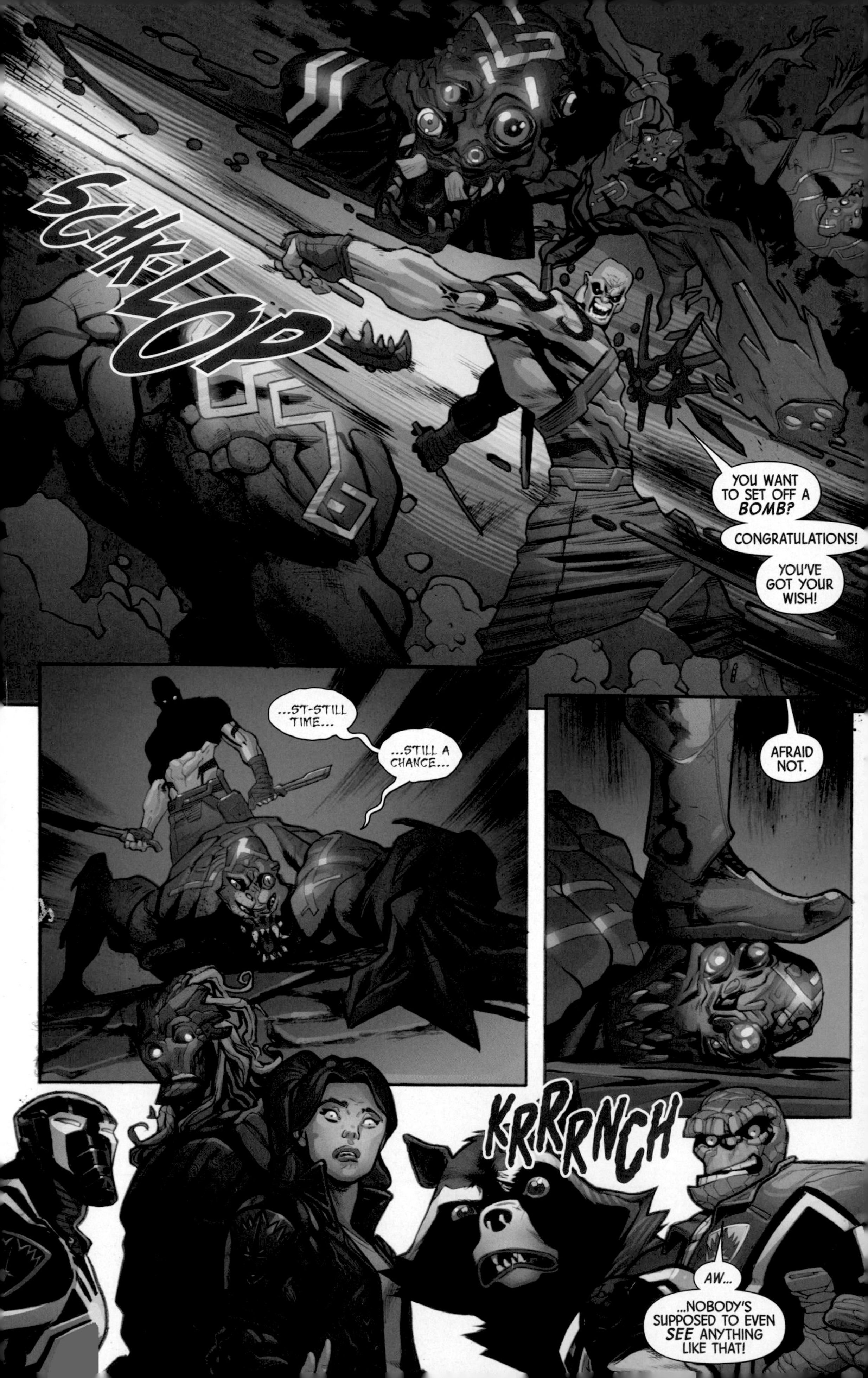
SCHKLOP
YOU WANT TO SET OFF A BOMB?
CONGRATULATIONS!
YOU'VE GOT YOUR WISH!
...ST-STILL TIME...
...STILL A CHANCE...
AFRAID NOT.
KRRRNCH
AW...
...NOBODY'S SUPPOSED TO EVEN SEE ANYTHING LIKE THAT!

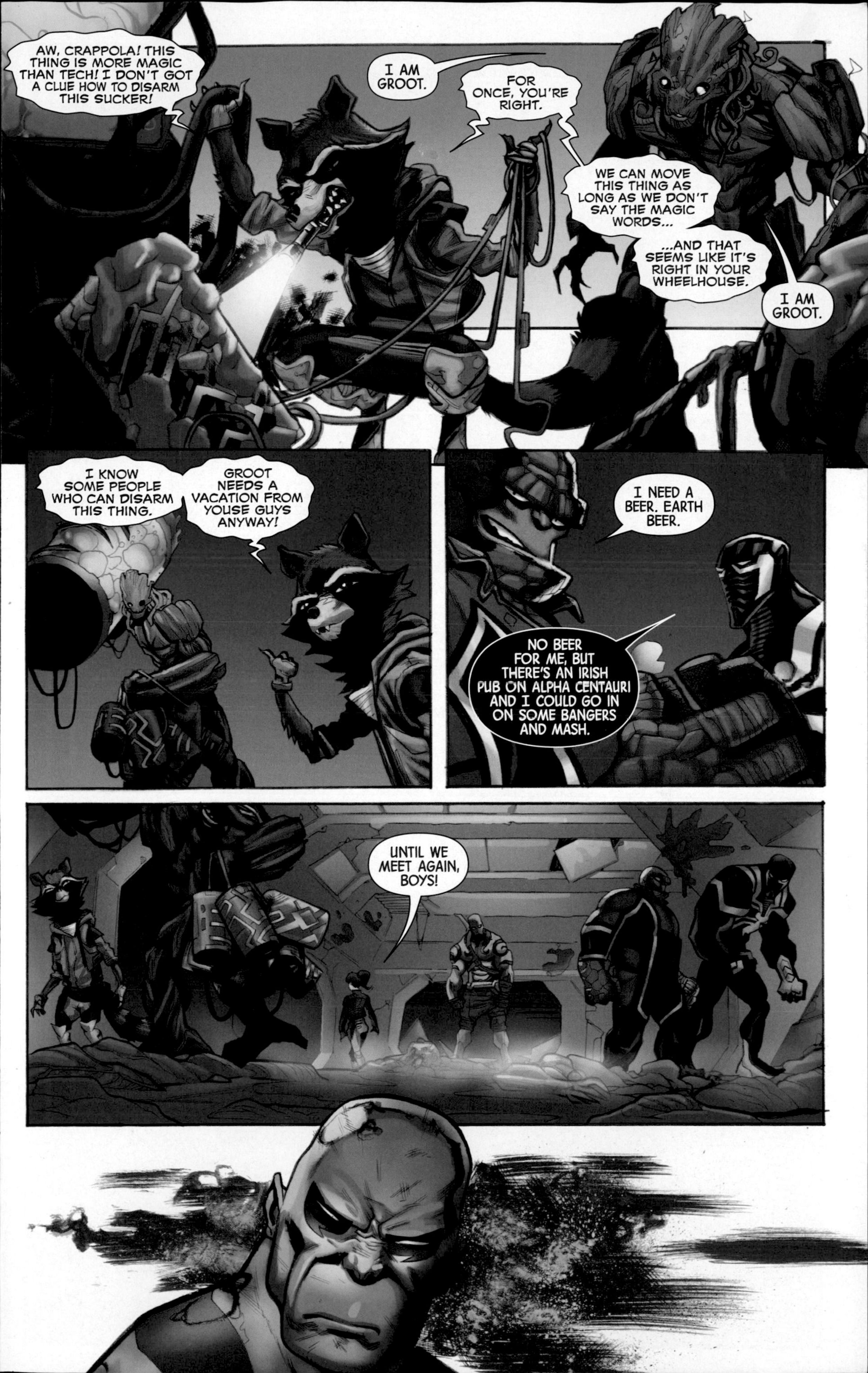
AW, CRAPPOLA! THIS THING IS MORE MAGIC THAN TECH! I DON'T GOT A CLUE HOW TO DISARM THIS SUCKER!
I AM GROOT.
FOR ONCE, YOU'RE RIGHT.
WE CAN MOVE THIS THING AS LONG AS WE DON'T SAY THE MAGIC WORDS...
...AND THAT SEEMS LIKE IT'S RIGHT IN YOUR WHEELHOUSE.
I AM GROOT.
I KNOW SOME PEOPLE WHO CAN DISARM THIS THING.
GROOT NEEDS A VACATION FROM YOUSE GUYS ANYWAY!
I NEED A BEER. EARTH BEER.
NO BEER FOR ME, BUT THERE'S AN IRISH PUB ON ALPHA CENTAURI AND I COULD GO IN ON SOME BANGERS AND MASH.
UNTIL WE MEET AGAIN, BOYS!

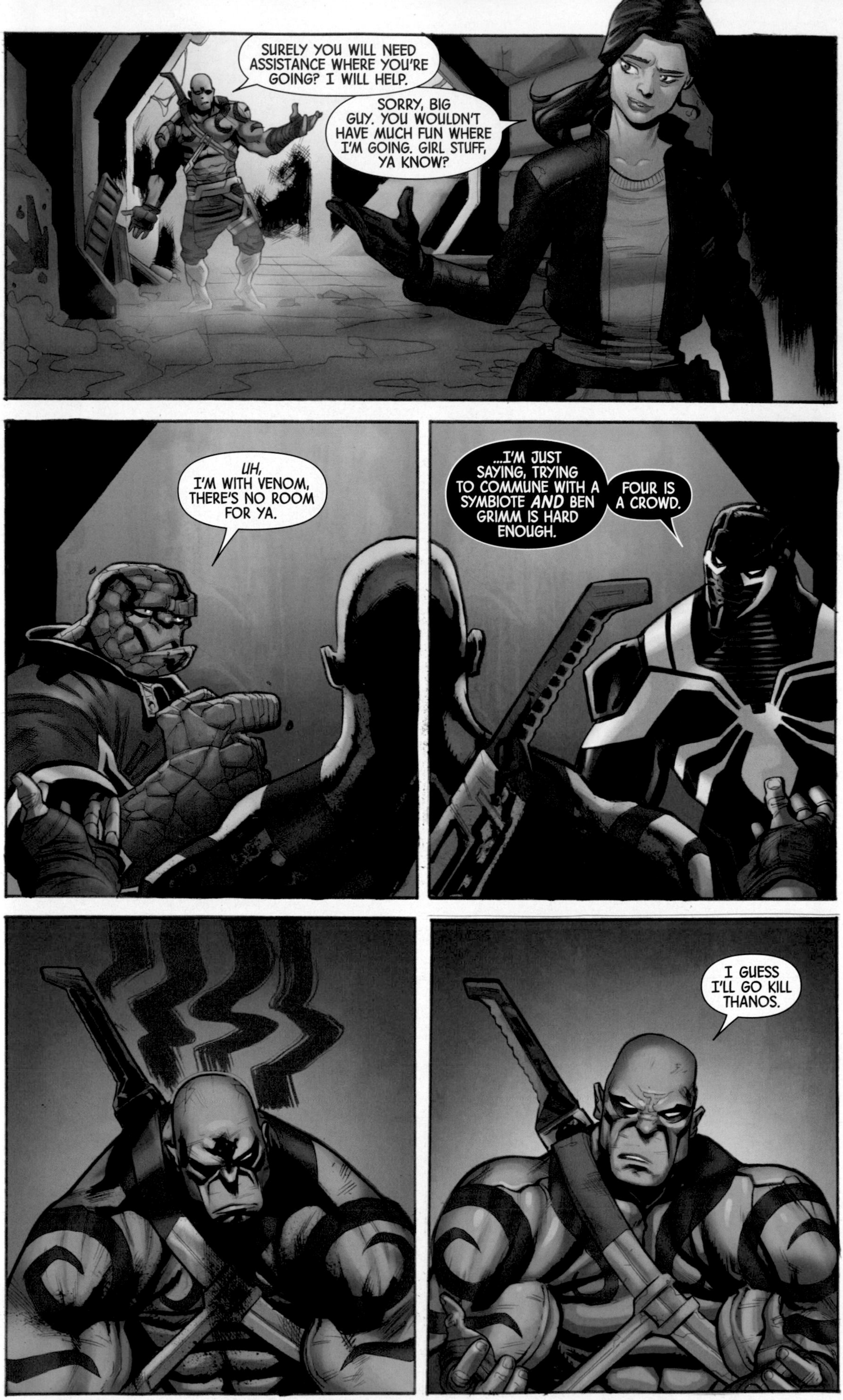
SURELY YOU WILL NEED ASSISTANCE WHERE YOU'RE GOING? I WILL HELP.
SORRY, BIG GUY. YOU WOULDN'T HAVE MUCH FUN WHERE I'M GOING. GIRL STUFF, YA KNOW?
UH, I'M WITH VENOM, THERE'S NO ROOM FOR YA.
...I'M JUST SAYING, TRYING TO COMMUNE WITH A SYMBIOTE AND BEN GRIMM IS HARD ENOUGH.
FOUR IS A CROWD.
I GUESS I'LL GO KILL THANOS.

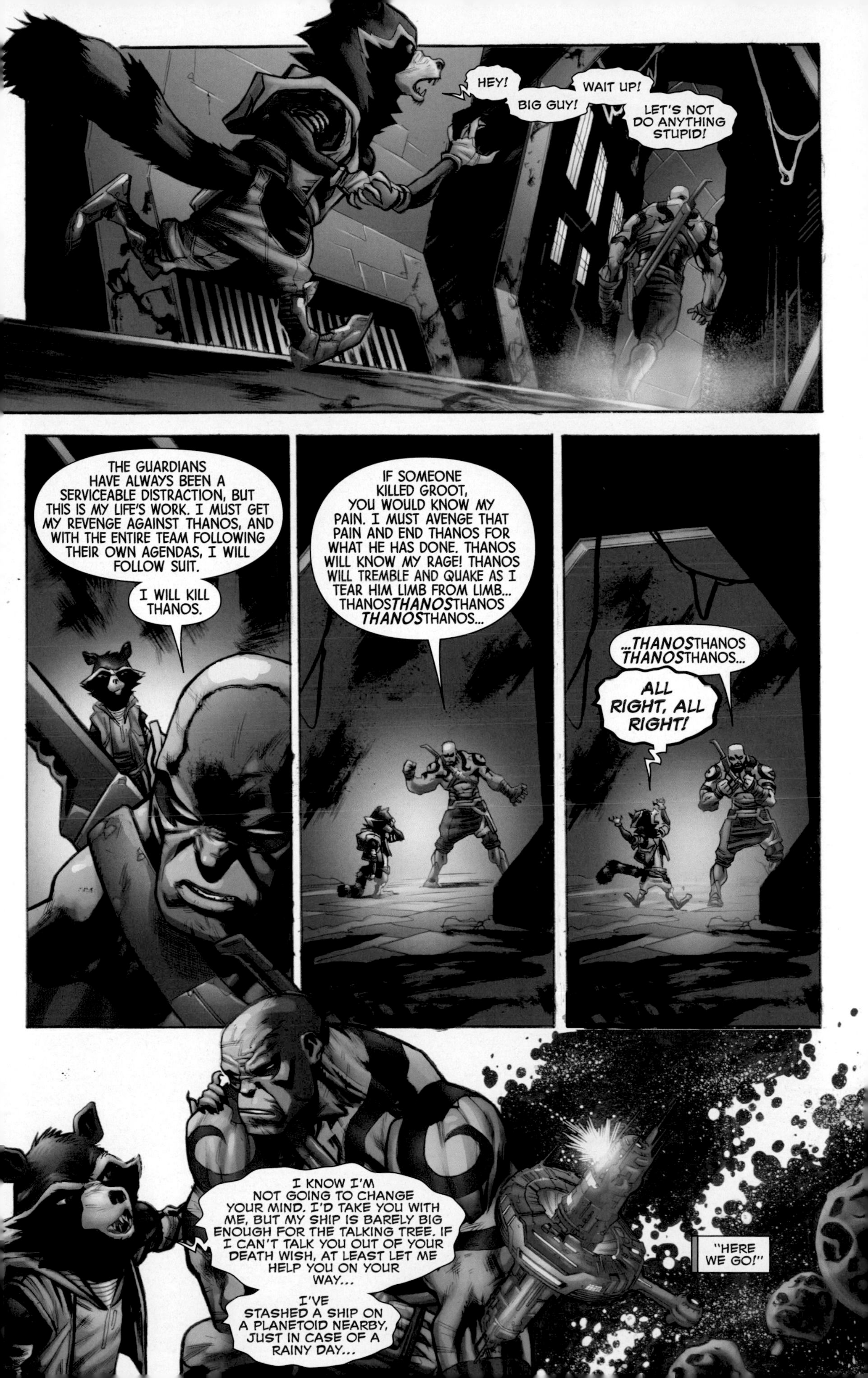
HEY!
BIG GUY!
WAIT UP!
LET'S NOT DO ANYTHING STUPID!
THE GUARDIANS HAVE ALWAYS BEEN A SERVICEABLE DISTRACTION, BUT THIS IS MY LIFE'S WORK. I MUST GET MY REVENGE AGAINST THANOS, AND WITH THE ENTIRE TEAM FOLLOWING THEIR OWN AGENDAS, I WILL FOLLOW SUIT.
I WILL KILL THANOS.
IF SOMEONE KILLED GROOT, YOU WOULD KNOW MY PAIN. I MUST AVENGE THAT PAIN AND END THANOS FOR WHAT HE HAS DONE. THANOS WILL KNOW MY RAGE! THANOS WILL TREMBLE AND QUAKE AS I TEAR HIM LIMB FROM LIMB... THANOS*THANOS*THANOS *THANOS*THANOS...
...*THANOS*THANOS *THANOS*THANOS...
ALL RIGHT, ALL RIGHT!
I KNOW I'M NOT GOING TO CHANGE YOUR MIND. I'D TAKE YOU WITH ME, BUT MY SHIP IS BARELY BIG ENOUGH FOR THE TALKING TREE. IF I CAN'T TALK YOU OUT OF YOUR DEATH WISH, AT LEAST LET ME HELP YOU ON YOUR WAY...
I'VE STASHED A SHIP ON A PLANETOID NEARBY, JUST IN CASE OF A RAINY DAY...
"HERE WE GO!"

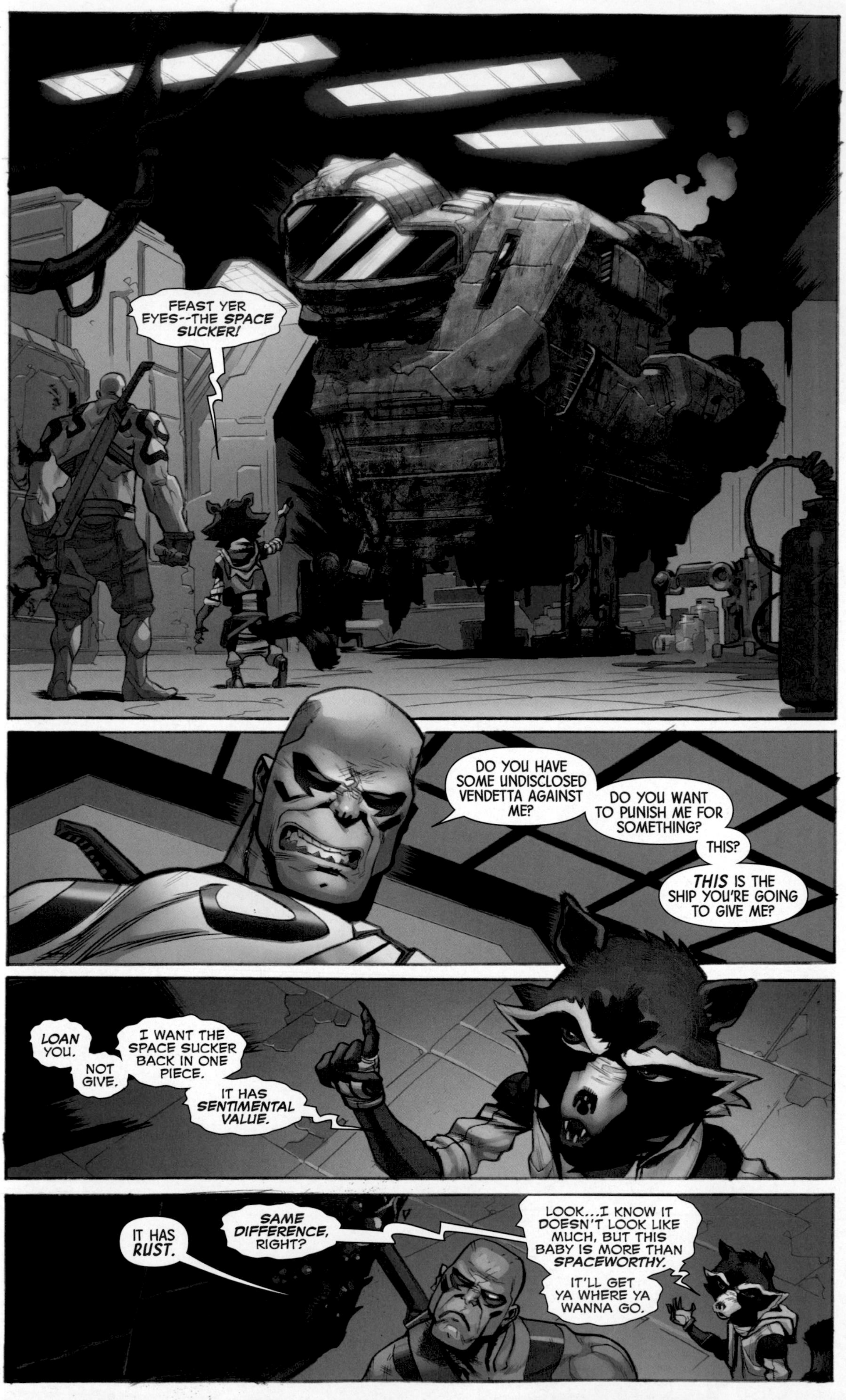
FEAST YER EYES--THE SPACE SUCKER!
DO YOU HAVE SOME UNDISCLOSED VENDETTA AGAINST ME?
DO YOU WANT TO PUNISH ME FOR SOMETHING?
THIS?
THIS IS THE SHIP YOU'RE GOING TO GIVE ME?
LOAN YOU.
NOT GIVE.
I WANT THE SPACE SUCKER BACK IN ONE PIECE.
IT HAS SENTIMENTAL VALUE.
IT HAS RUST.
SAME DIFFERENCE, RIGHT?
LOOK...I KNOW IT DOESN'T LOOK LIKE MUCH, BUT THIS BABY IS MORE THAN SPACEWORTHY.
IT'LL GET YA WHERE YA WANNA GO.

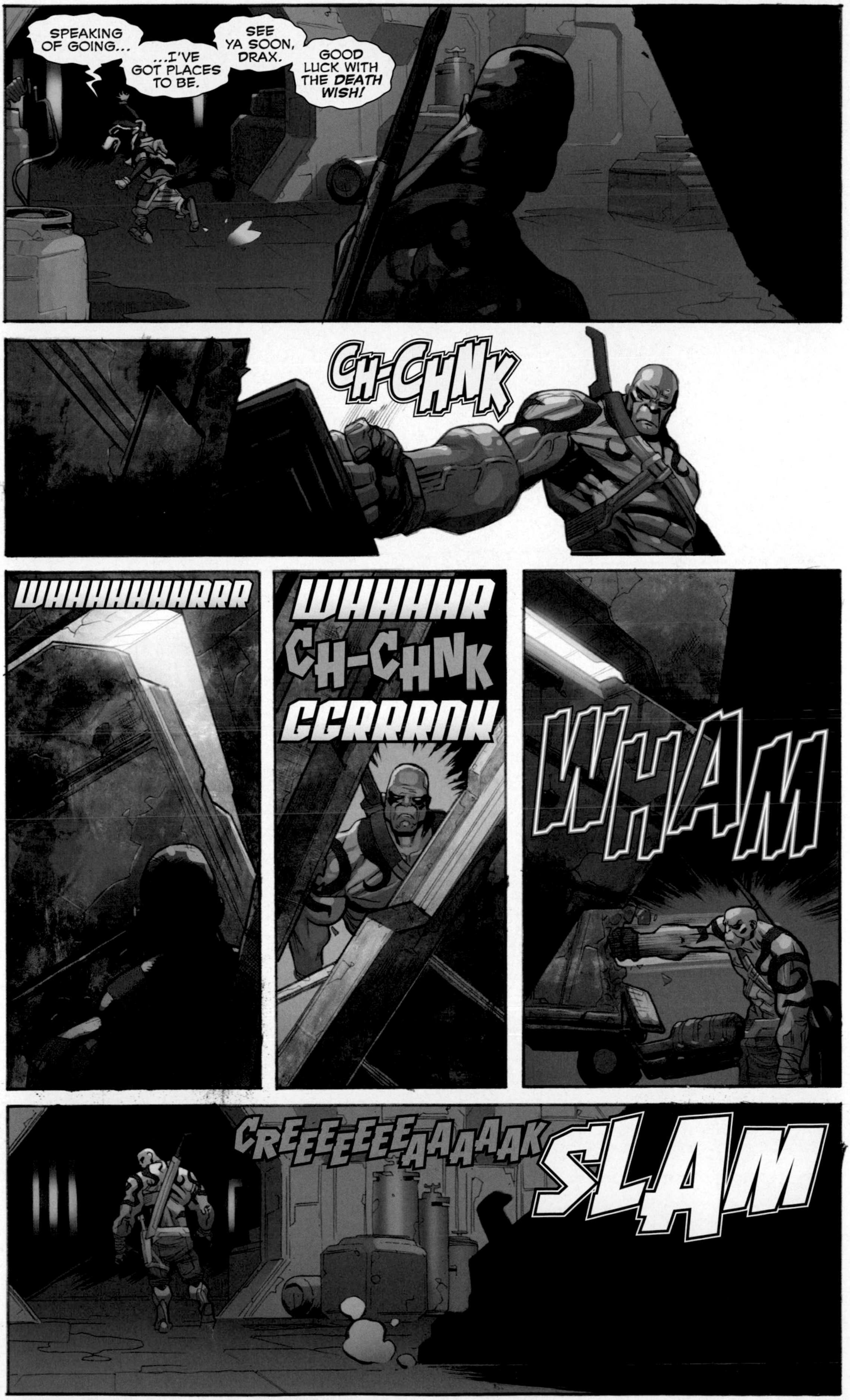
SPEAKING OF GOING...
...I'VE GOT PLACES TO BE.
SEE YA SOON, DRAX.
GOOD LUCK WITH THE DEATH WISH!
CH-CHNK
WHHHHHHHHRRR
WHHHHR
CH-CHNK
CCRRRRNK
WHAM
CREEEEEEEAAAAAK
SLAM

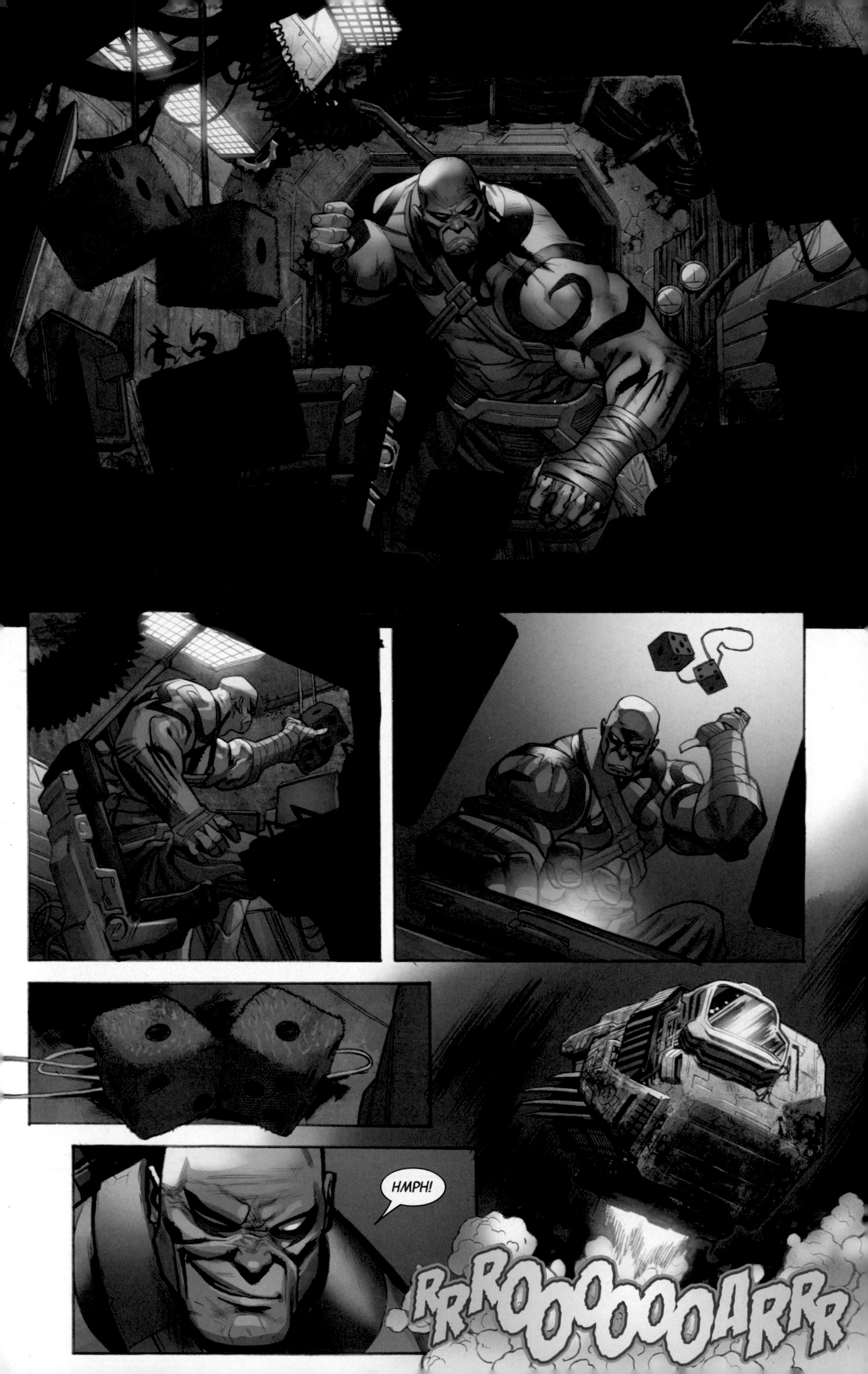
HMPH!
RRROOOOOOOARRR

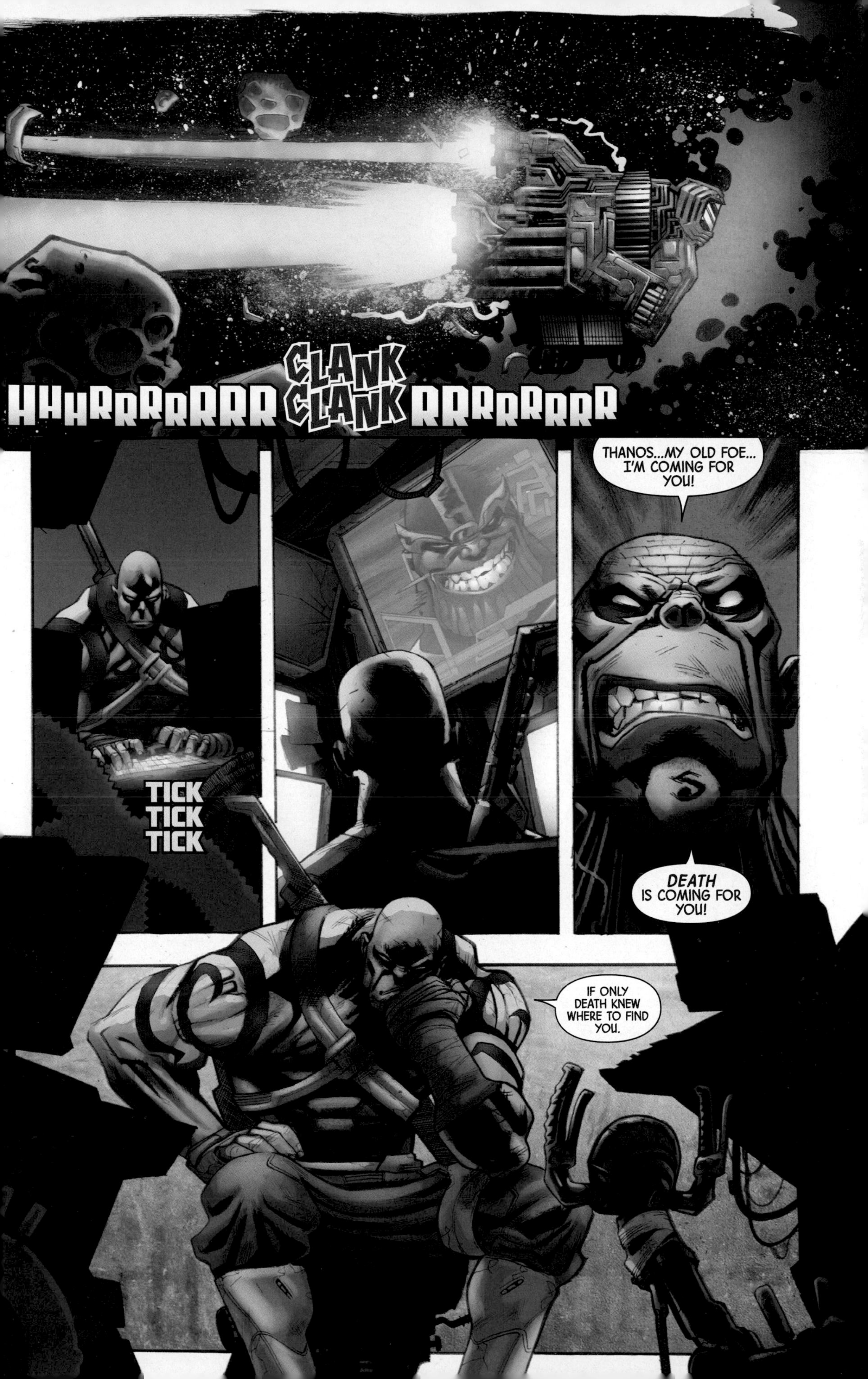
HHHRRRRRRR CLANK CLANK RRRRRRRRR
TICK TICK TICK
THANOS...MY OLD FOE... I'M COMING FOR YOU!
DEATH IS COMING FOR YOU!
IF ONLY DEATH KNEW WHERE TO FIND YOU.

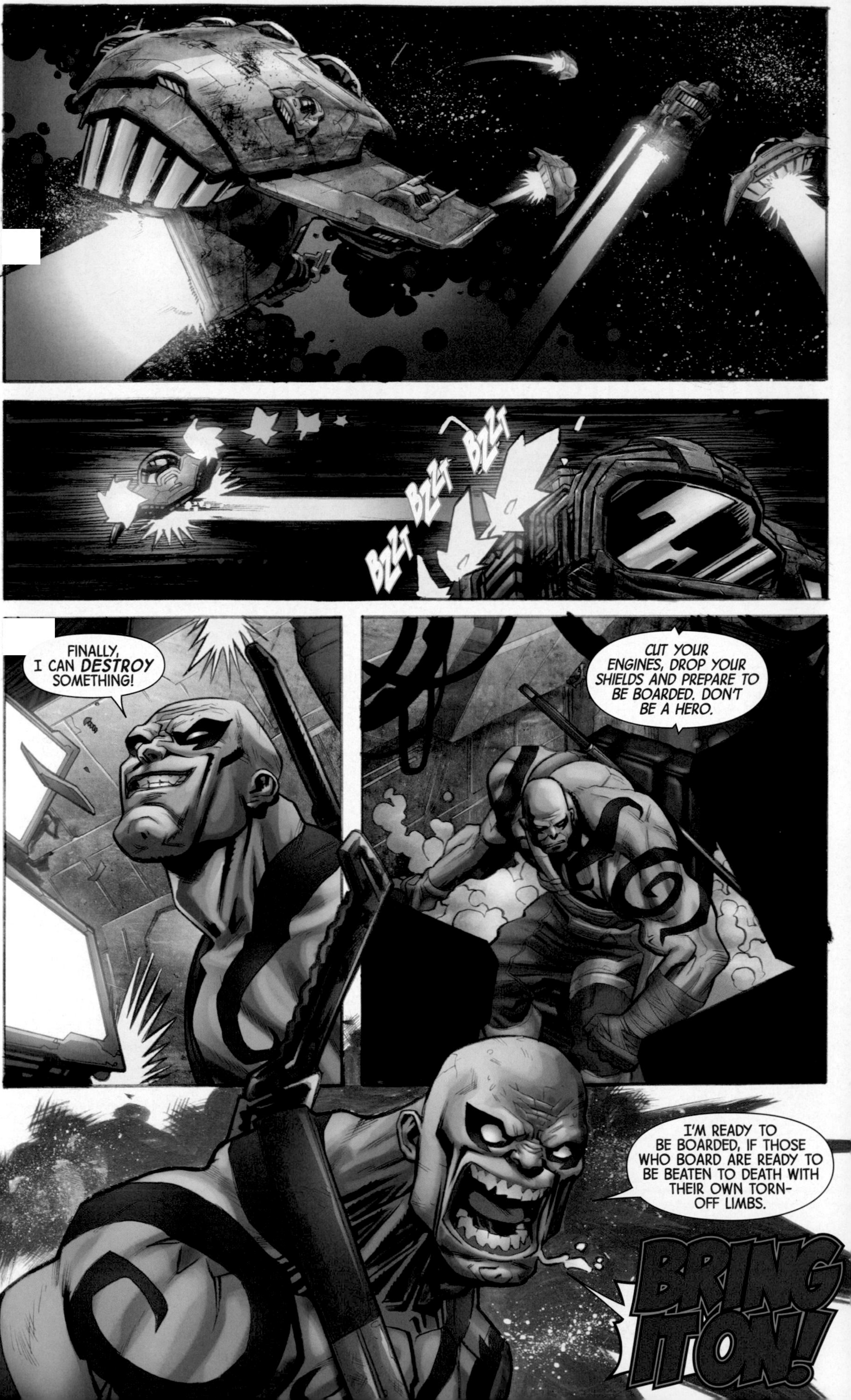
BZZT BZZT BZZT
FINALLY, I CAN DESTROY SOMETHING!
CUT YOUR ENGINES, DROP YOUR SHIELDS AND PREPARE TO BE BOARDED. DON'T BE A HERO.
I'M READY TO BE BOARDED, IF THOSE WHO BOARD ARE READY TO BE BEATEN TO DEATH WITH THEIR OWN TORN-OFF LIMBS.
BRING IT ON!

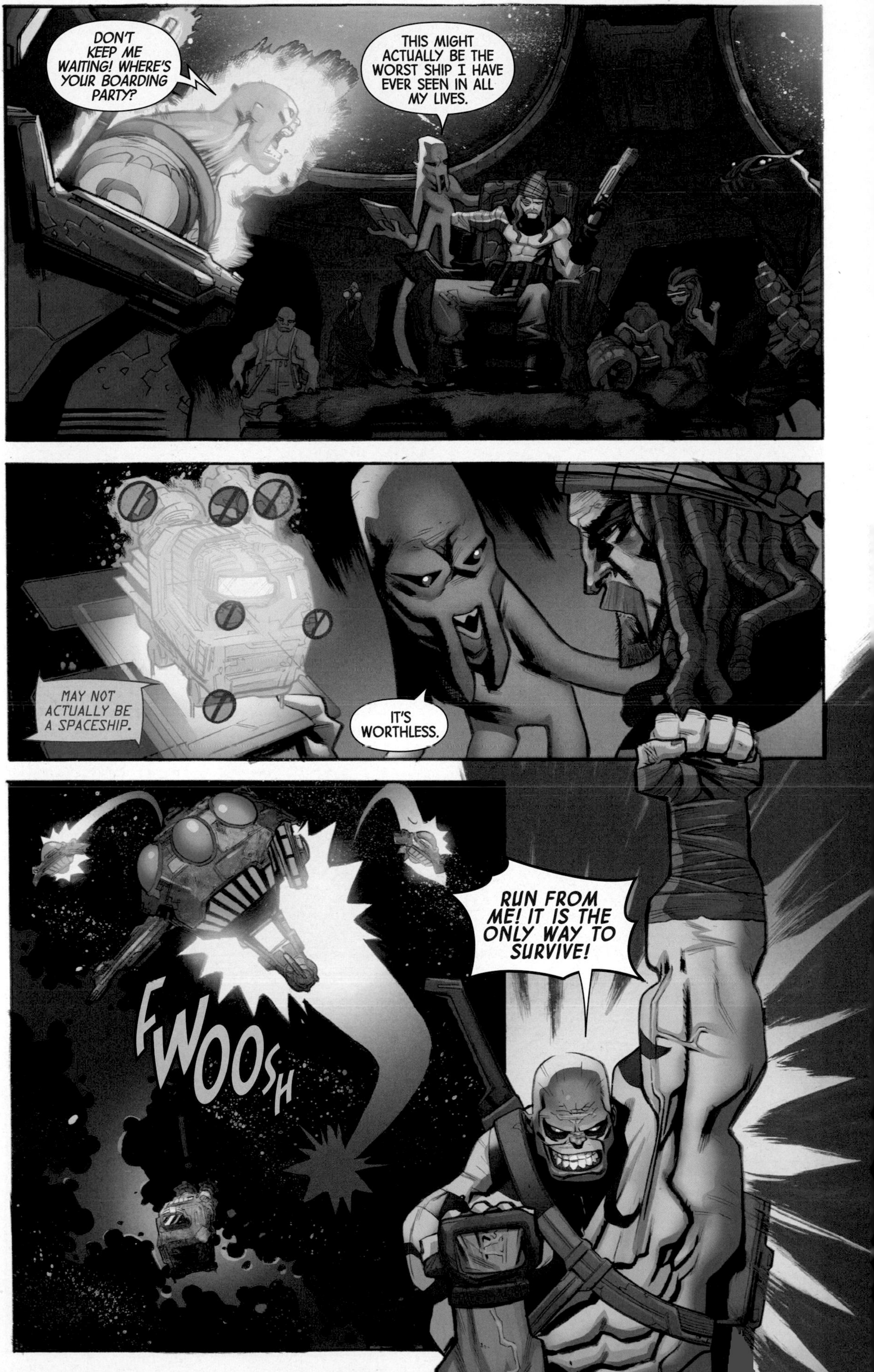
DON'T KEEP ME WAITING! WHERE'S YOUR BOARDING PARTY?
THIS MIGHT ACTUALLY BE THE WORST SHIP I HAVE EVER SEEN IN ALL MY LIVES.
MAY NOT ACTUALLY BE A SPACESHIP.
IT'S WORTHLESS.
RUN FROM ME! IT IS THE ONLY WAY TO SURVIVE!
FWOOSH

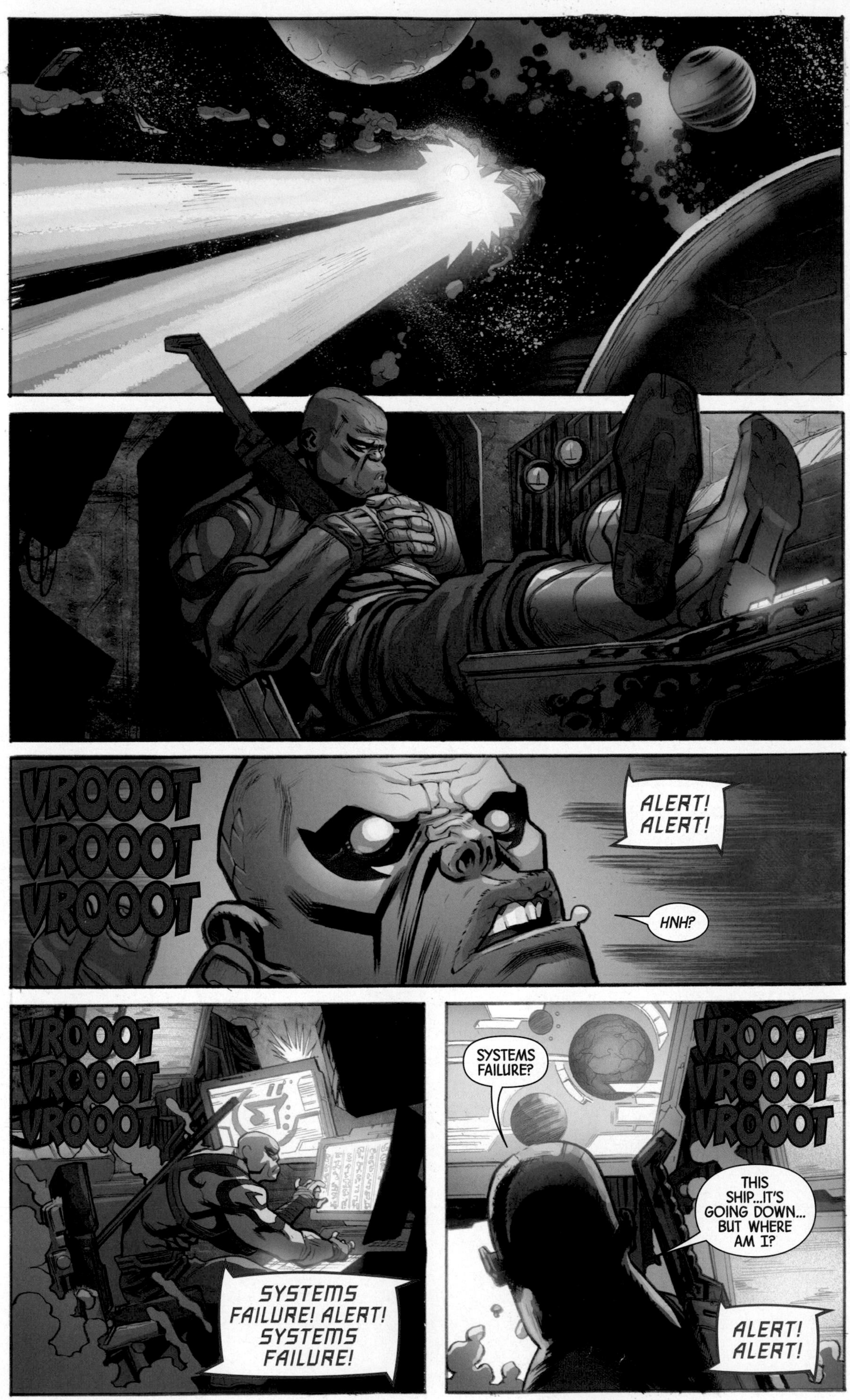
VROOOT VROOOT VROOOT
ALERT! ALERT!
HNH?
VROOOT VROOOT VROOOT
SYSTEMS FAILURE! ALERT! SYSTEMS FAILURE!
SYSTEMS FAILURE?
VROOOT VROOOT VROOOT
THIS SHIP...IT'S GOING DOWN... BUT WHERE AM I?
ALERT! ALERT!

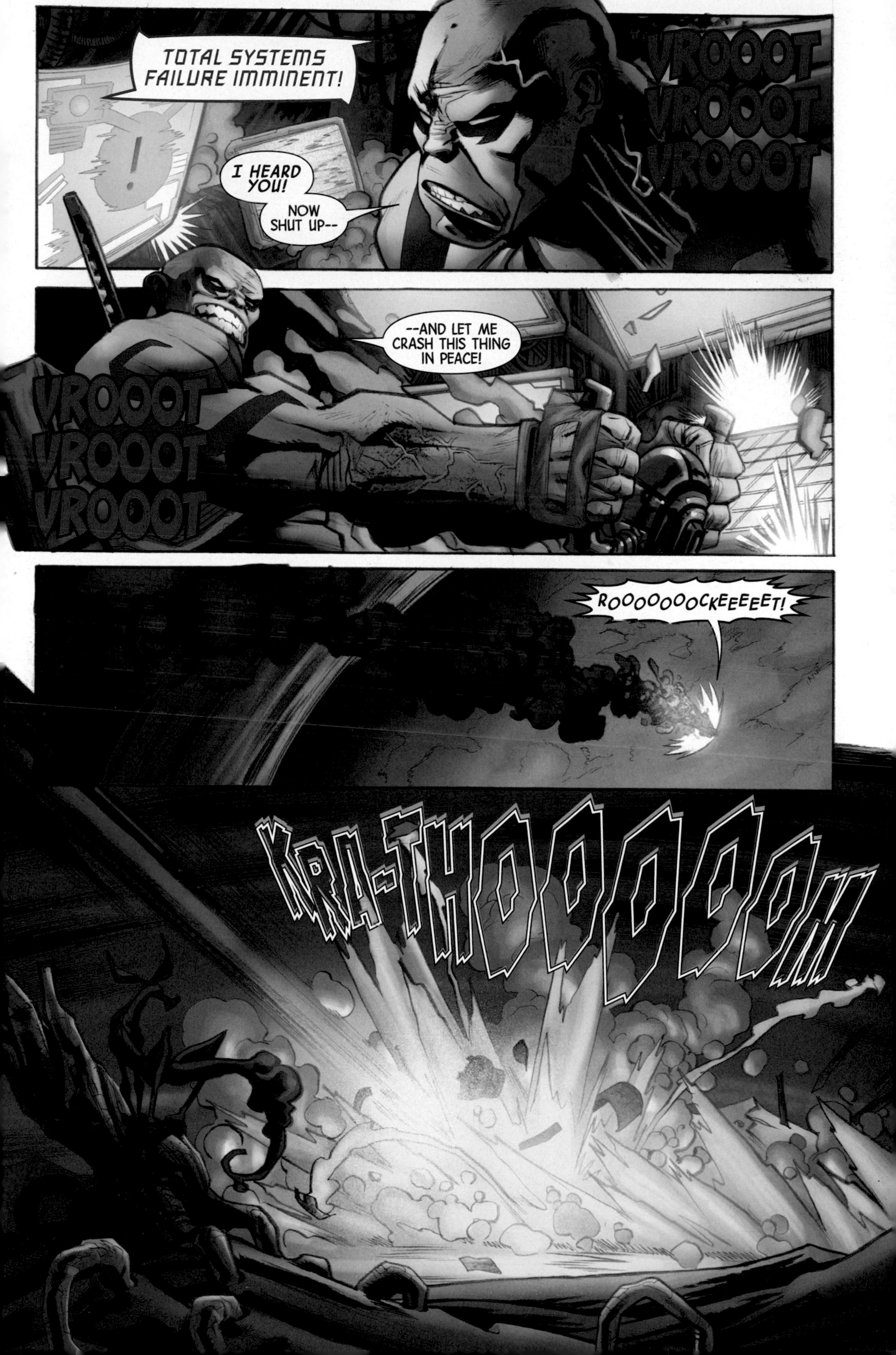
TOTAL SYSTEMS FAILURE IMMINENT!
VROOOT VROOOT VROOOT
I HEARD YOU!
NOW SHUT UP--
--AND LET ME CRASH THIS THING IN PEACE!
VROOOT VROOOT VROOOT
ROOOOOOOCKEEEEET!
KRA-THOOOOOOM

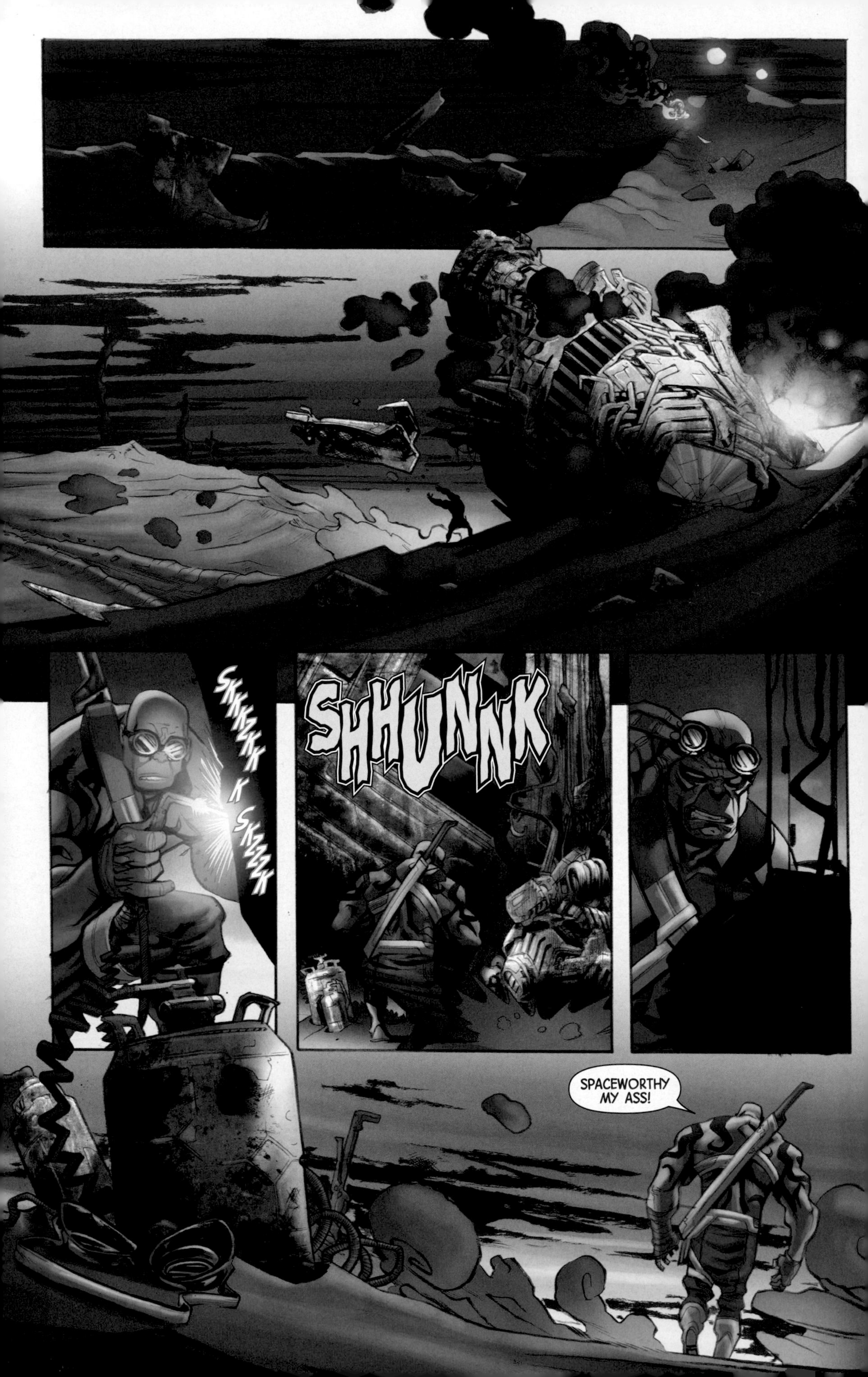
SKKKZKKK K SKZZZK
SHHUNNK
SPACEWORTHY MY ASS!

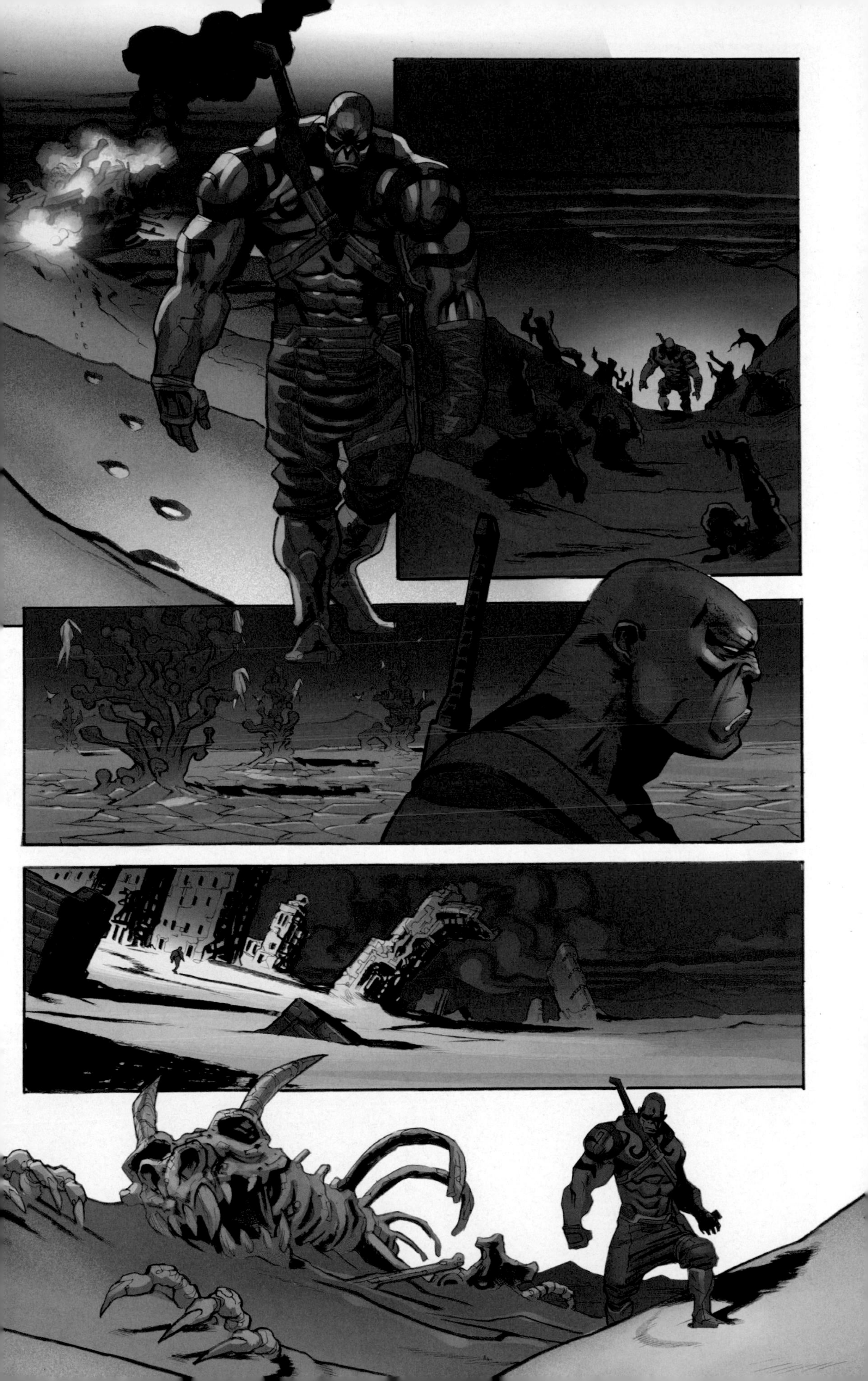

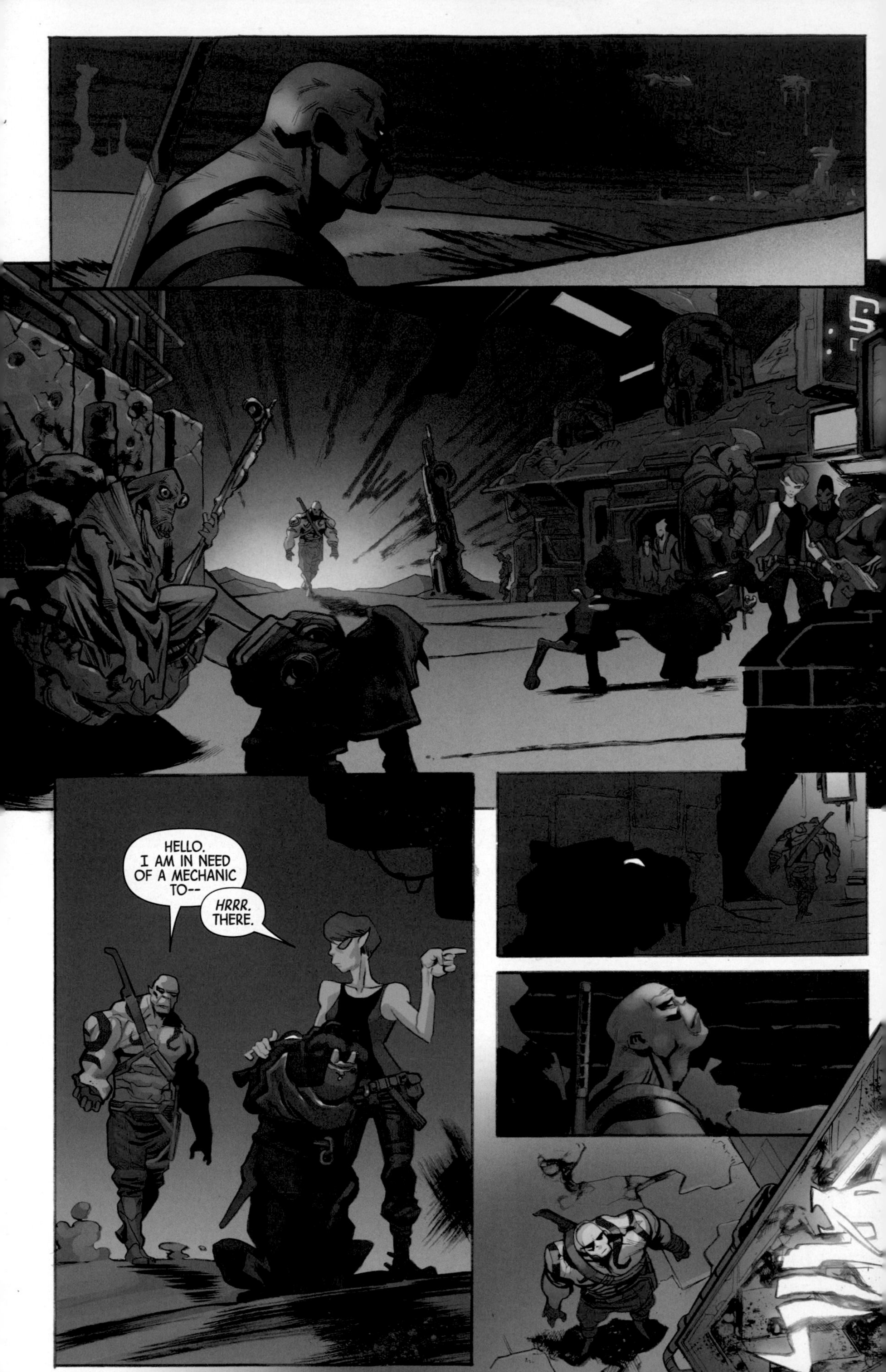
HELLO. I AM IN NEED OF A MECHANIC TO--
HRRR. THERE.

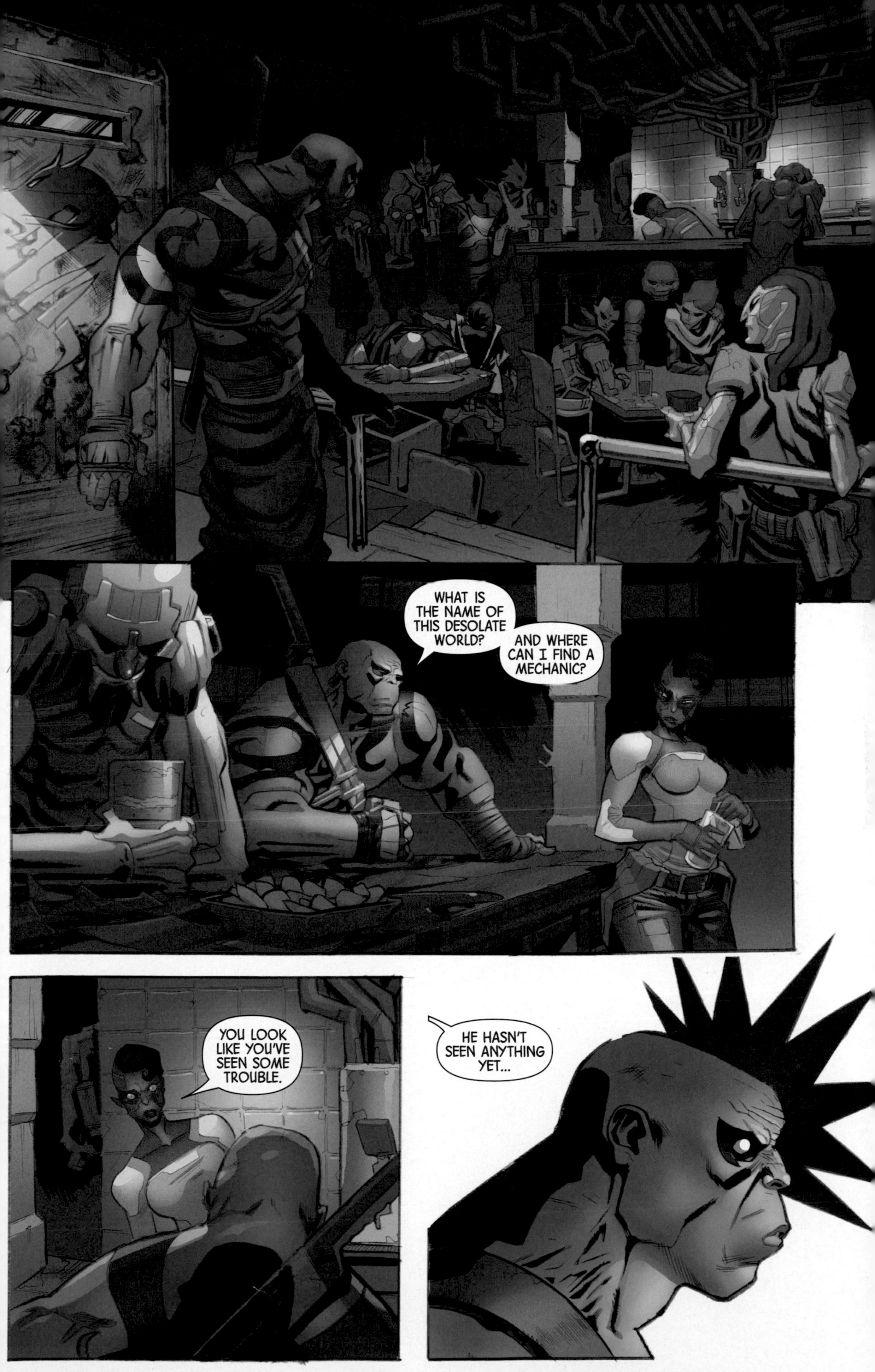
WHAT IS THE NAME OF THIS DESOLATE WORLD?
AND WHERE CAN I FIND A MECHANIC?
YOU LOOK LIKE YOU'VE SEEN SOME TROUBLE.
HE HASN'T SEEN ANYTHING YET...

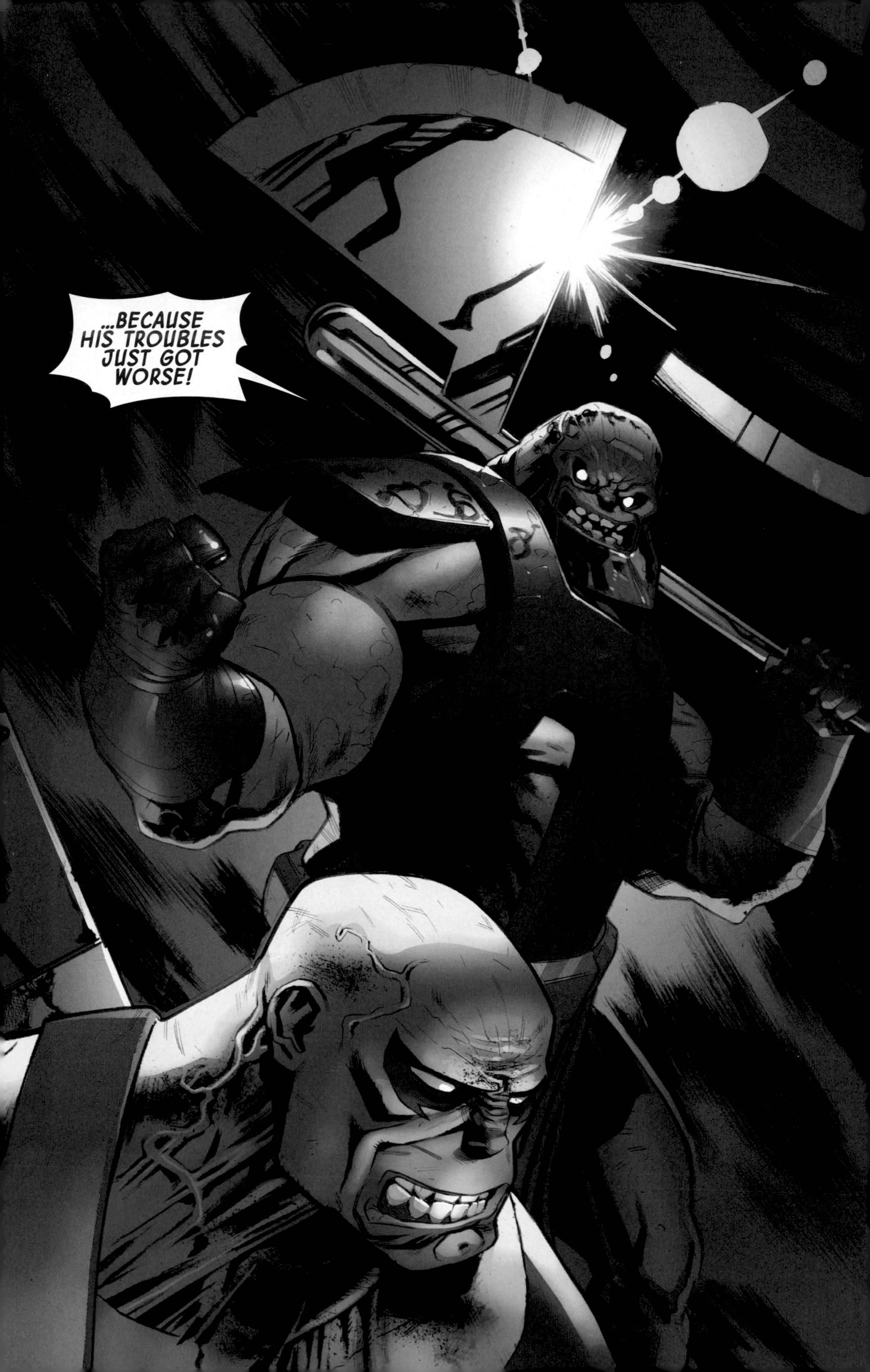
...BECAUSE HIS TROUBLES JUST GOT WORSE!

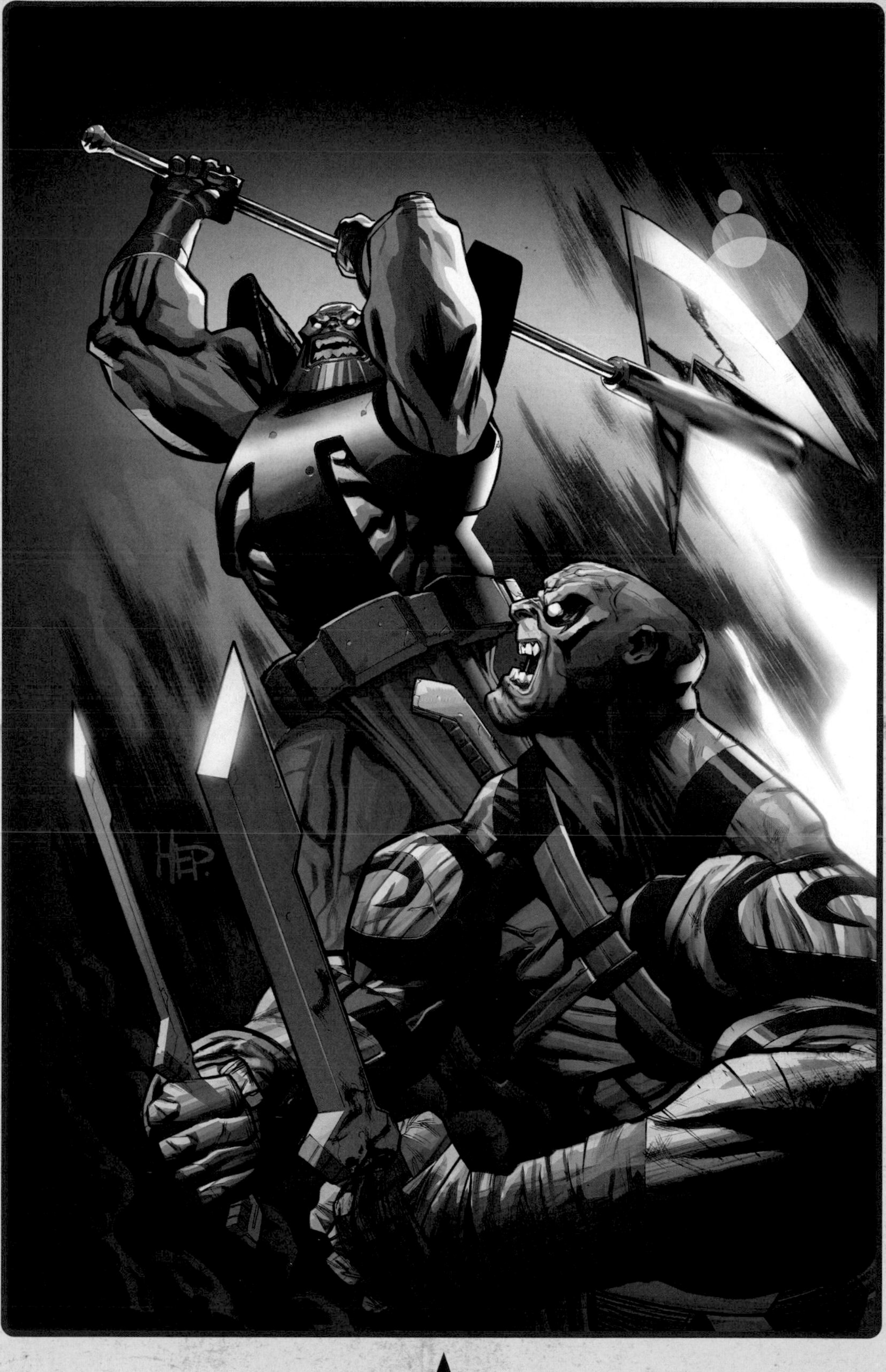
HEP.

2

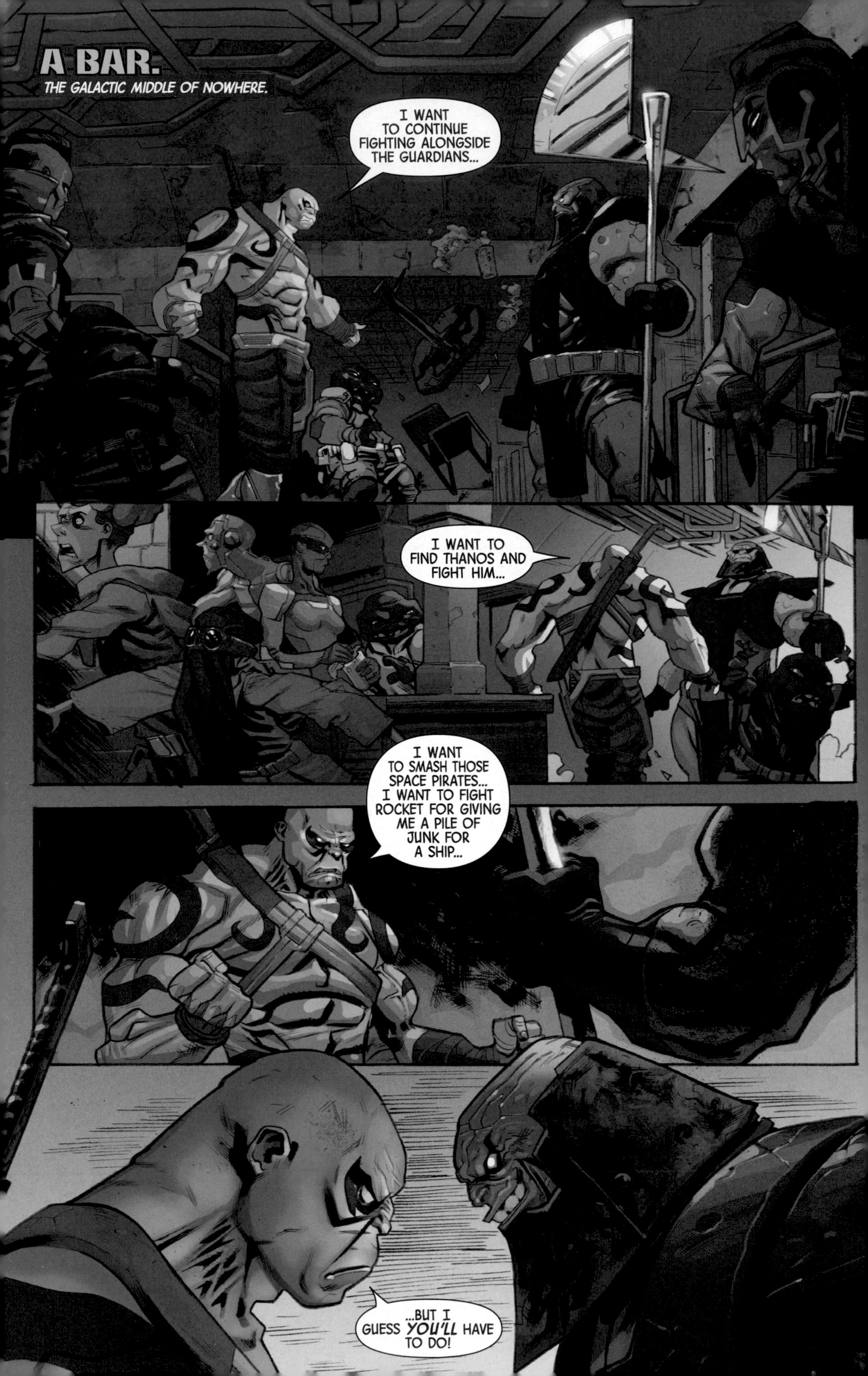
A BAR.
THE GALACTIC MIDDLE OF NOWHERE.
I WANT TO CONTINUE FIGHTING ALONGSIDE THE GUARDIANS...
I WANT TO FIND THANOS AND FIGHT HIM...
I WANT TO SMASH THOSE SPACE PIRATES... I WANT TO FIGHT ROCKET FOR GIVING ME A PILE OF JUNK FOR A SHIP...
...BUT I GUESS YOU'LL HAVE TO DO!

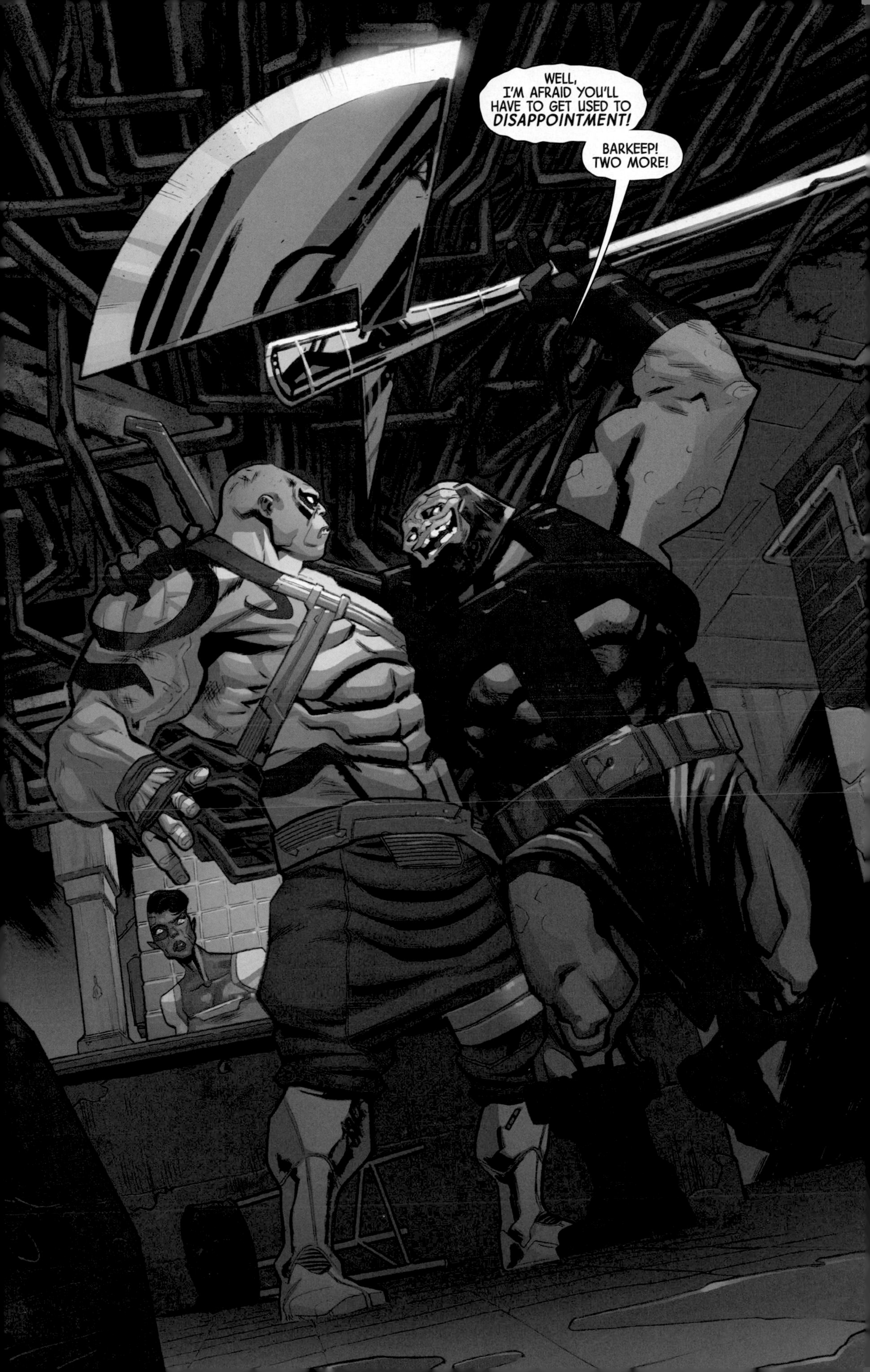
WELL, I'M AFRAID YOU'LL HAVE TO GET USED TO DISAPPOINTMENT!
BARKEEP! TWO MORE!

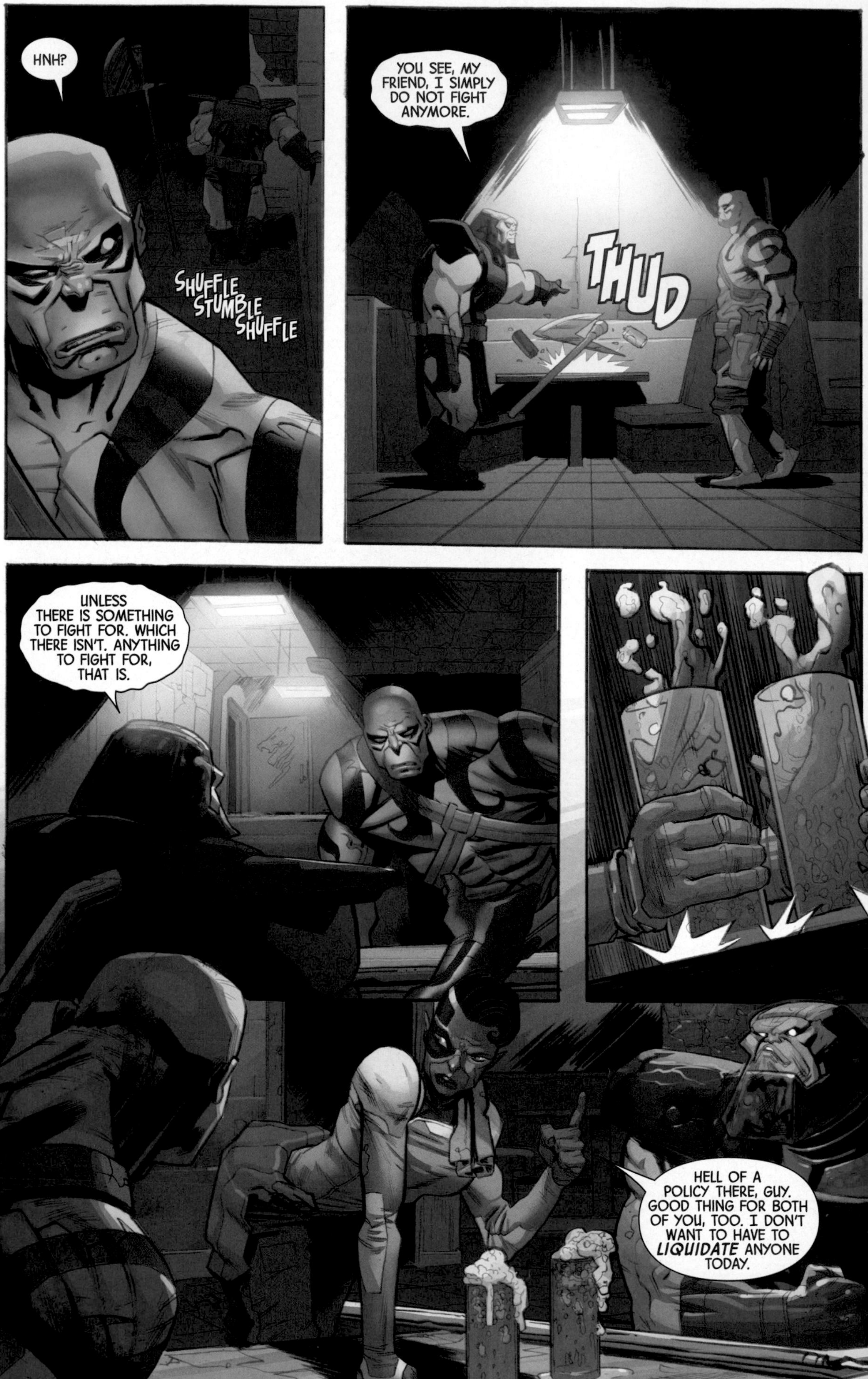
HNH?
SHUFFLE STUMBLE SHUFFLE
YOU SEE, MY FRIEND, I SIMPLY DO NOT FIGHT ANYMORE.
THUD
UNLESS THERE IS SOMETHING TO FIGHT FOR. WHICH THERE ISN'T. ANYTHING TO FIGHT FOR, THAT IS.
HELL OF A POLICY THERE, GUY. GOOD THING FOR BOTH OF YOU, TOO. I DON'T WANT TO HAVE TO LIQUIDATE ANYONE TODAY.

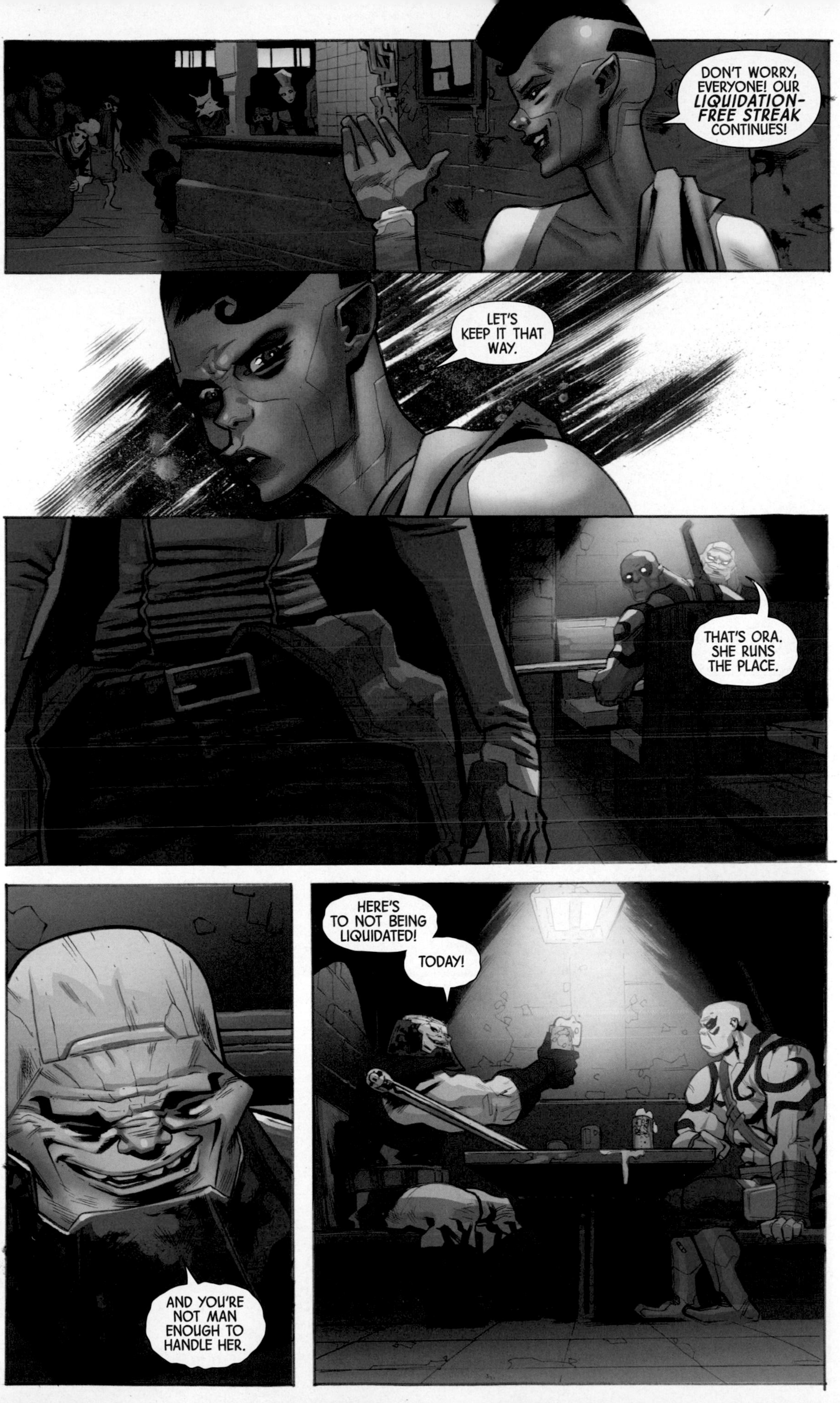
DON'T WORRY, EVERYONE! OUR LIQUIDATION-FREE STREAK CONTINUES!
LET'S KEEP IT THAT WAY.
THAT'S ORA. SHE RUNS THE PLACE.
AND YOU'RE NOT MAN ENOUGH TO HANDLE HER.
HERE'S TO NOT BEING LIQUIDATED!
TODAY!

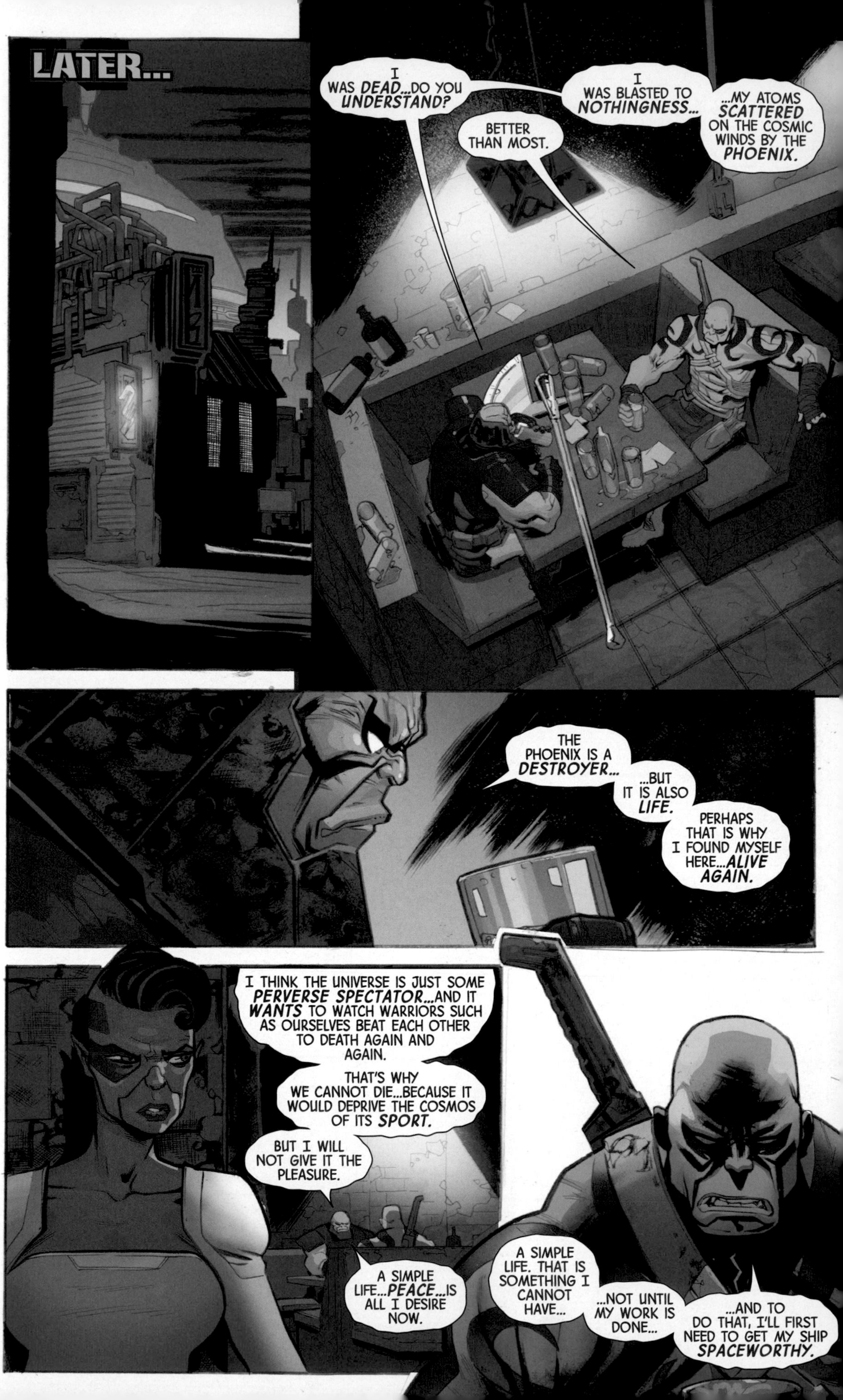
LATER...
I WAS DEAD...DO YOU UNDERSTAND?
BETTER THAN MOST.
I WAS BLASTED TO NOTHINGNESS...
...MY ATOMS SCATTERED ON THE COSMIC WINDS BY THE PHOENIX.
THE PHOENIX IS A DESTROYER...
...BUT IT IS ALSO LIFE.
PERHAPS THAT IS WHY I FOUND MYSELF HERE...ALIVE AGAIN.
I THINK THE UNIVERSE IS JUST SOME PERVERSE SPECTATOR...AND IT WANTS TO WATCH WARRIORS SUCH AS OURSELVES BEAT EACH OTHER TO DEATH AGAIN AND AGAIN.
THAT'S WHY WE CANNOT DIE...BECAUSE IT WOULD DEPRIVE THE COSMOS OF ITS SPORT.
BUT I WILL NOT GIVE IT THE PLEASURE.
A SIMPLE LIFE...PEACE...IS ALL I DESIRE NOW.
A SIMPLE LIFE. THAT IS SOMETHING I CANNOT HAVE...
...NOT UNTIL MY WORK IS DONE...
...AND TO DO THAT, I'LL FIRST NEED TO GET MY SHIP SPACEWORTHY.

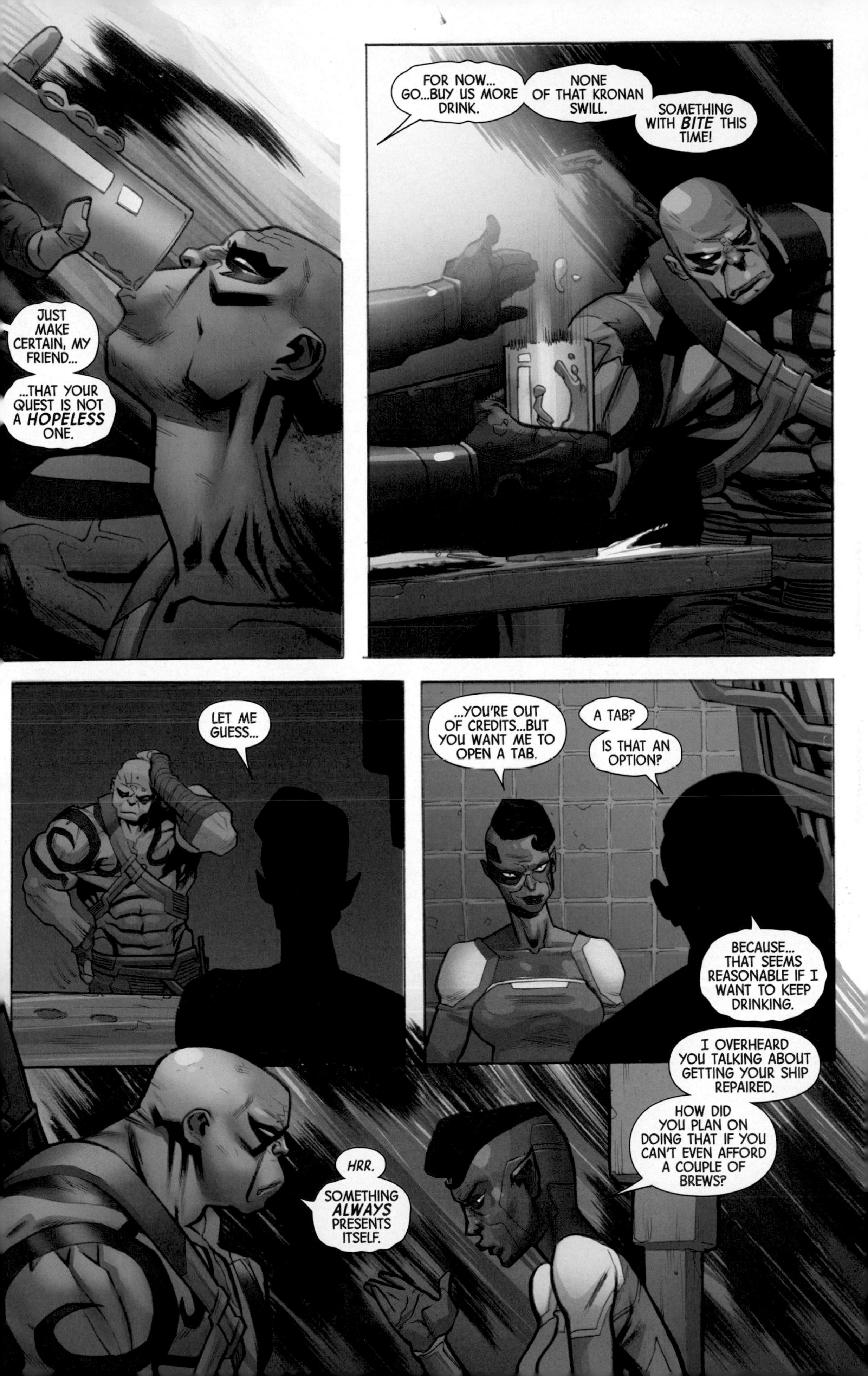
JUST MAKE CERTAIN, MY FRIEND...
...THAT YOUR QUEST IS NOT A *HOPELESS* ONE.
FOR NOW... GO...BUY US MORE DRINK.
NONE OF THAT KRONAN SWILL.
SOMETHING WITH *BITE* THIS TIME!
LET ME GUESS...
...YOU'RE OUT OF CREDITS...BUT YOU WANT ME TO OPEN A TAB.
A TAB?
IS THAT AN OPTION?
BECAUSE... THAT SEEMS REASONABLE IF I WANT TO KEEP DRINKING.
I OVERHEARD YOU TALKING ABOUT GETTING YOUR SHIP REPAIRED.
HOW DID YOU PLAN ON DOING THAT IF YOU CAN'T EVEN AFFORD A COUPLE OF BREWS?
HRR.
SOMETHING *ALWAYS* PRESENTS ITSELF.

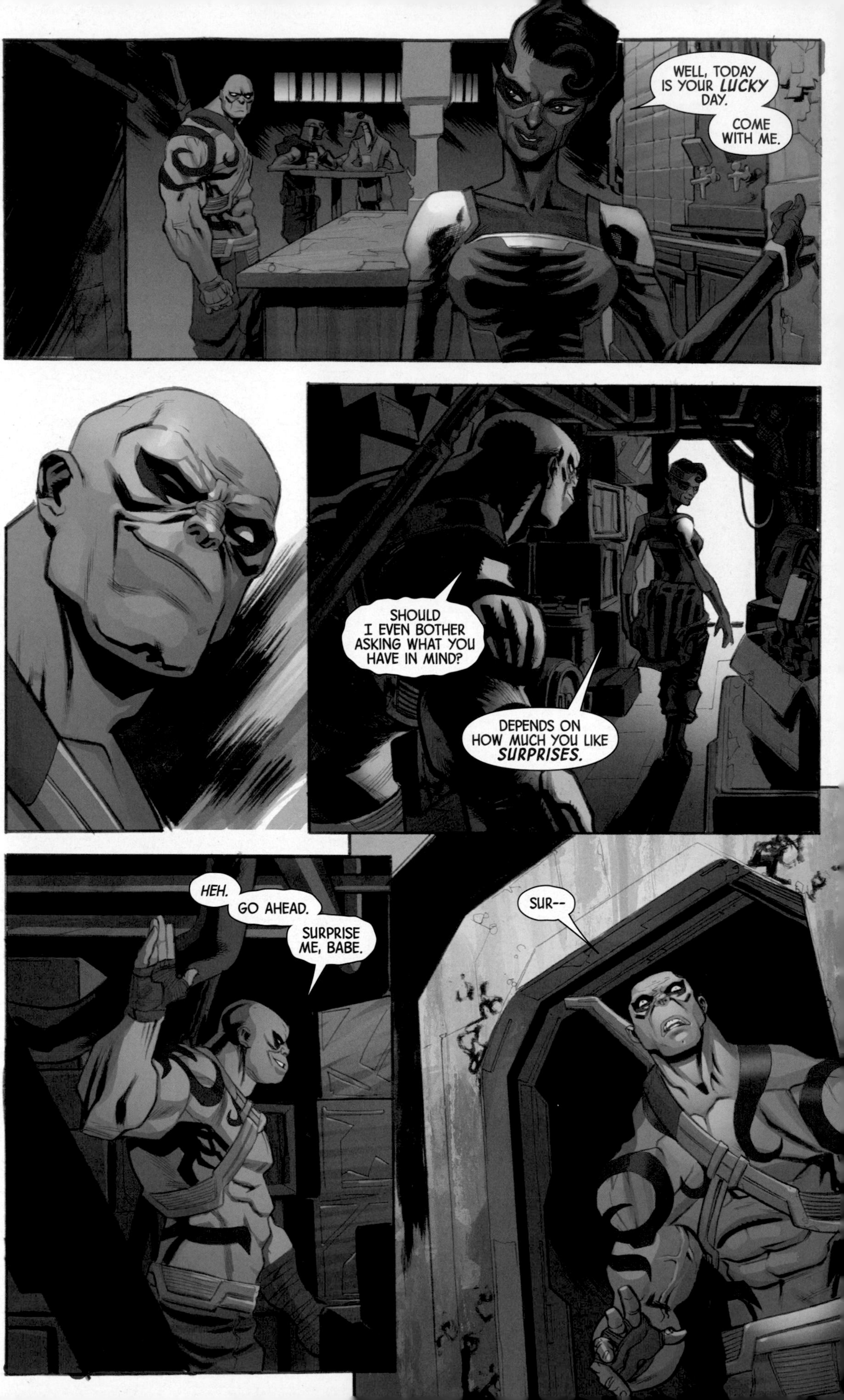
WELL, TODAY IS YOUR *LUCKY* DAY.
COME WITH ME.
SHOULD I EVEN BOTHER ASKING WHAT YOU HAVE IN MIND?
DEPENDS ON HOW MUCH YOU LIKE *SURPRISES.*
HEH.
GO AHEAD.
SURPRISE ME, BABE.
SUR--

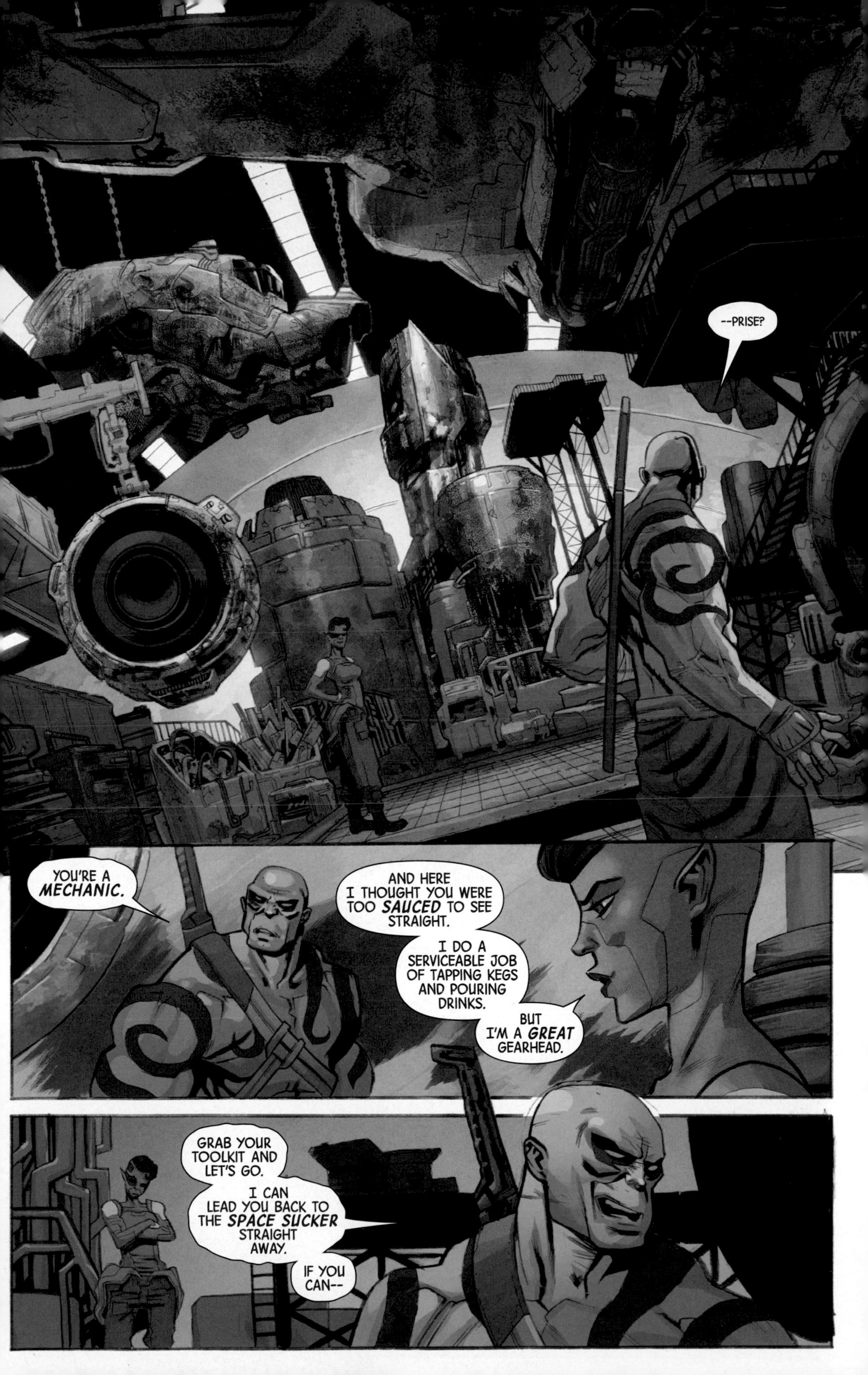
--PRISE?
YOU'RE A MECHANIC.
AND HERE I THOUGHT YOU WERE TOO SAUCED TO SEE STRAIGHT.
I DO A SERVICEABLE JOB OF TAPPING KEGS AND POURING DRINKS.
BUT I'M A GREAT GEARHEAD.
GRAB YOUR TOOLKIT AND LET'S GO.
I CAN LEAD YOU BACK TO THE SPACE SUCKER STRAIGHT AWAY.
IF YOU CAN--

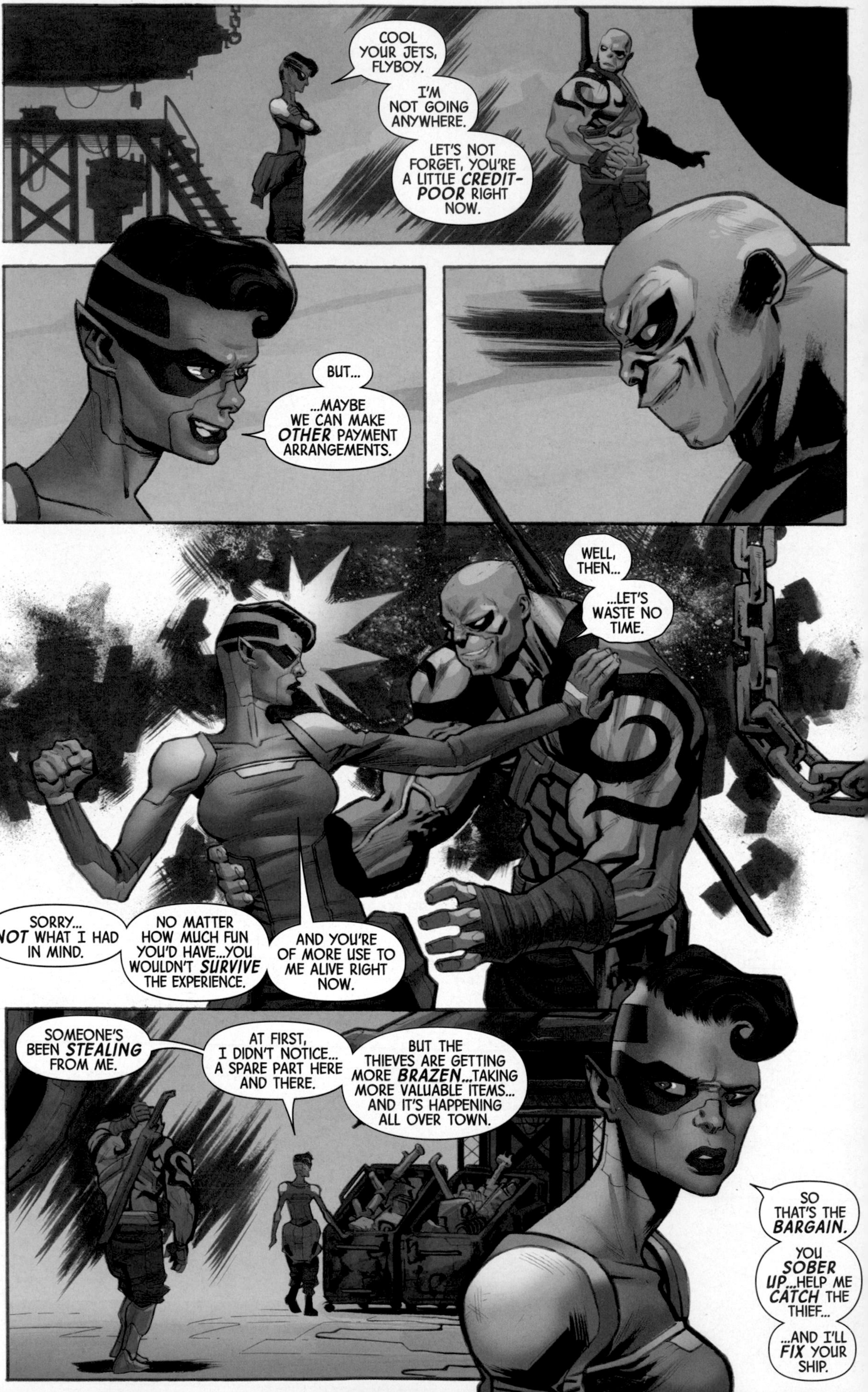
COOL YOUR JETS, FLYBOY.
I'M NOT GOING ANYWHERE.
LET'S NOT FORGET, YOU'RE A LITTLE CREDIT-POOR RIGHT NOW.
BUT...
...MAYBE WE CAN MAKE OTHER PAYMENT ARRANGEMENTS.
WELL, THEN...
...LET'S WASTE NO TIME.
SORRY... NOT WHAT I HAD IN MIND.
NO MATTER HOW MUCH FUN YOU'D HAVE...YOU WOULDN'T SURVIVE THE EXPERIENCE.
AND YOU'RE OF MORE USE TO ME ALIVE RIGHT NOW.
SOMEONE'S BEEN STEALING FROM ME.
AT FIRST, I DIDN'T NOTICE... A SPARE PART HERE AND THERE.
BUT THE THIEVES ARE GETTING MORE BRAZEN...TAKING MORE VALUABLE ITEMS... AND IT'S HAPPENING ALL OVER TOWN.
SO THAT'S THE BARGAIN.
YOU SOBER UP...HELP ME CATCH THE THIEF...
...AND I'LL FIX YOUR SHIP.

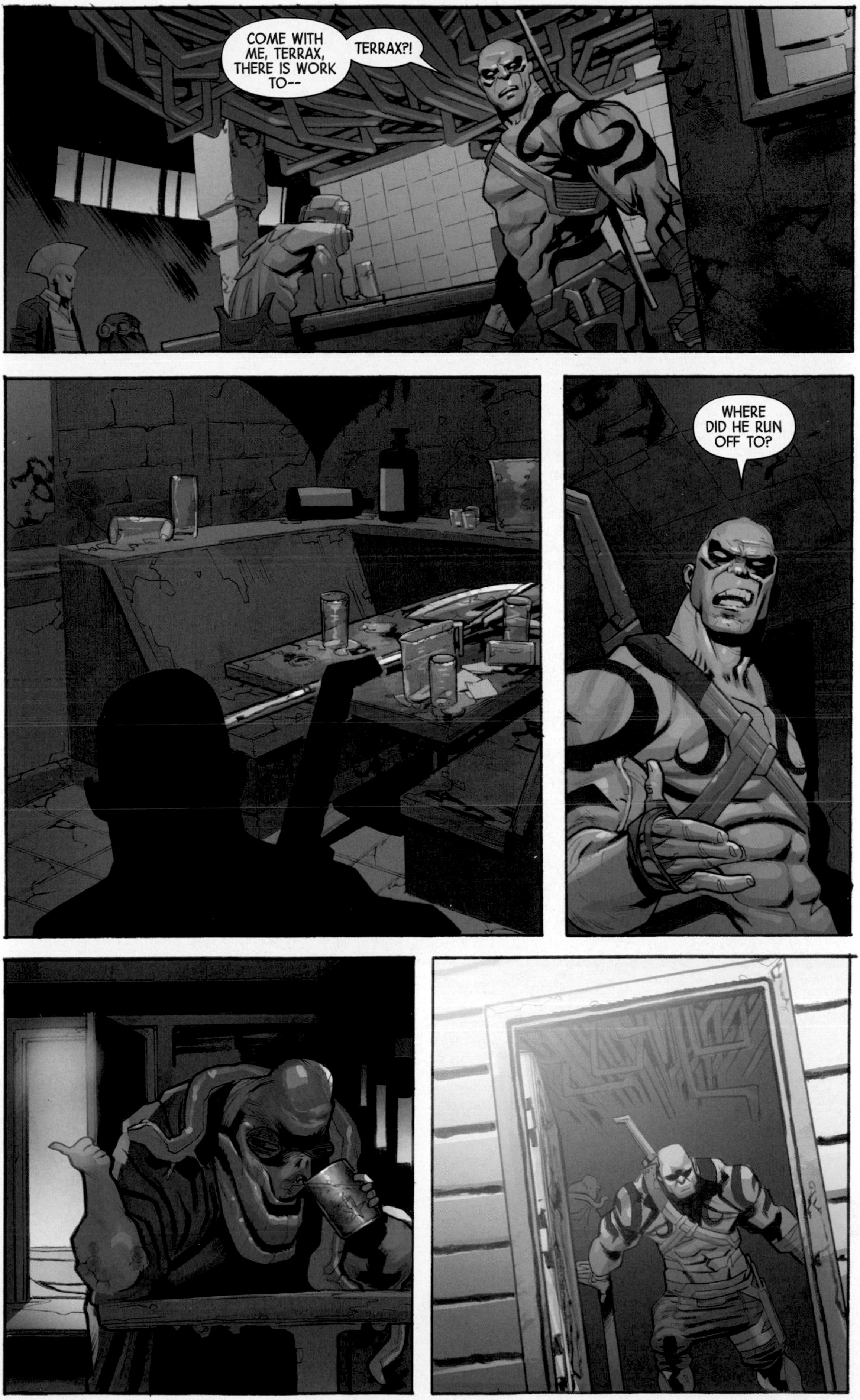
COME WITH ME, TERRAX, THERE IS WORK TO--
TERRAX?!
WHERE DID HE RUN OFF TO?

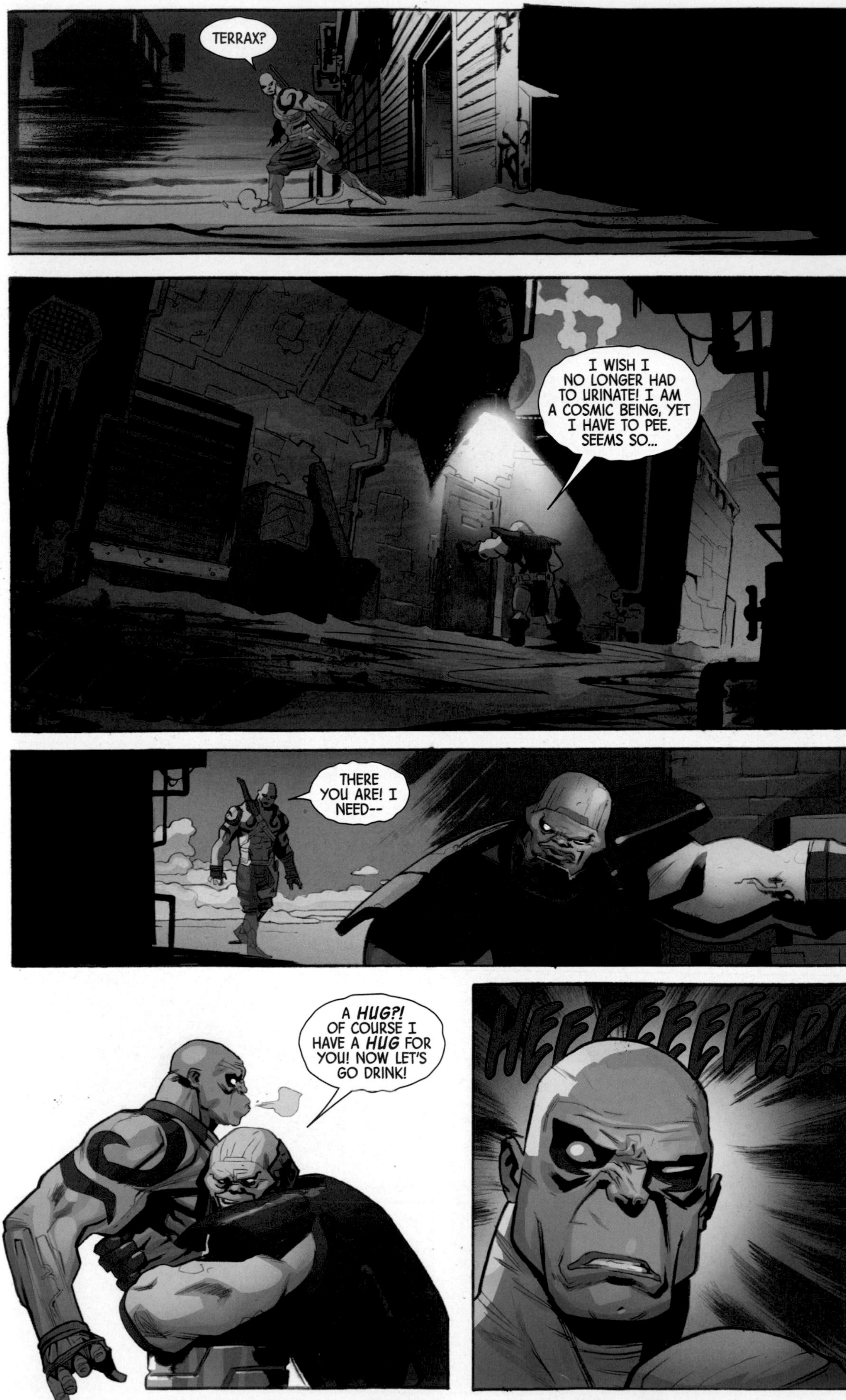
TERRAX?
I WISH I NO LONGER HAD TO URINATE! I AM A COSMIC BEING, YET I HAVE TO PEE. SEEMS SO...
THERE YOU ARE! I NEED--
A HUG?! OF COURSE I HAVE A HUG FOR YOU! NOW LET'S GO DRINK!
HEEEEEEELP!

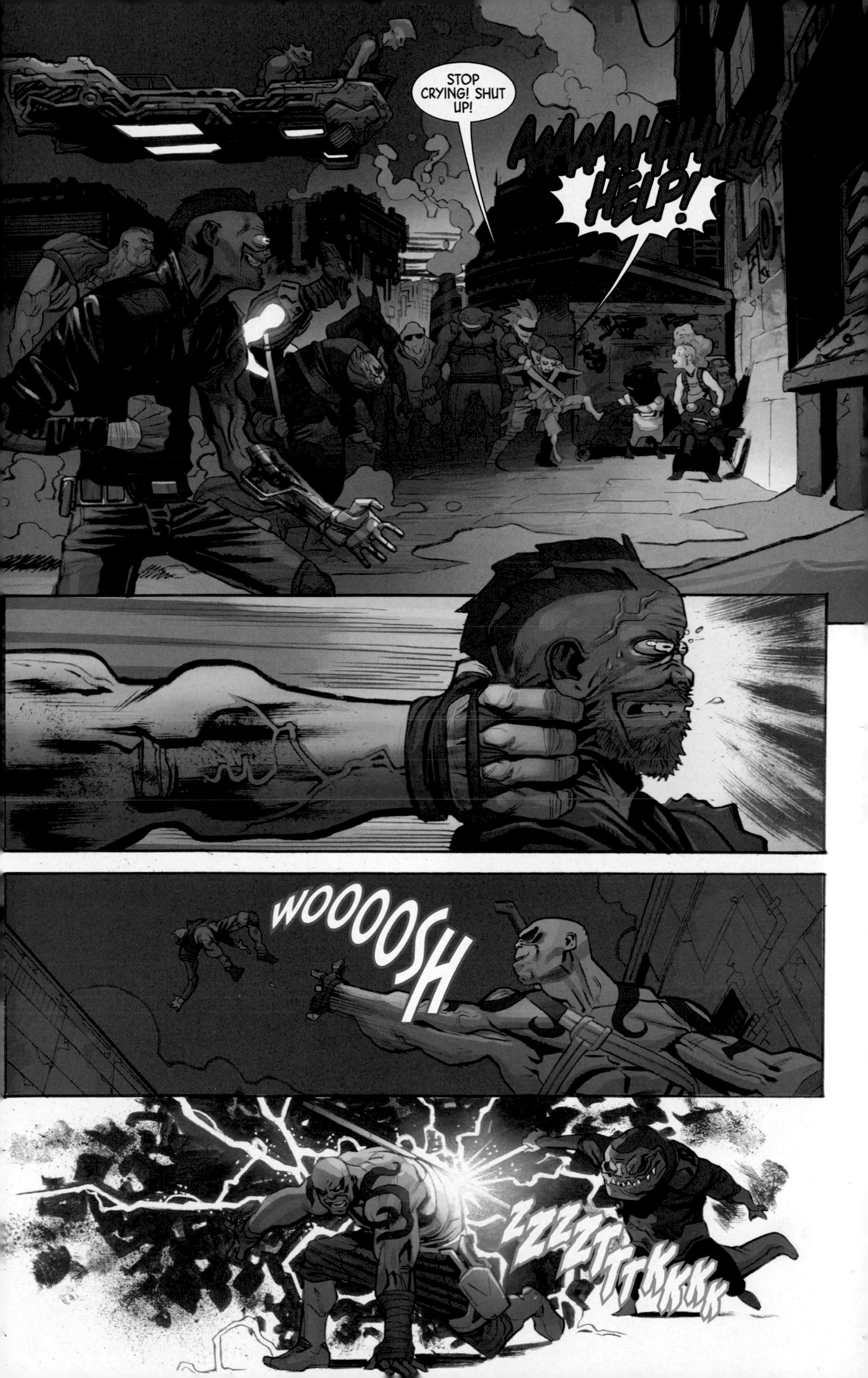
STOP CRYING! SHUT UP!
AAAAAHHHHH! HELP!
WOOOOSH
ZZZZTTTKKKK

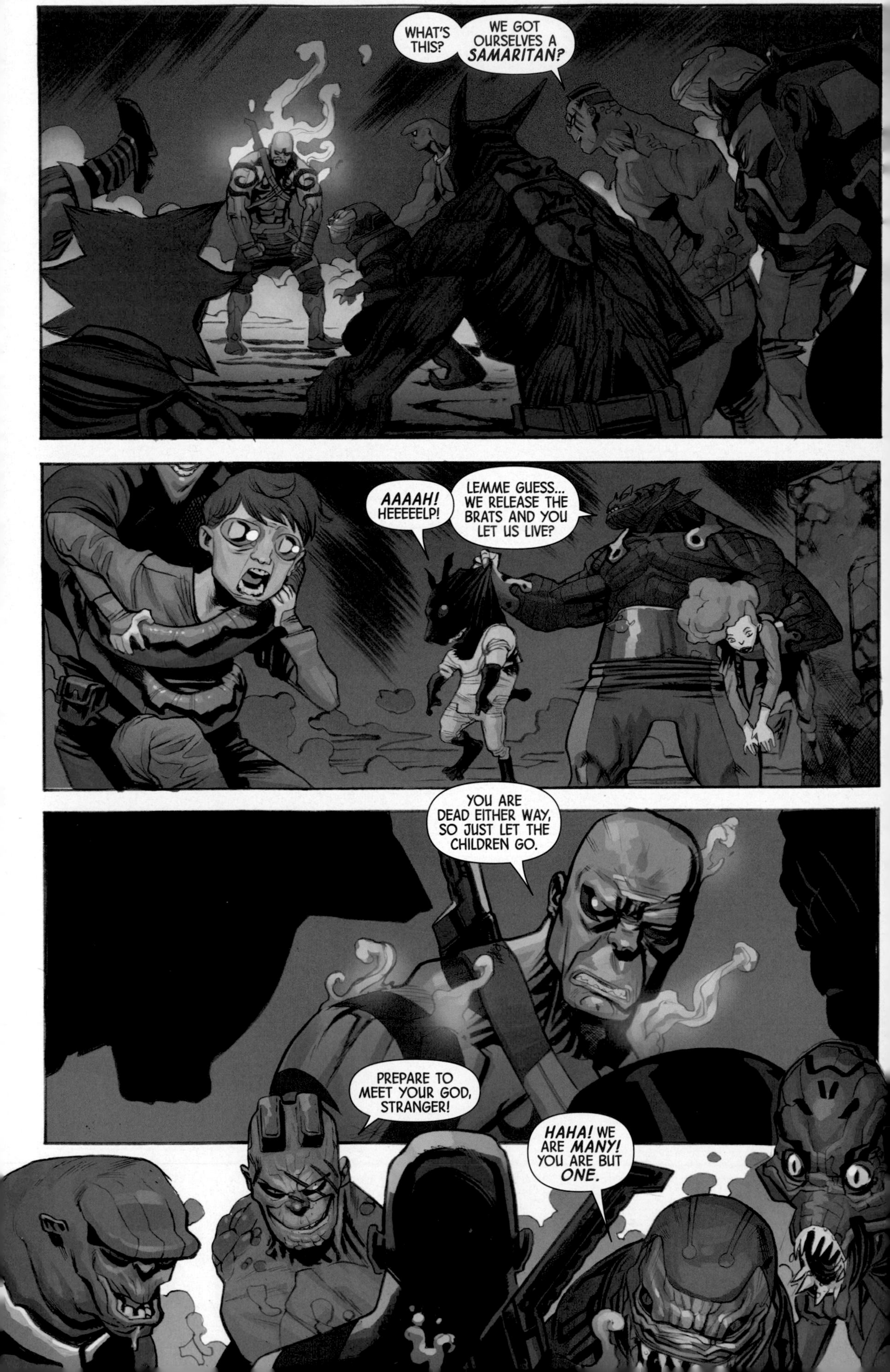
WHAT'S THIS?
WE GOT OURSELVES A SAMARITAN?
AAAAH! HEEEEELP!
LEMME GUESS... WE RELEASE THE BRATS AND YOU LET US LIVE?
YOU ARE DEAD EITHER WAY, SO JUST LET THE CHILDREN GO.
PREPARE TO MEET YOUR GOD, STRANGER!
HAHA! WE ARE MANY! YOU ARE BUT ONE.

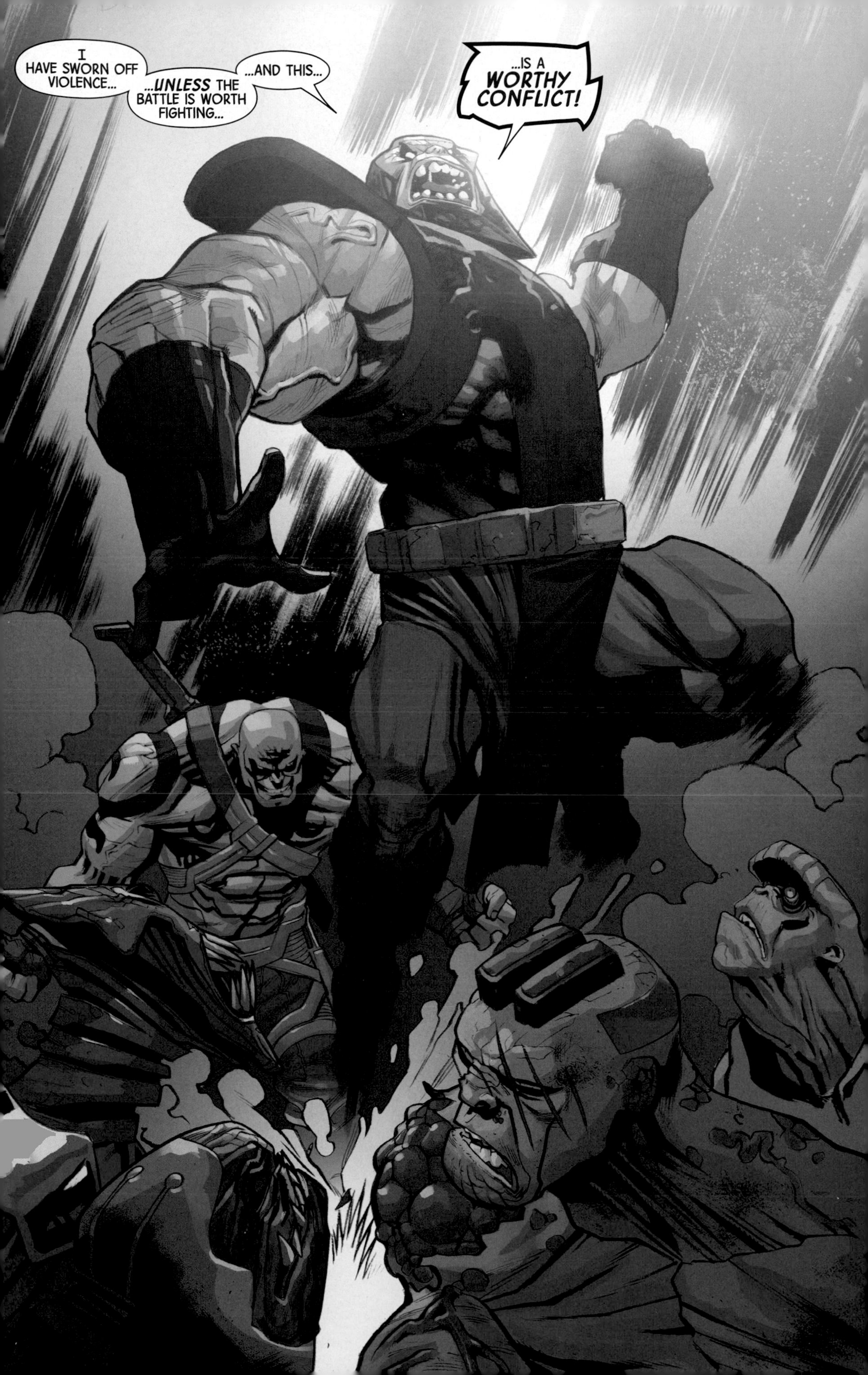
I HAVE SWORN OFF VIOLENCE...
...UNLESS THE BATTLE IS WORTH FIGHTING...
...AND THIS...
...IS A WORTHY CONFLICT!

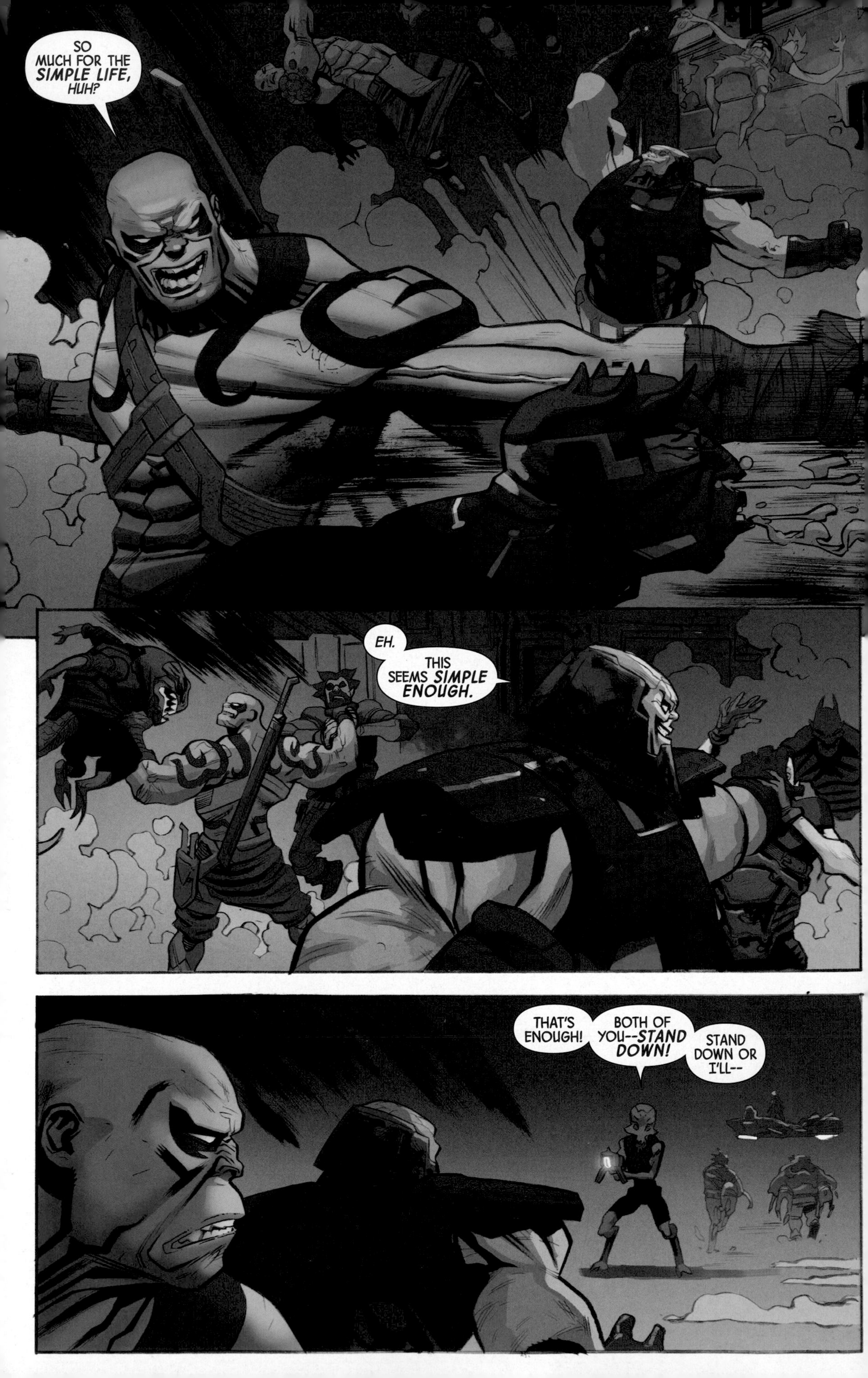

SO MUCH FOR THE SIMPLE LIFE, HUH?
EH.
THIS SEEMS SIMPLE ENOUGH.
THAT'S ENOUGH!
BOTH OF YOU--STAND DOWN!
STAND DOWN OR I'LL--

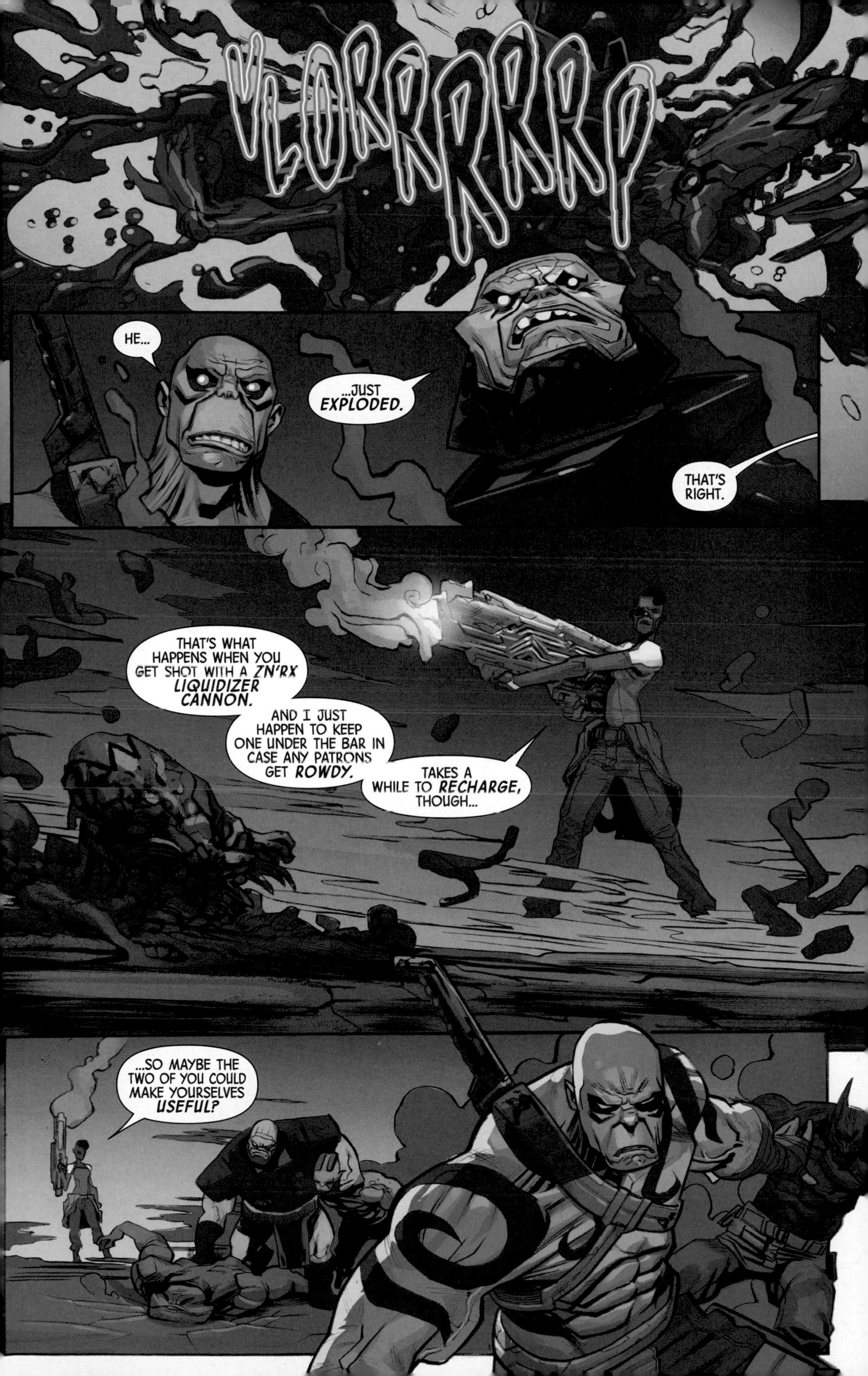
VLORRRRRP
HE...
...JUST EXPLODED.
THAT'S RIGHT.
THAT'S WHAT HAPPENS WHEN YOU GET SHOT WITH A ZN'RX LIQUIDIZER CANNON.
AND I JUST HAPPEN TO KEEP ONE UNDER THE BAR IN CASE ANY PATRONS GET ROWDY.
TAKES A WHILE TO RECHARGE, THOUGH...
...SO MAYBE THE TWO OF YOU COULD MAKE YOURSELVES USEFUL?

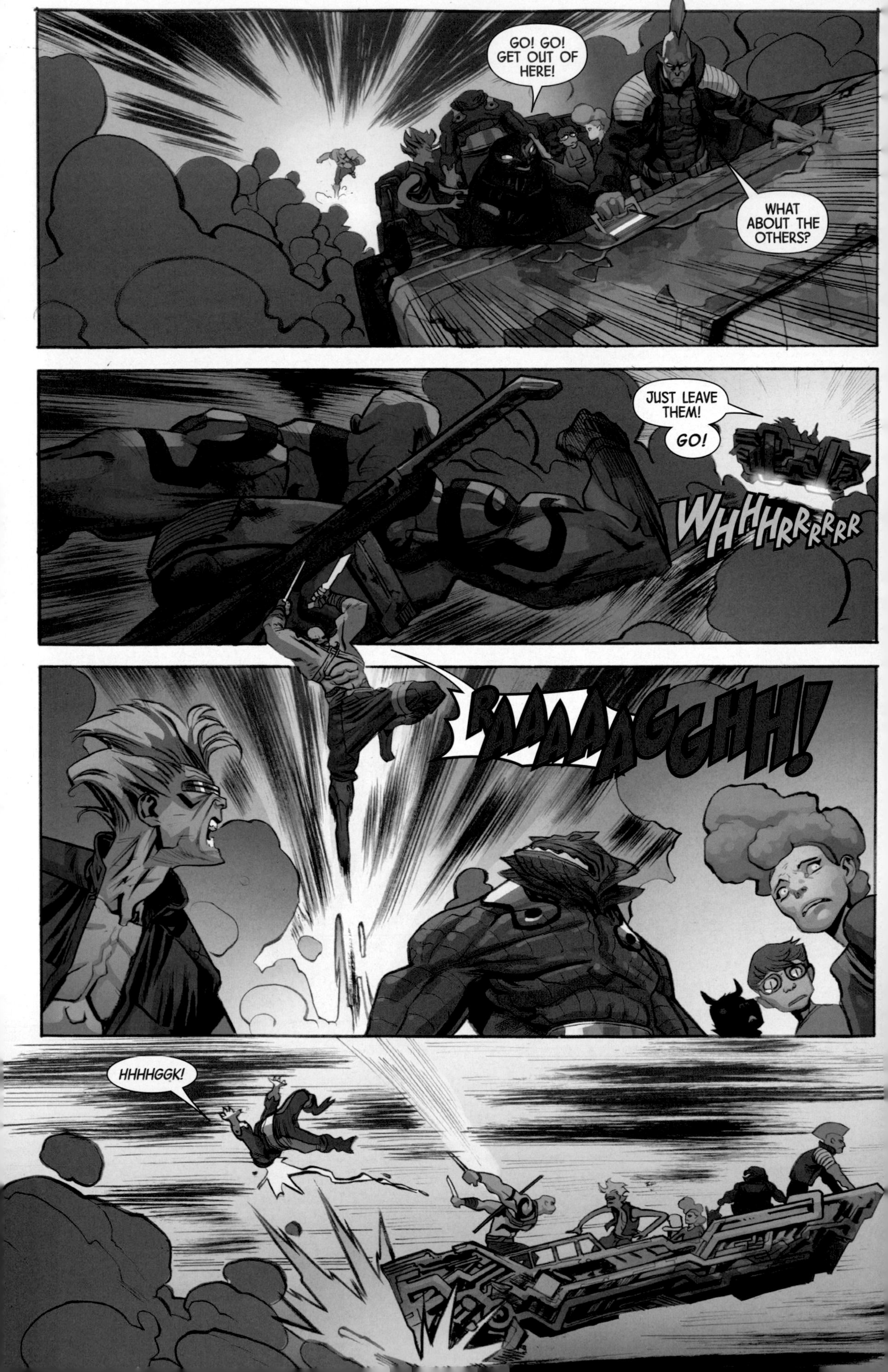
GO! GO! GET OUT OF HERE!
WHAT ABOUT THE OTHERS?
JUST LEAVE THEM!
GO!
WHHHRRRRRR
RAAAAAGGHH!
HHHHGGK!

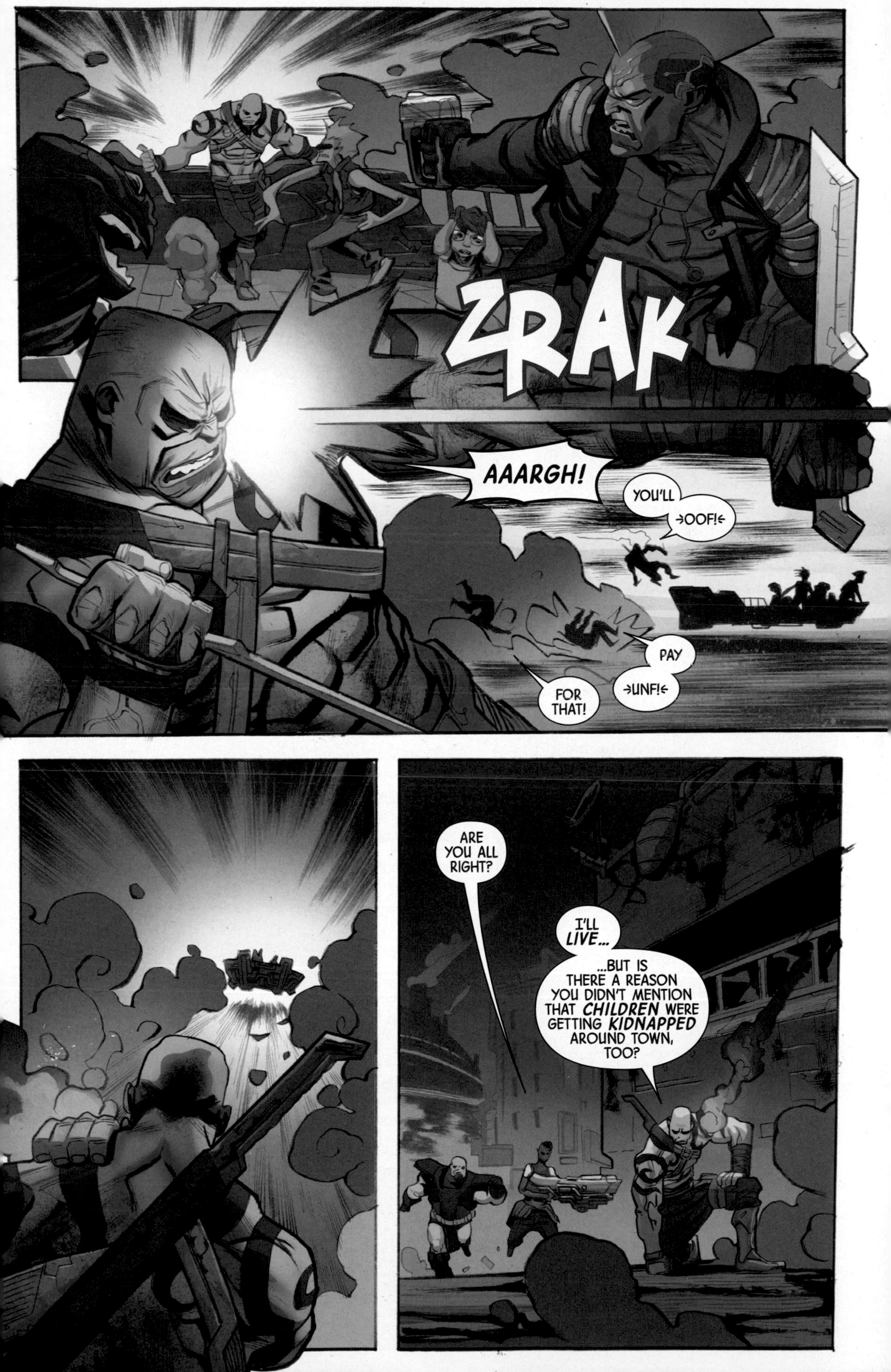
ZRAK
AAARGH!
YOU'LL
OOF!
PAY
UNF!
FOR THAT!
ARE YOU ALL RIGHT?
I'LL *LIVE*...
...BUT IS THERE A REASON YOU DIDN'T MENTION THAT *CHILDREN* WERE GETTING *KIDNAPPED* AROUND TOWN, TOO?

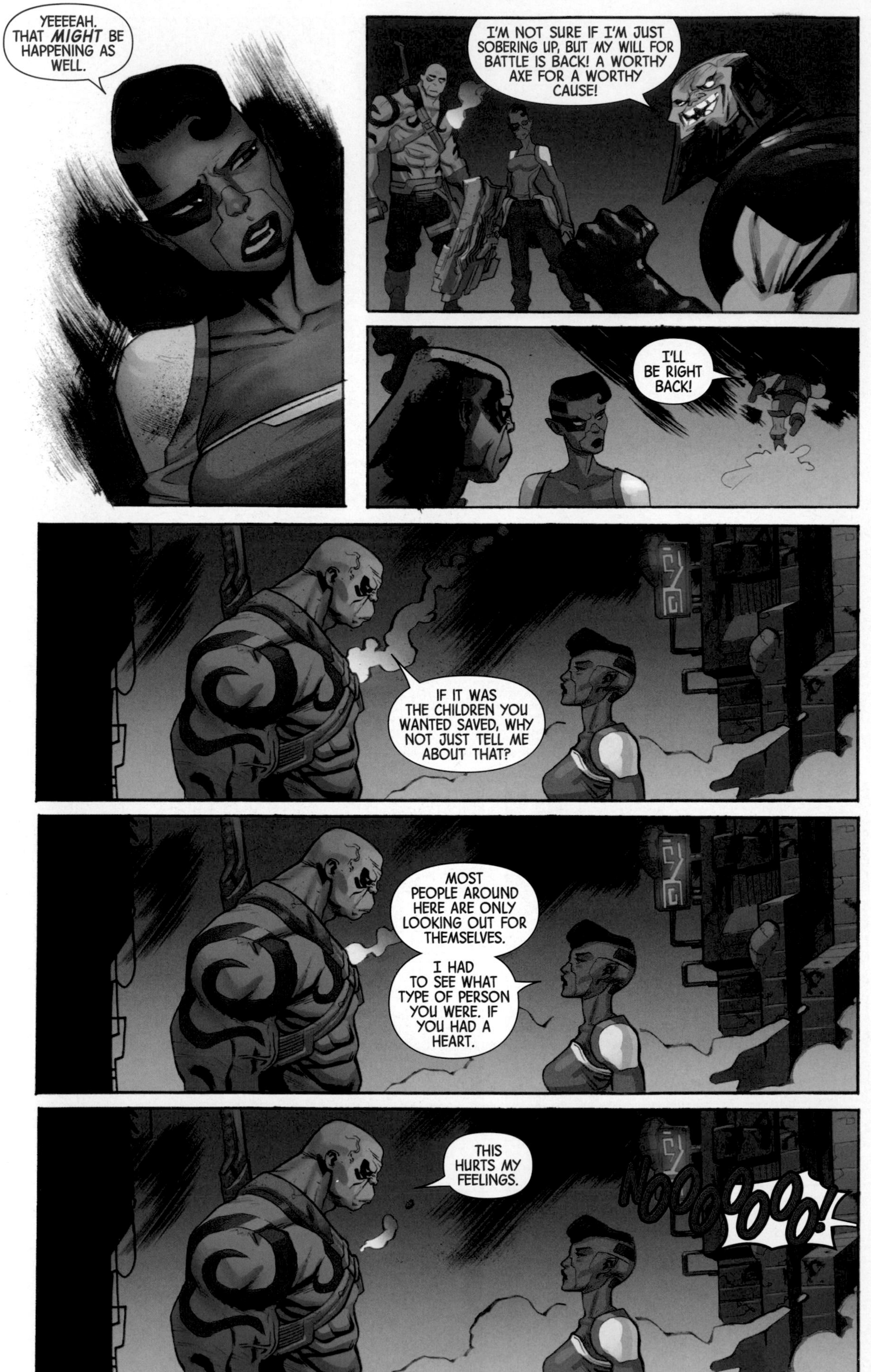
YEEEEAH. THAT MIGHT BE HAPPENING AS WELL.
I'M NOT SURE IF I'M JUST SOBERING UP, BUT MY WILL FOR BATTLE IS BACK! A WORTHY AXE FOR A WORTHY CAUSE!
I'LL BE RIGHT BACK!
IF IT WAS THE CHILDREN YOU WANTED SAVED, WHY NOT JUST TELL ME ABOUT THAT?
MOST PEOPLE AROUND HERE ARE ONLY LOOKING OUT FOR THEMSELVES.
I HAD TO SEE WHAT TYPE OF PERSON YOU WERE. IF YOU HAD A HEART.
THIS HURTS MY FEELINGS.
NOOOOOOOO!

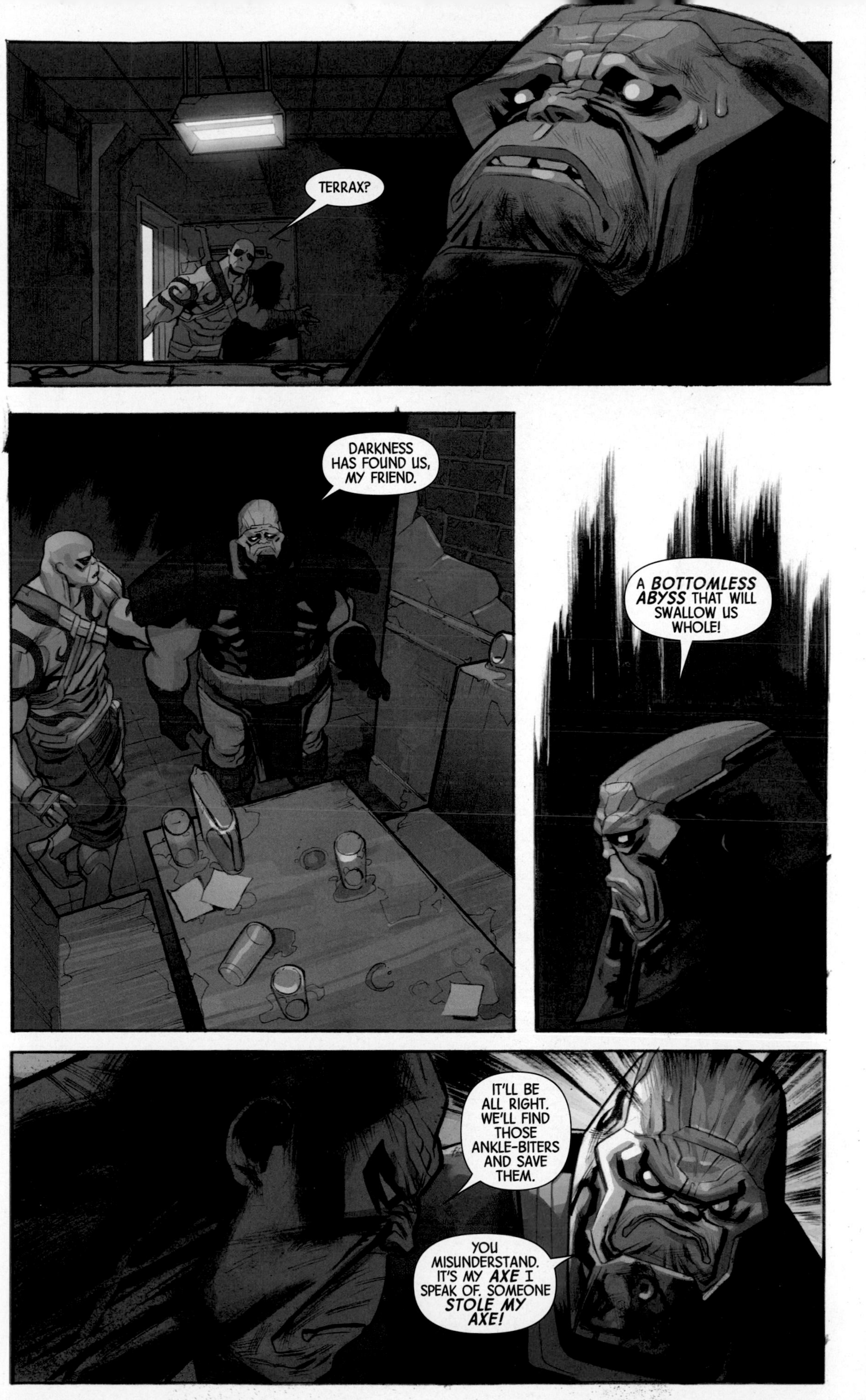
TERRAX?
DARKNESS HAS FOUND US, MY FRIEND.
A BOTTOMLESS ABYSS THAT WILL SWALLOW US WHOLE!
IT'LL BE ALL RIGHT. WE'LL FIND THOSE ANKLE-BITERS AND SAVE THEM.
YOU MISUNDERSTAND. IT'S MY AXE I SPEAK OF. SOMEONE STOLE MY AXE!

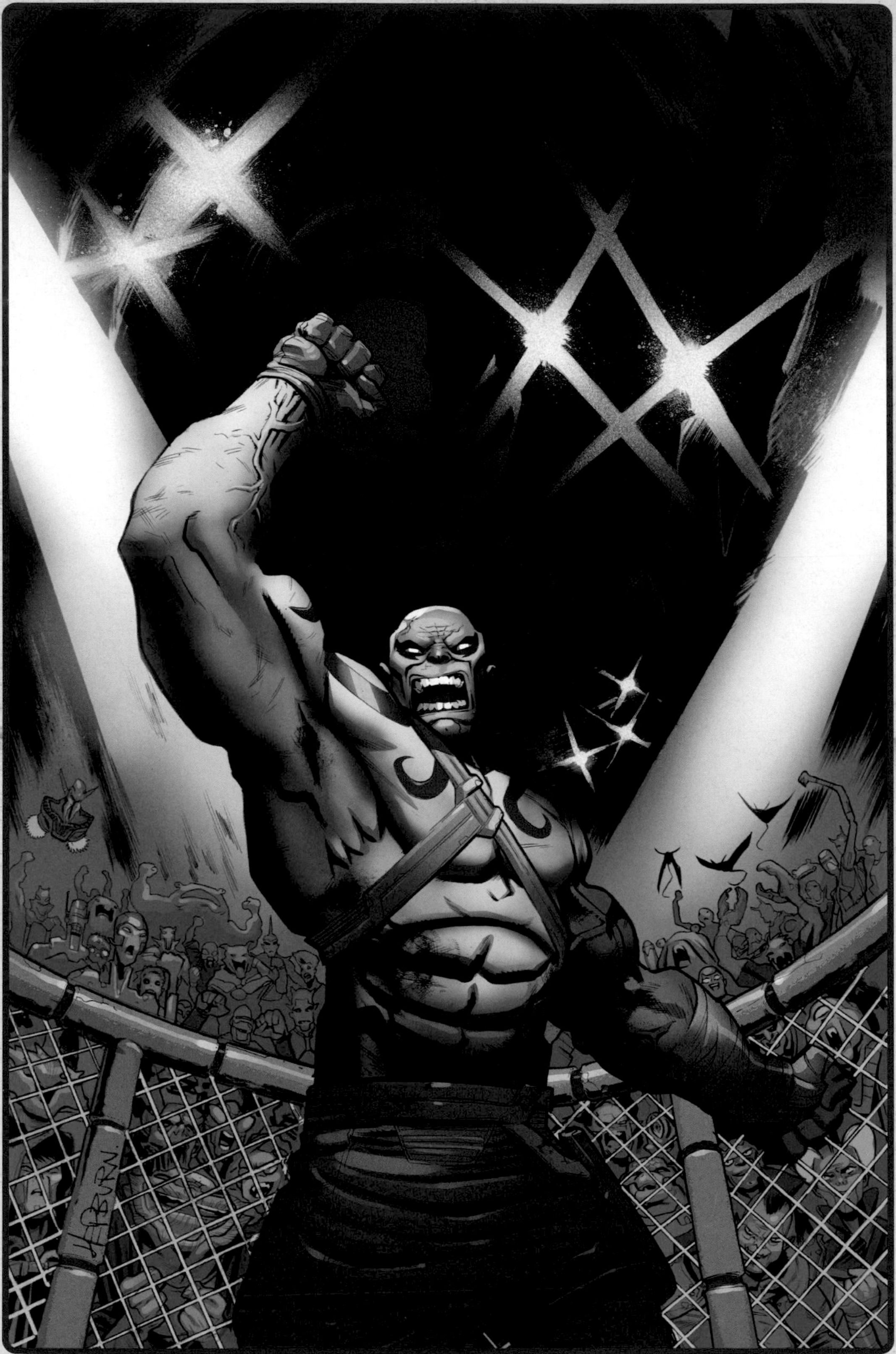

3

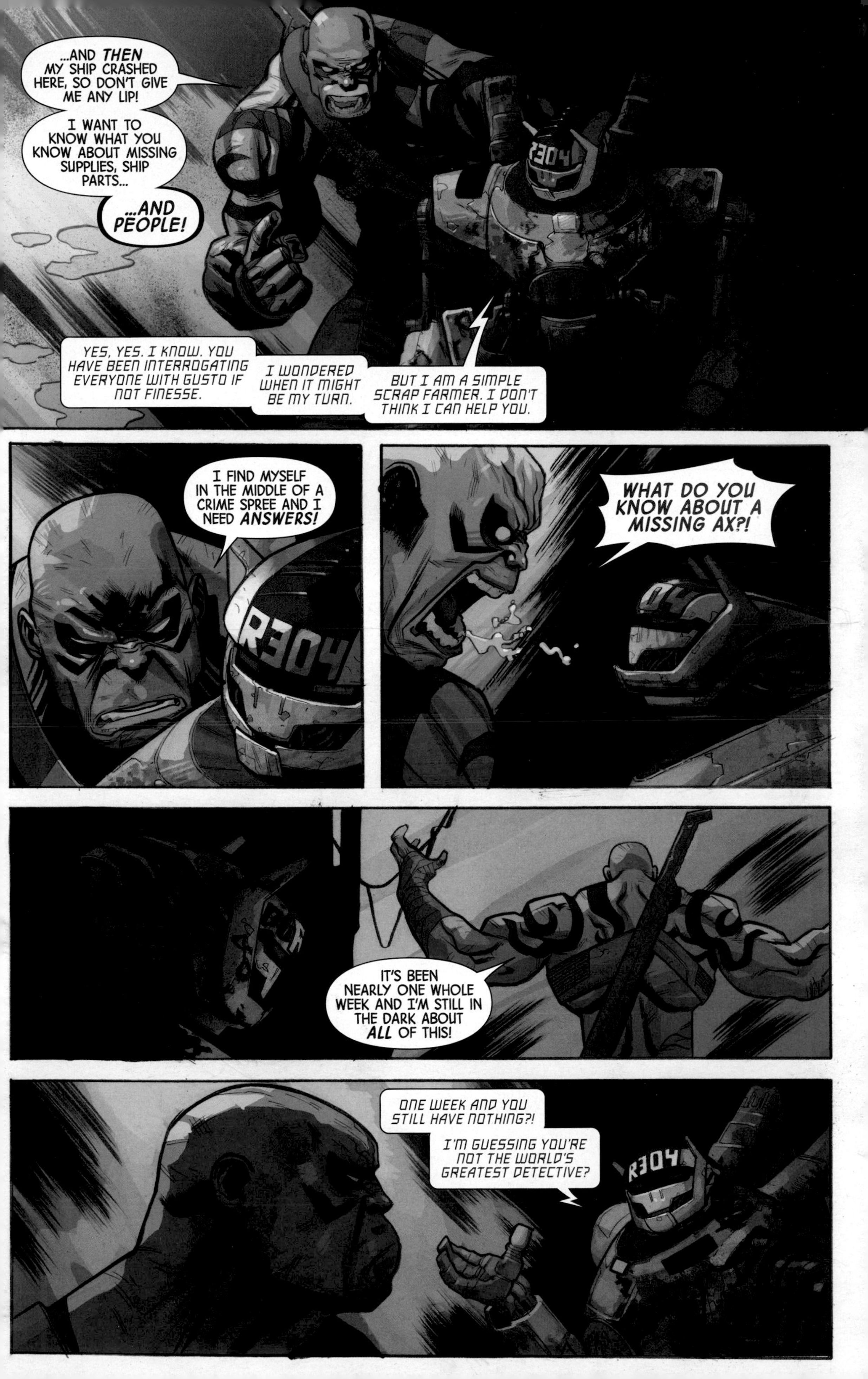
...AND THEN MY SHIP CRASHED HERE, SO DON'T GIVE ME ANY LIP!
I WANT TO KNOW WHAT YOU KNOW ABOUT MISSING SUPPLIES, SHIP PARTS...
...AND PEOPLE!
YES, YES. I KNOW. YOU HAVE BEEN INTERROGATING EVERYONE WITH GUSTO IF NOT FINESSE.
I WONDERED WHEN IT MIGHT BE MY TURN.
BUT I AM A SIMPLE SCRAP FARMER. I DON'T THINK I CAN HELP YOU.
I FIND MYSELF IN THE MIDDLE OF A CRIME SPREE AND I NEED ANSWERS!
R304
WHAT DO YOU KNOW ABOUT A MISSING AX?!
IT'S BEEN NEARLY ONE WHOLE WEEK AND I'M STILL IN THE DARK ABOUT ALL OF THIS!
ONE WEEK AND YOU STILL HAVE NOTHING?!
I'M GUESSING YOU'RE NOT THE WORLD'S GREATEST DETECTIVE?

THIS ENTIRE CITY HAS BECOME A GHOST TOWN. THE FEW PEOPLE THAT HAVEN'T DISAPPEARED REMAIN INDOORS.

SHEET METAL MISSING FROM BUILDINGS. GARBAGE IS LITTERING THE STREETS. THIS HOUSE IS MISSING ENTIRE WALLS!

IT'S AS IF SOMEONE IS STEALING THE ENTIRE CITY FROM UNDER YOUR NOSE!

AH-HA! IF IT WAS UNDER MY NOSE, I WOULD SEE IT HAPPENING AND DESTROY THE COWARDLY THIEVES!

PERHAPS YOU DON'T KNOW ANYTHING AFTER ALL.

I CAN'T EVEN TELL IF YOU'RE SERIOUS RIGHT NOW.

I AM DRAX THE DESTROYER! I AM ALWAYS SERIOUS! AND RIGHT NOW, I NEED ANSWERS!

I KNOW THE THUGS I FOUGHT ARE BEHIND ALL THIS, TELL ME WHO THEY ARE! TELL ME WHAT YOU KNOW OF THEM!!

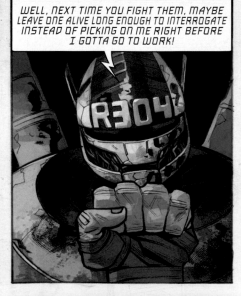

WELL, NEXT TIME YOU FIGHT THEM, MAYBE LEAVE ONE ALIVE LONG ENOUGH TO INTERROGATE INSTEAD OF PICKING ON ME RIGHT BEFORE I GOTTA GO TO WORK!

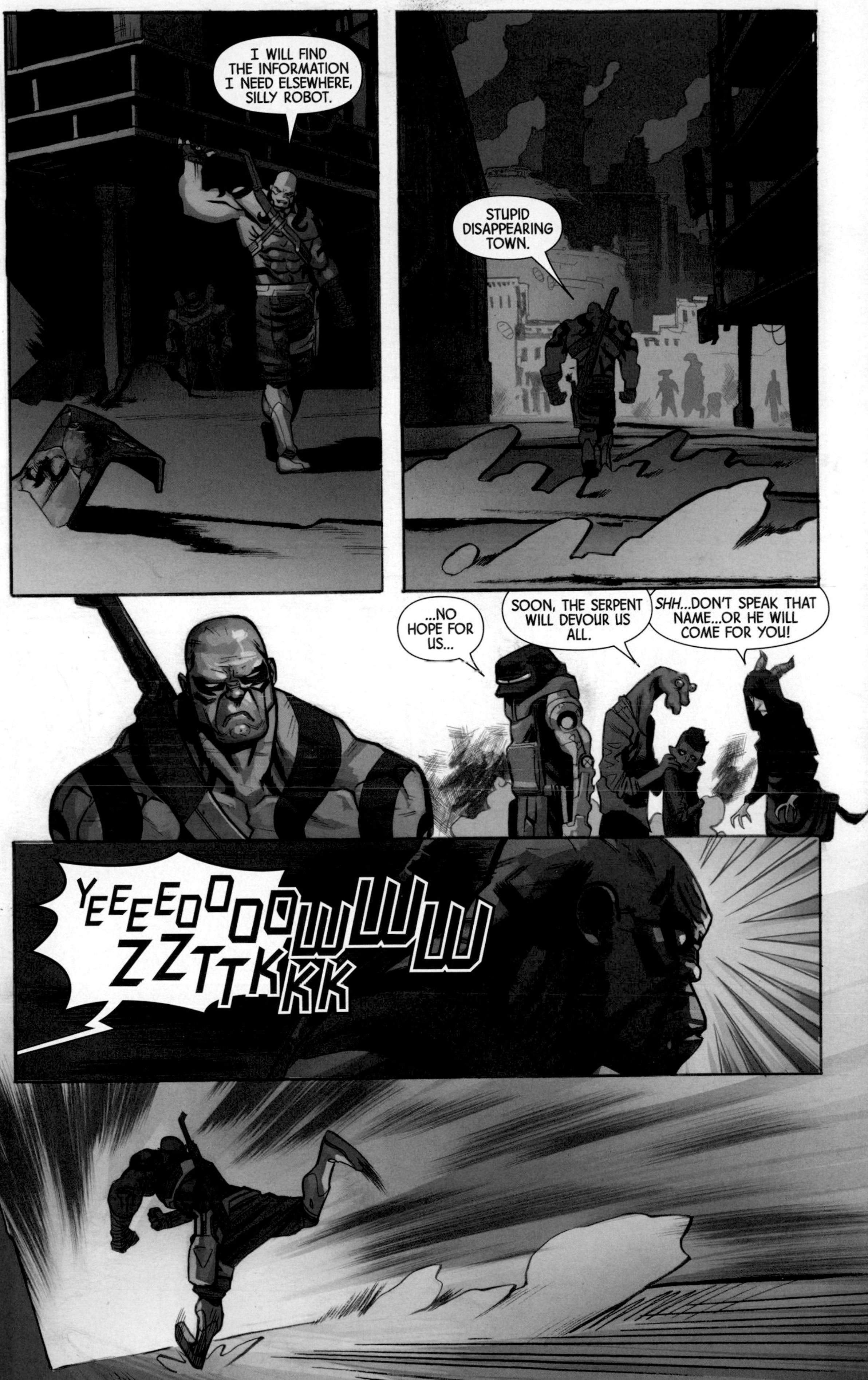

I WILL FIND THE INFORMATION I NEED ELSEWHERE, SILLY ROBOT.
STUPID DISAPPEARING TOWN.
...NO HOPE FOR US...
SOON, THE SERPENT WILL DEVOUR US ALL.
SHH...DON'T SPEAK THAT NAME...OR HE WILL COME FOR YOU!
YEEEOOOOWWWW
ZZTTKKK

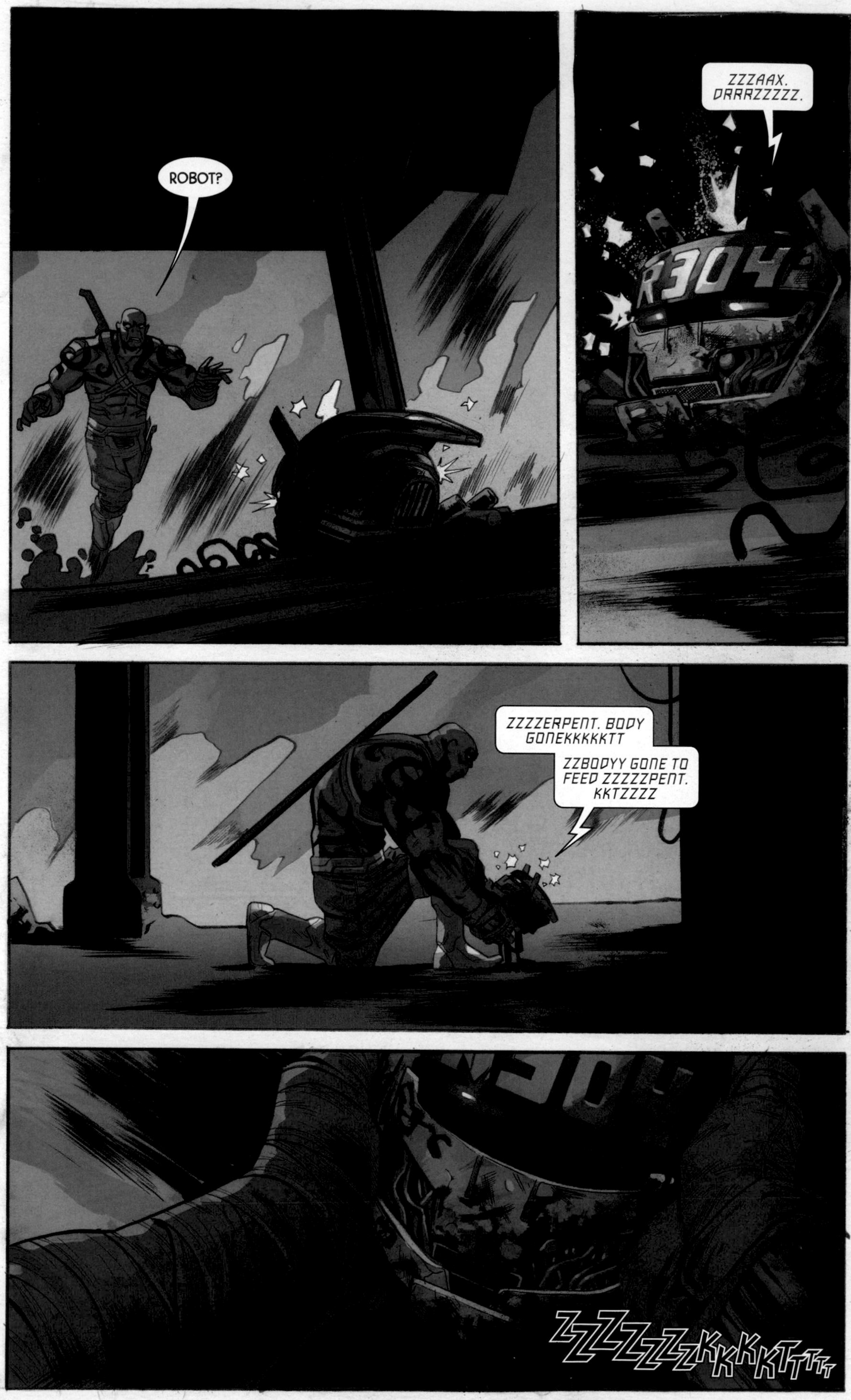
ROBOT?
ZZZAAX. DRRRZZZZZ.
ZZZZERPENT. BODY GONEKKKKKKTT
ZZBODYY GONE TO FEED ZZZZZPENT. KKTZZZZ
ZZZZZZZKKKKKTTTTT

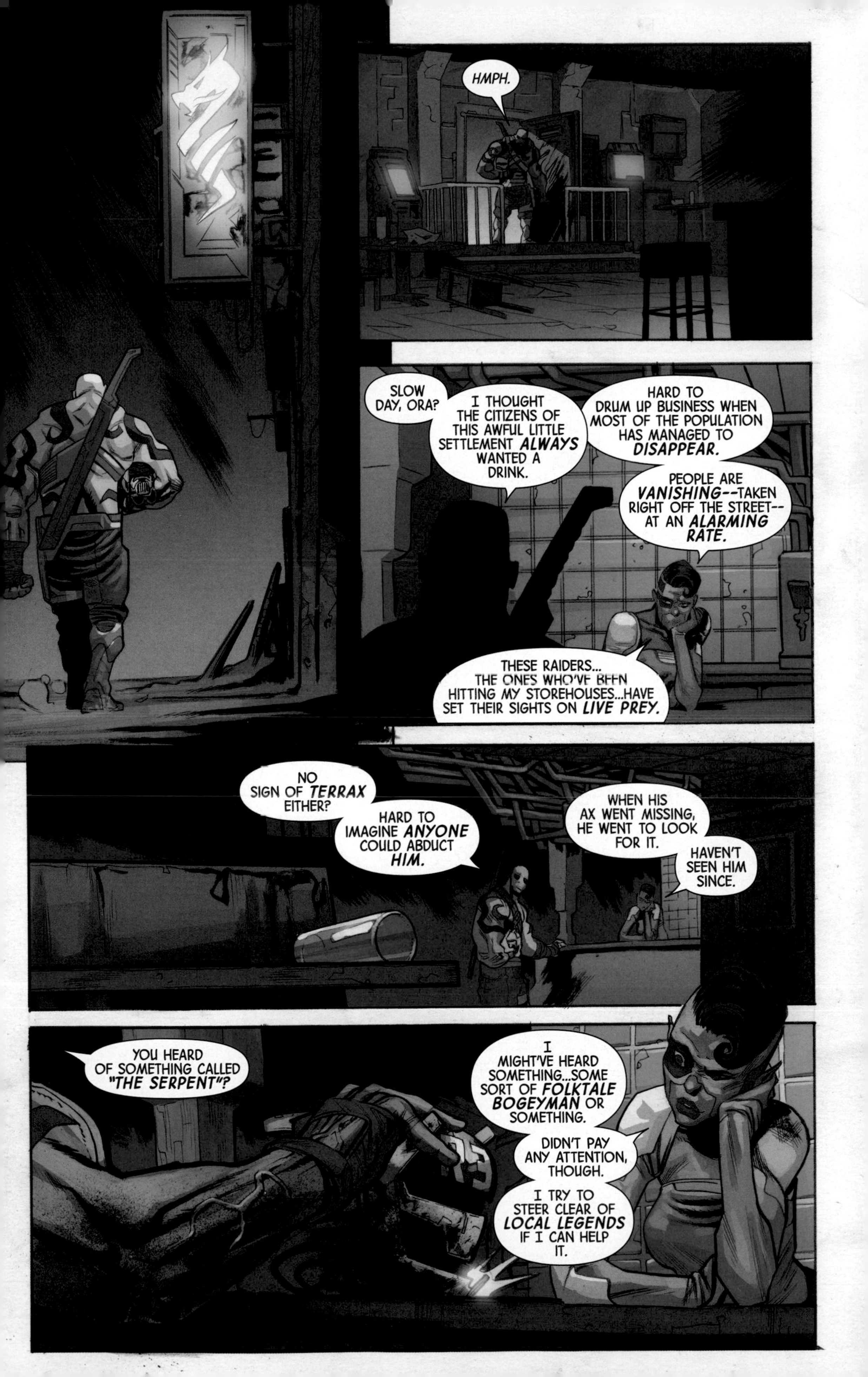
HMPH.
SLOW DAY, ORA?
I THOUGHT THE CITIZENS OF THIS AWFUL LITTLE SETTLEMENT ALWAYS WANTED A DRINK.
HARD TO DRUM UP BUSINESS WHEN MOST OF THE POPULATION HAS MANAGED TO DISAPPEAR.
PEOPLE ARE VANISHING--TAKEN RIGHT OFF THE STREET--AT AN ALARMING RATE.
THESE RAIDERS... THE ONES WHO'VE BEEN HITTING MY STOREHOUSES...HAVE SET THEIR SIGHTS ON LIVE PREY.
NO SIGN OF TERRAX EITHER?
HARD TO IMAGINE ANYONE COULD ABDUCT HIM.
WHEN HIS AX WENT MISSING, HE WENT TO LOOK FOR IT.
HAVEN'T SEEN HIM SINCE.
YOU HEARD OF SOMETHING CALLED "THE SERPENT"?
I MIGHT'VE HEARD SOMETHING...SOME SORT OF FOLKTALE BOGEYMAN OR SOMETHING.
DIDN'T PAY ANY ATTENTION, THOUGH.
I TRY TO STEER CLEAR OF LOCAL LEGENDS IF I CAN HELP IT.

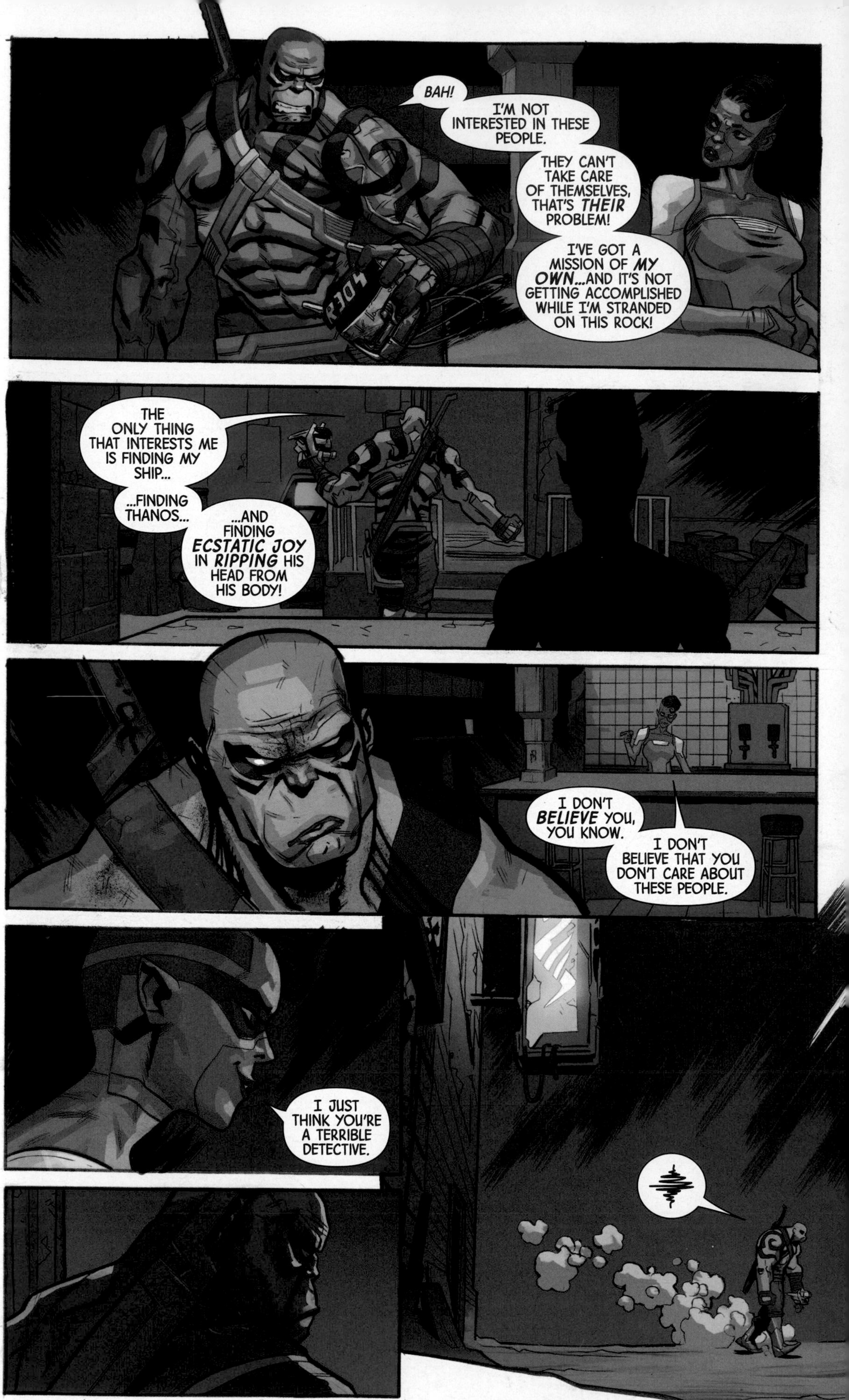

BAH!
I'M NOT INTERESTED IN THESE PEOPLE.
THEY CAN'T TAKE CARE OF THEMSELVES, THAT'S THEIR PROBLEM!
I'VE GOT A MISSION OF MY OWN...AND IT'S NOT GETTING ACCOMPLISHED WHILE I'M STRANDED ON THIS ROCK!
THE ONLY THING THAT INTERESTS ME IS FINDING MY SHIP...
...FINDING THANOS...
...AND FINDING ECSTATIC JOY IN RIPPING HIS HEAD FROM HIS BODY!
I DON'T BELIEVE YOU, YOU KNOW.
I DON'T BELIEVE THAT YOU DON'T CARE ABOUT THESE PEOPLE.
I JUST THINK YOU'RE A TERRIBLE DETECTIVE.

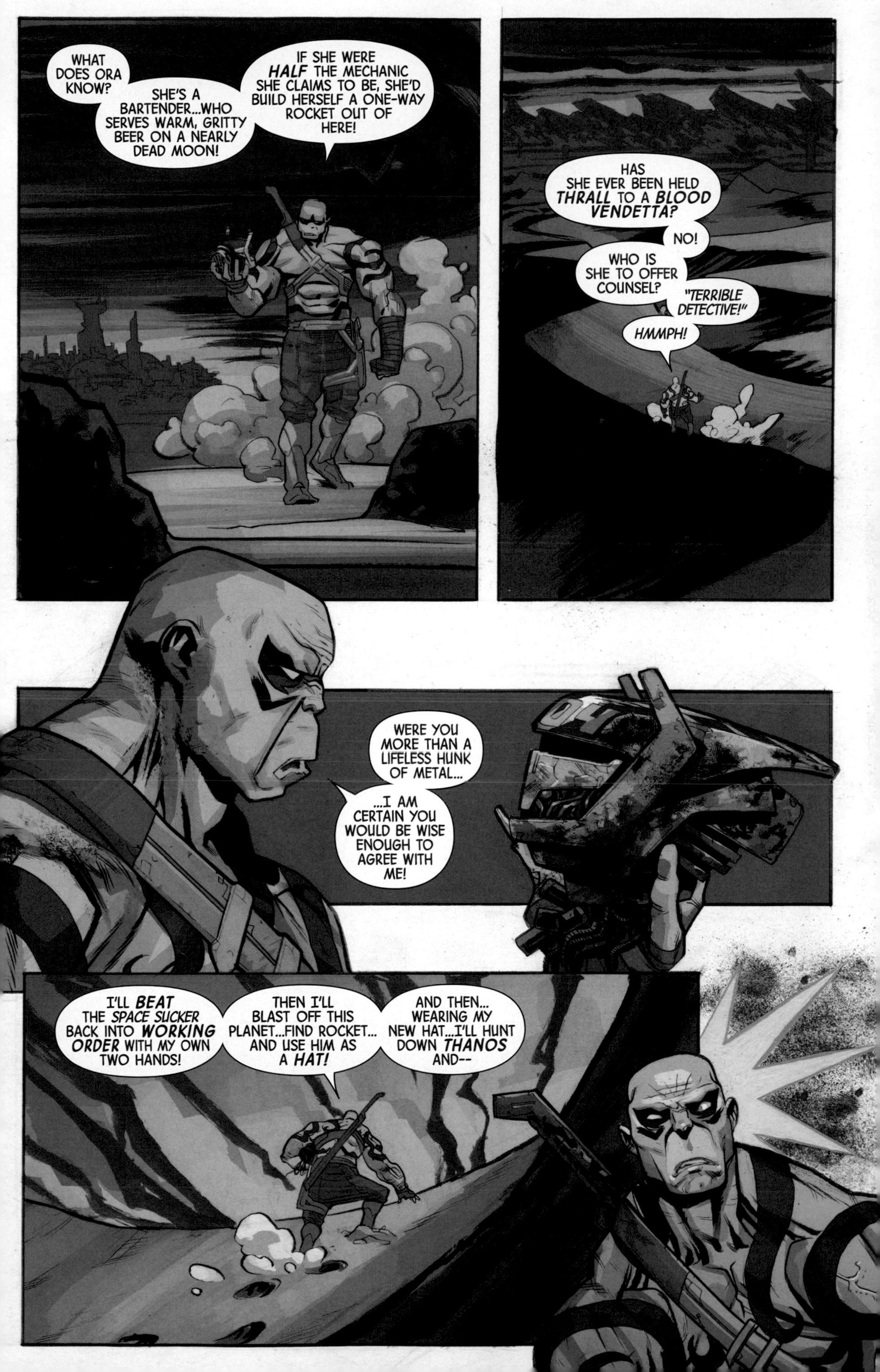
WHAT DOES ORA KNOW?
SHE'S A BARTENDER...WHO SERVES WARM, GRITTY BEER ON A NEARLY DEAD MOON!
IF SHE WERE HALF THE MECHANIC SHE CLAIMS TO BE, SHE'D BUILD HERSELF A ONE-WAY ROCKET OUT OF HERE!
HAS SHE EVER BEEN HELD THRALL TO A BLOOD VENDETTA?
NO!
WHO IS SHE TO OFFER COUNSEL?
"TERRIBLE DETECTIVE!"
HMMPH!
WERE YOU MORE THAN A LIFELESS HUNK OF METAL...
...I AM CERTAIN YOU WOULD BE WISE ENOUGH TO AGREE WITH ME!
I'LL BEAT THE SPACE SUCKER BACK INTO WORKING ORDER WITH MY OWN TWO HANDS!
THEN I'LL BLAST OFF THIS PLANET...FIND ROCKET... AND USE HIM AS A HAT!
AND THEN... WEARING MY NEW HAT...I'LL HUNT DOWN THANOS AND--

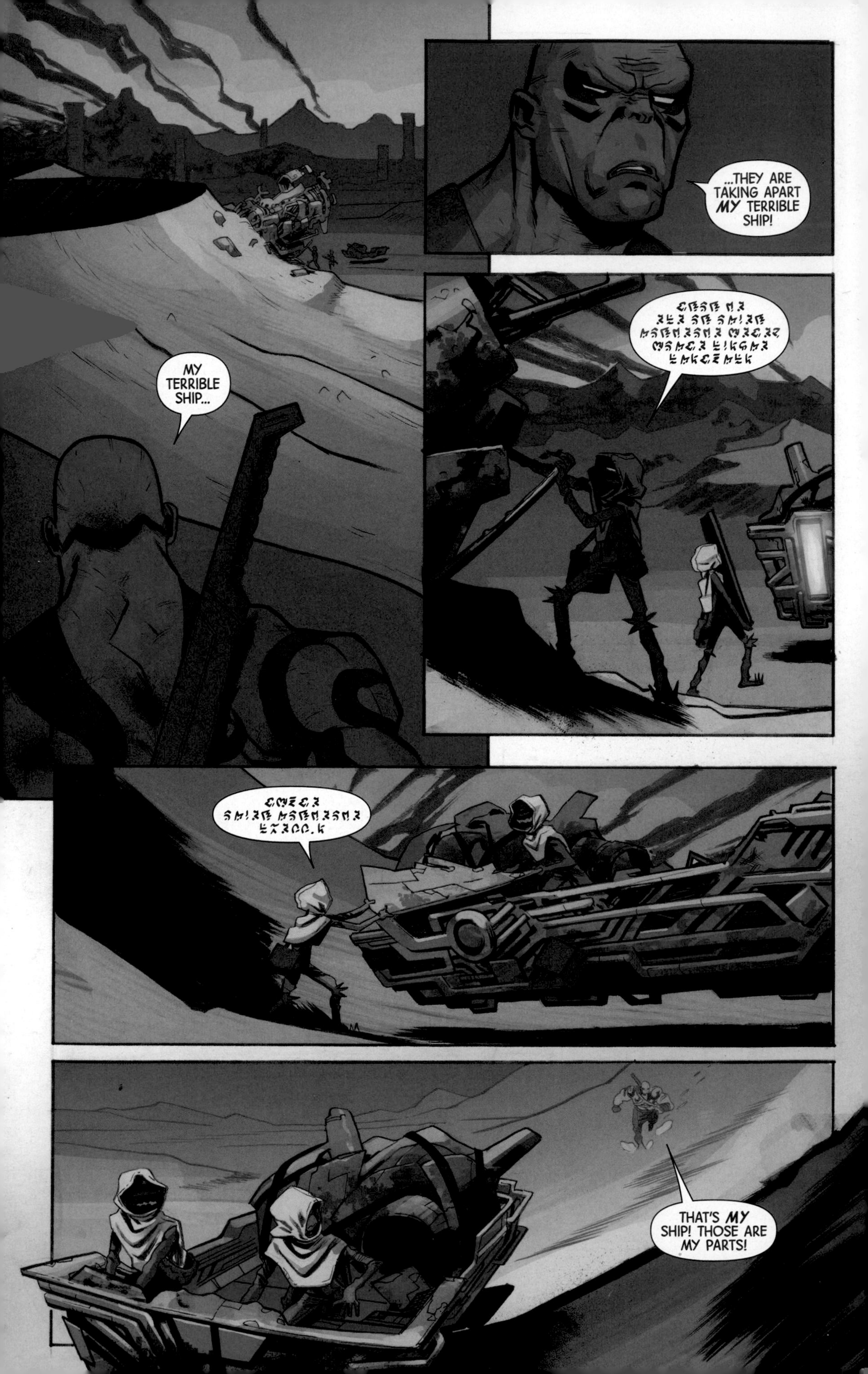
MY TERRIBLE SHIP...
...THEY ARE TAKING APART MY TERRIBLE SHIP!
THAT'S MY SHIP! THOSE ARE MY PARTS!

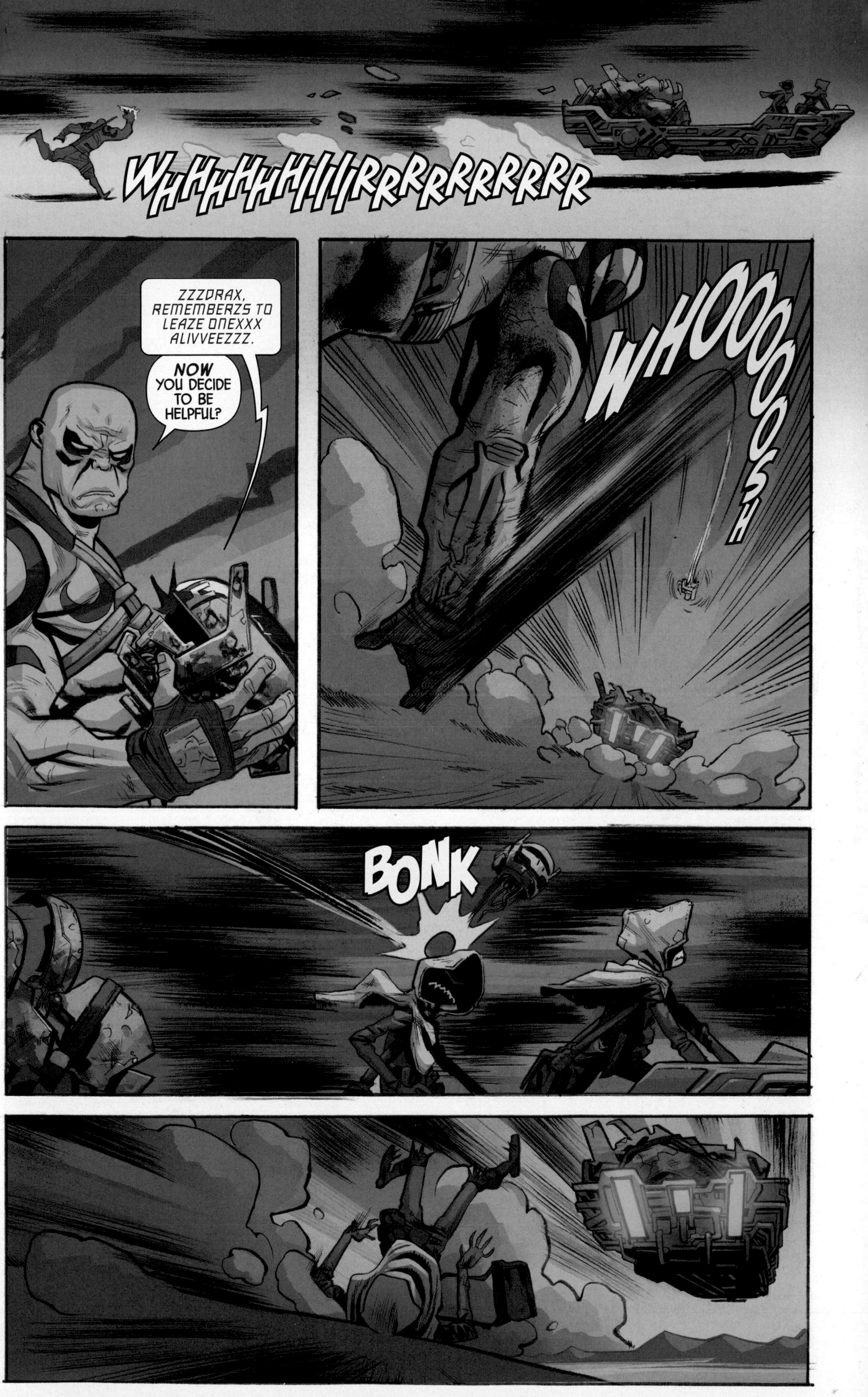
WHHHHHIIIIRRRRRRRRRR
ZZZDRAX, REMEMBERZS TO LEAZE ONEXXX ALIVVEEZZZ.
NOW YOU DECIDE TO BE HELPFUL?
WHOOOOOSH
BONK

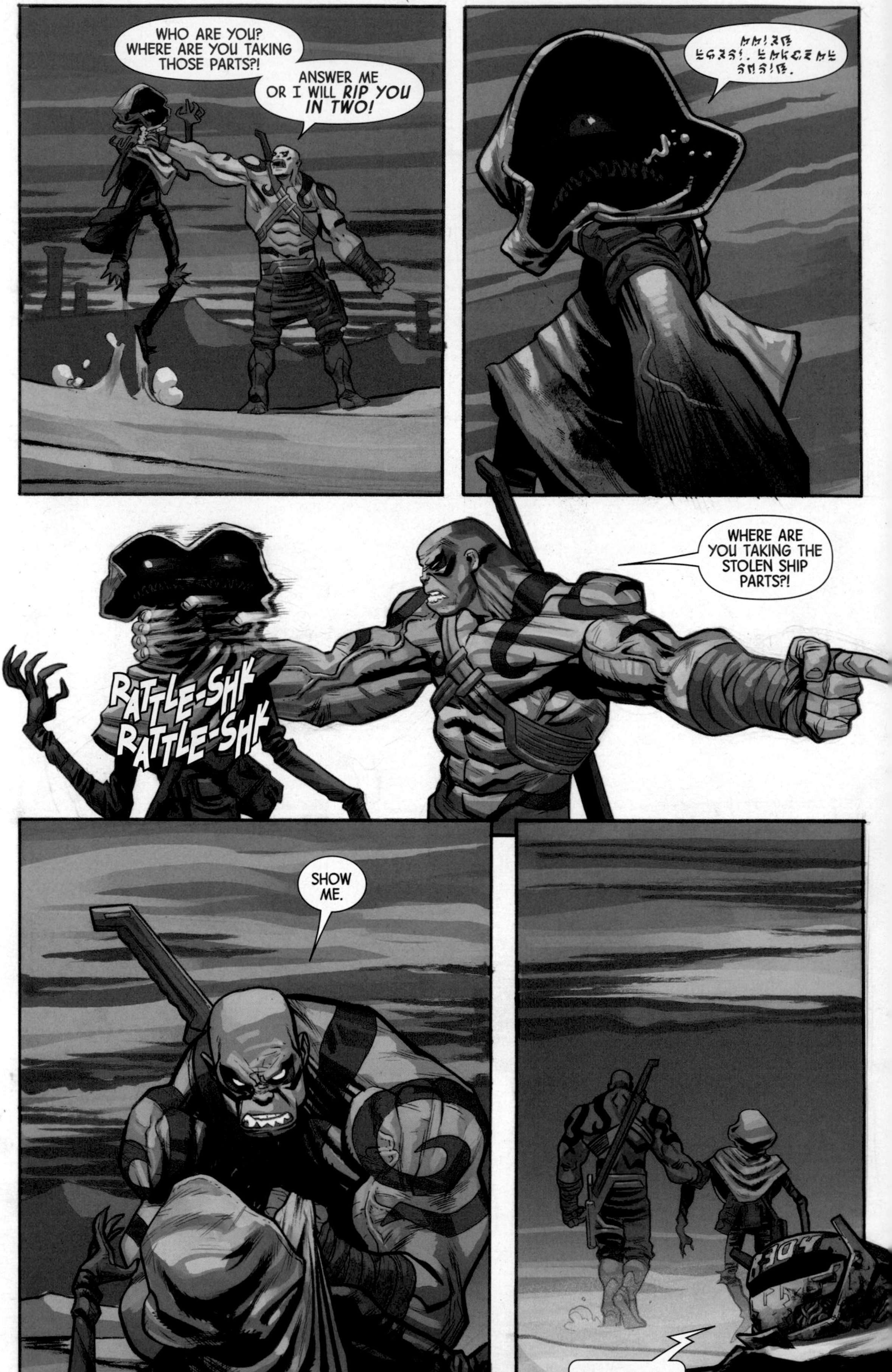
WHO ARE YOU? WHERE ARE YOU TAKING THOSE PARTS?!
ANSWER ME OR I WILL RIP YOU IN TWO!
WHERE ARE YOU TAKING THE STOLEN SHIP PARTS?!
RATTLE-SHK RATTLE-SHK
SHOW ME.
ZZZZERPENT. SSKKZZERS

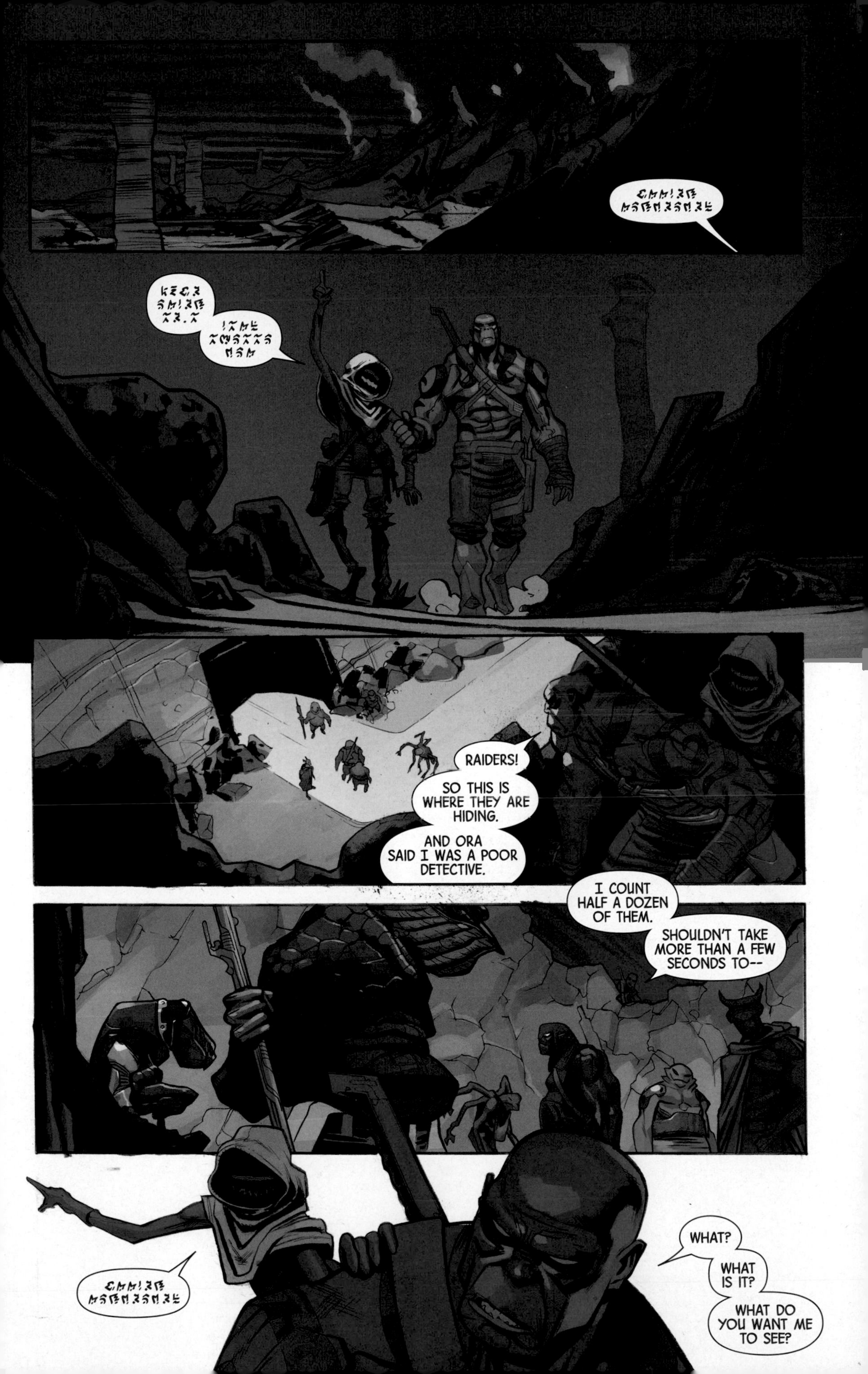

RAIDERS!
SO THIS IS WHERE THEY ARE HIDING.
AND ORA SAID I WAS A POOR DETECTIVE.
I COUNT HALF A DOZEN OF THEM.
SHOULDN'T TAKE MORE THAN A FEW SECONDS TO--
WHAT?
WHAT IS IT?
WHAT DO YOU WANT ME TO SEE?

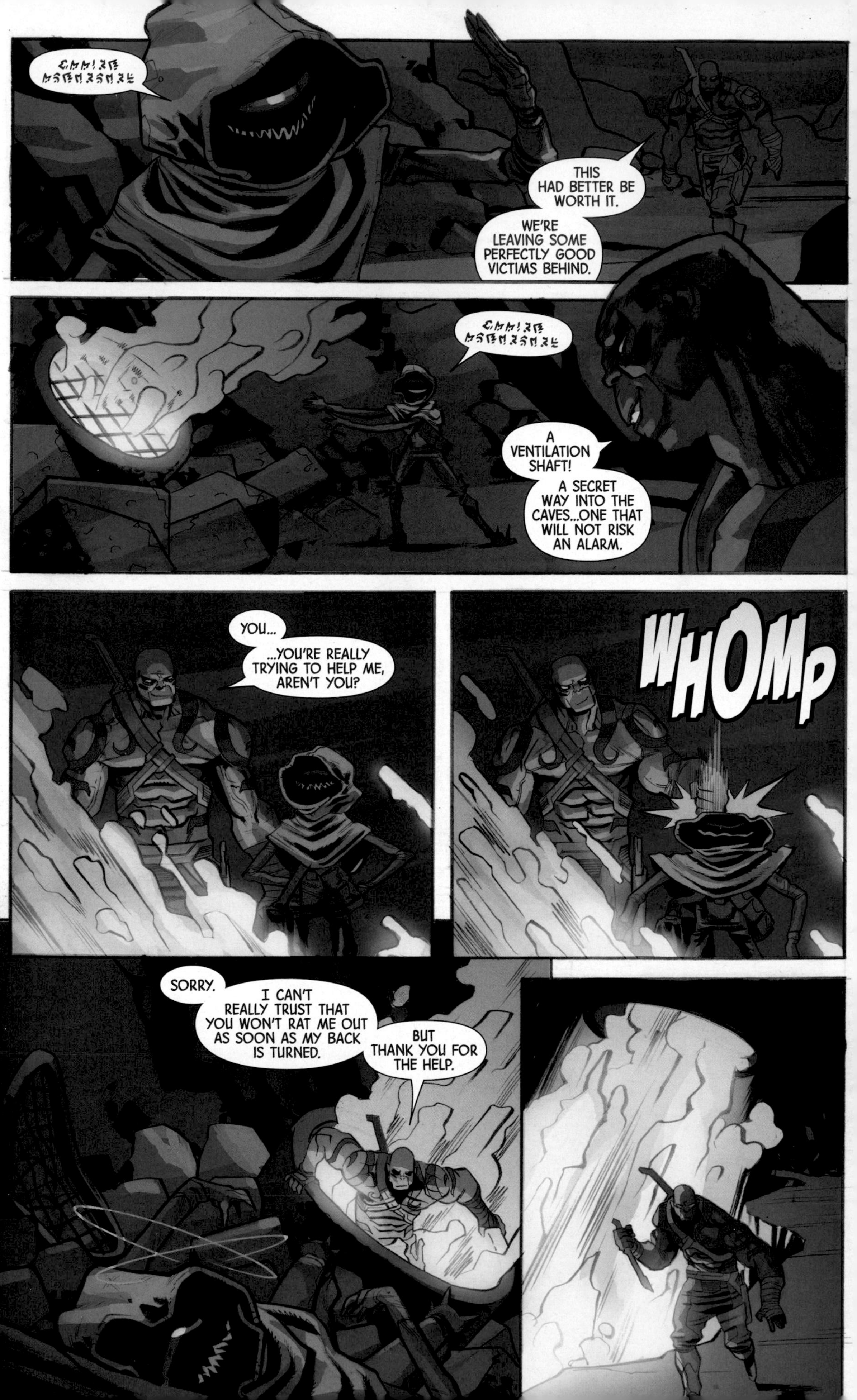
THIS HAD BETTER BE WORTH IT.
WE'RE LEAVING SOME PERFECTLY GOOD VICTIMS BEHIND.
A VENTILATION SHAFT!
A SECRET WAY INTO THE CAVES...ONE THAT WILL NOT RISK AN ALARM.
YOU...
...YOU'RE REALLY TRYING TO HELP ME, AREN'T YOU?
WHOMP
SORRY.
I CAN'T REALLY TRUST THAT YOU WON'T RAT ME OUT AS SOON AS MY BACK IS TURNED.
BUT THANK YOU FOR THE HELP.

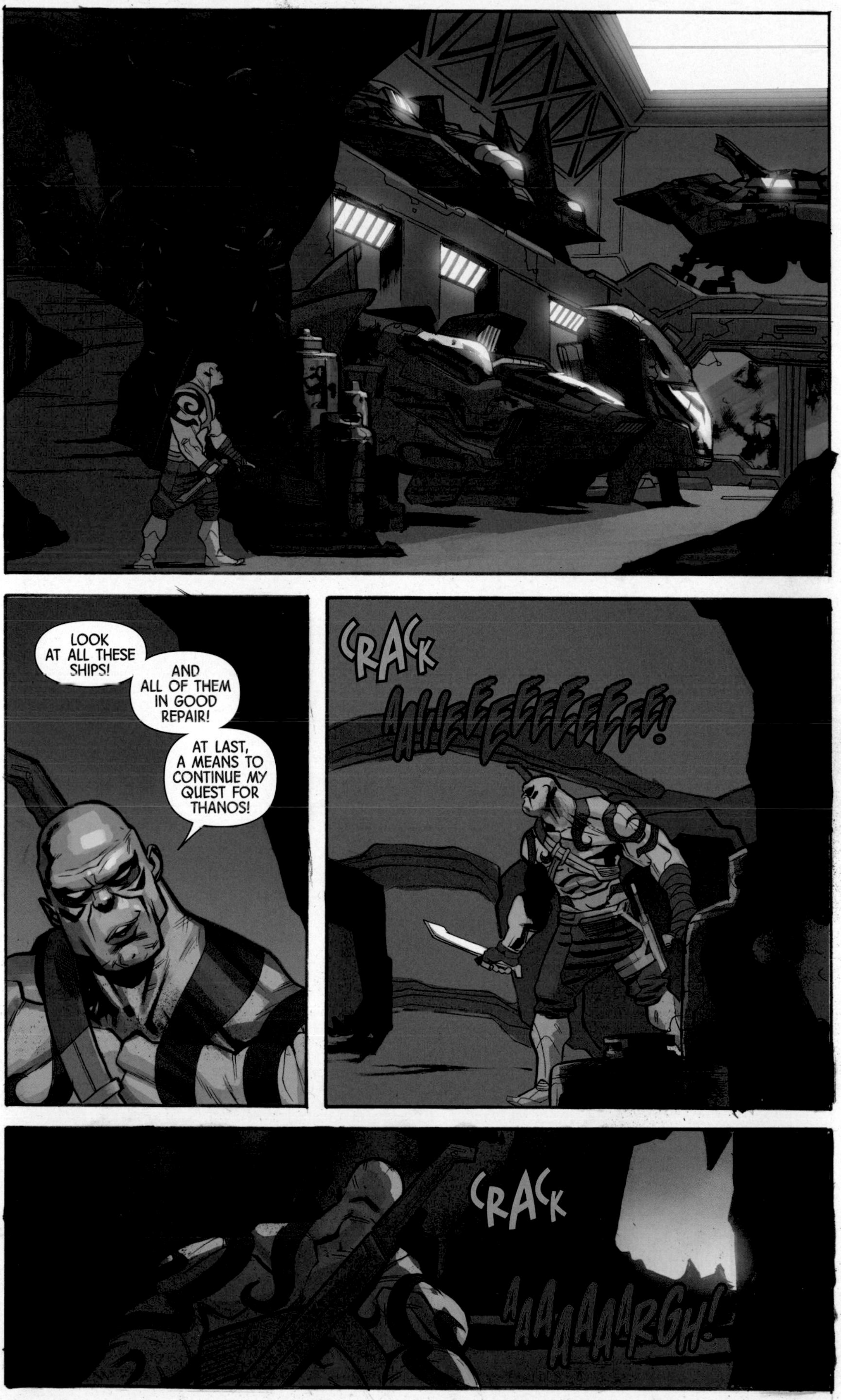
LOOK AT ALL THESE SHIPS!
AND ALL OF THEM IN GOOD REPAIR!
AT LAST, A MEANS TO CONTINUE MY QUEST FOR THANOS!
CRACK
AAIIEEEEEEEEEE!
CRACK
AAAAAAARGH!

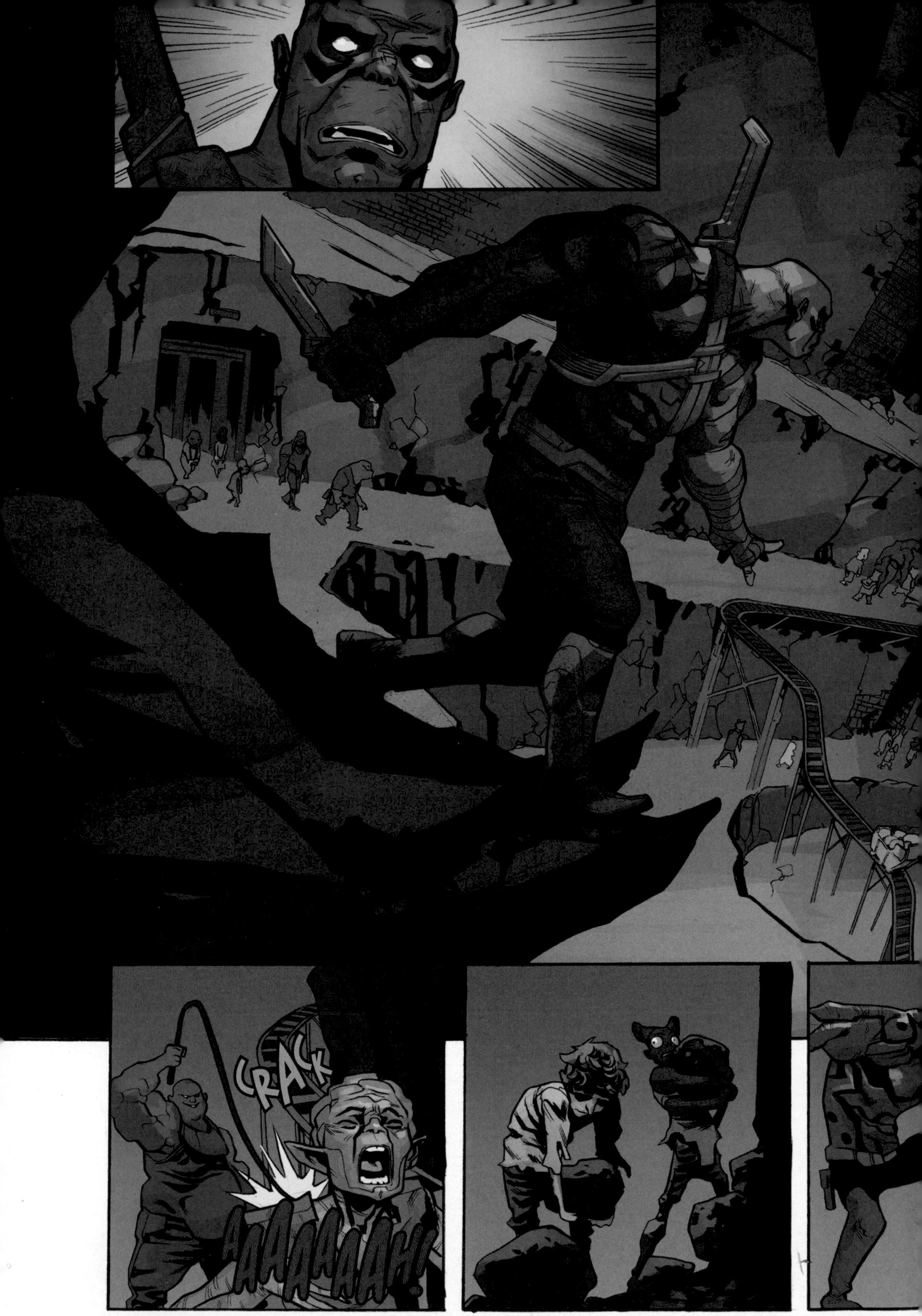
CRACK
AAAAAAAAAH!

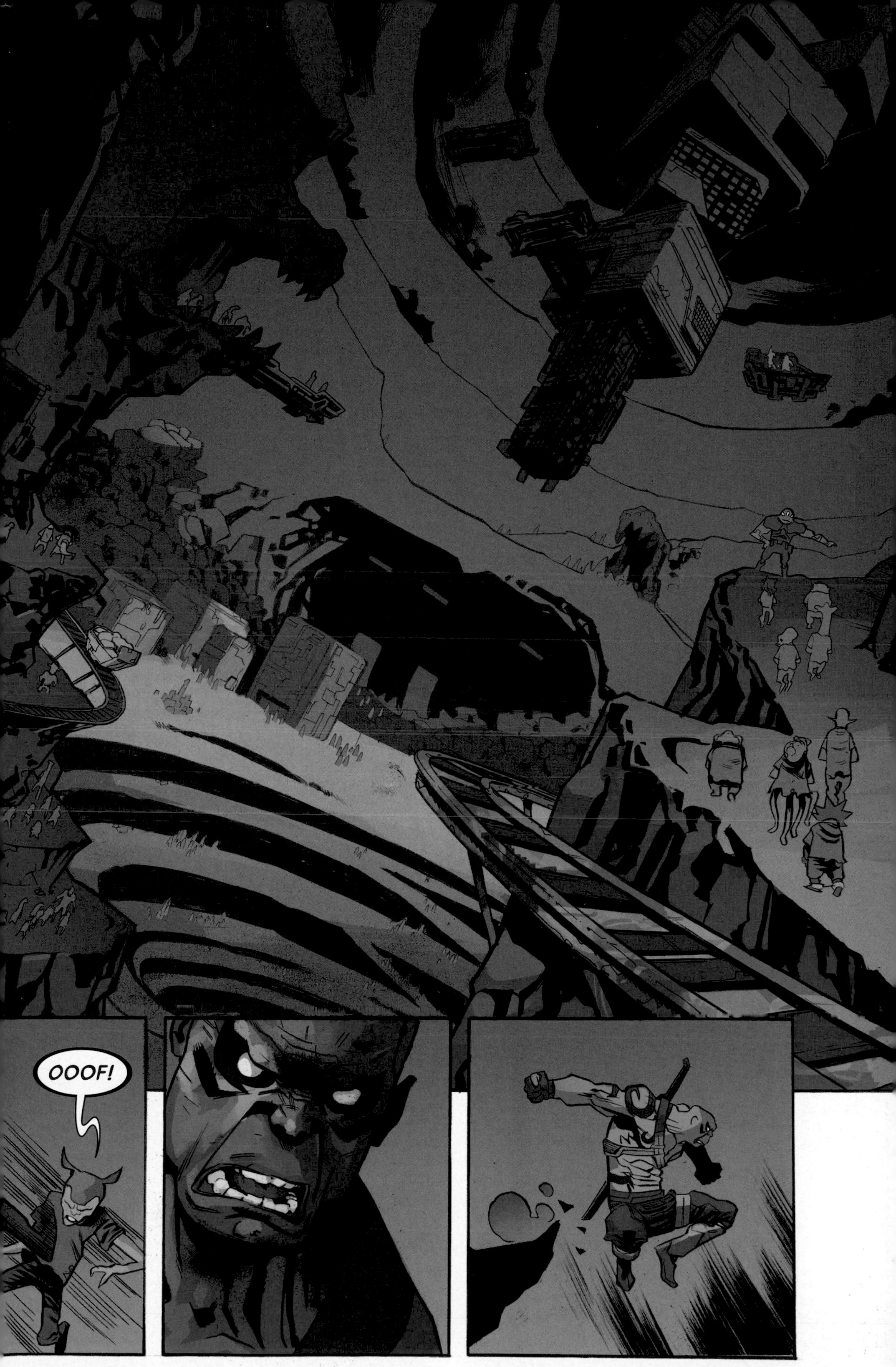
OOOF!

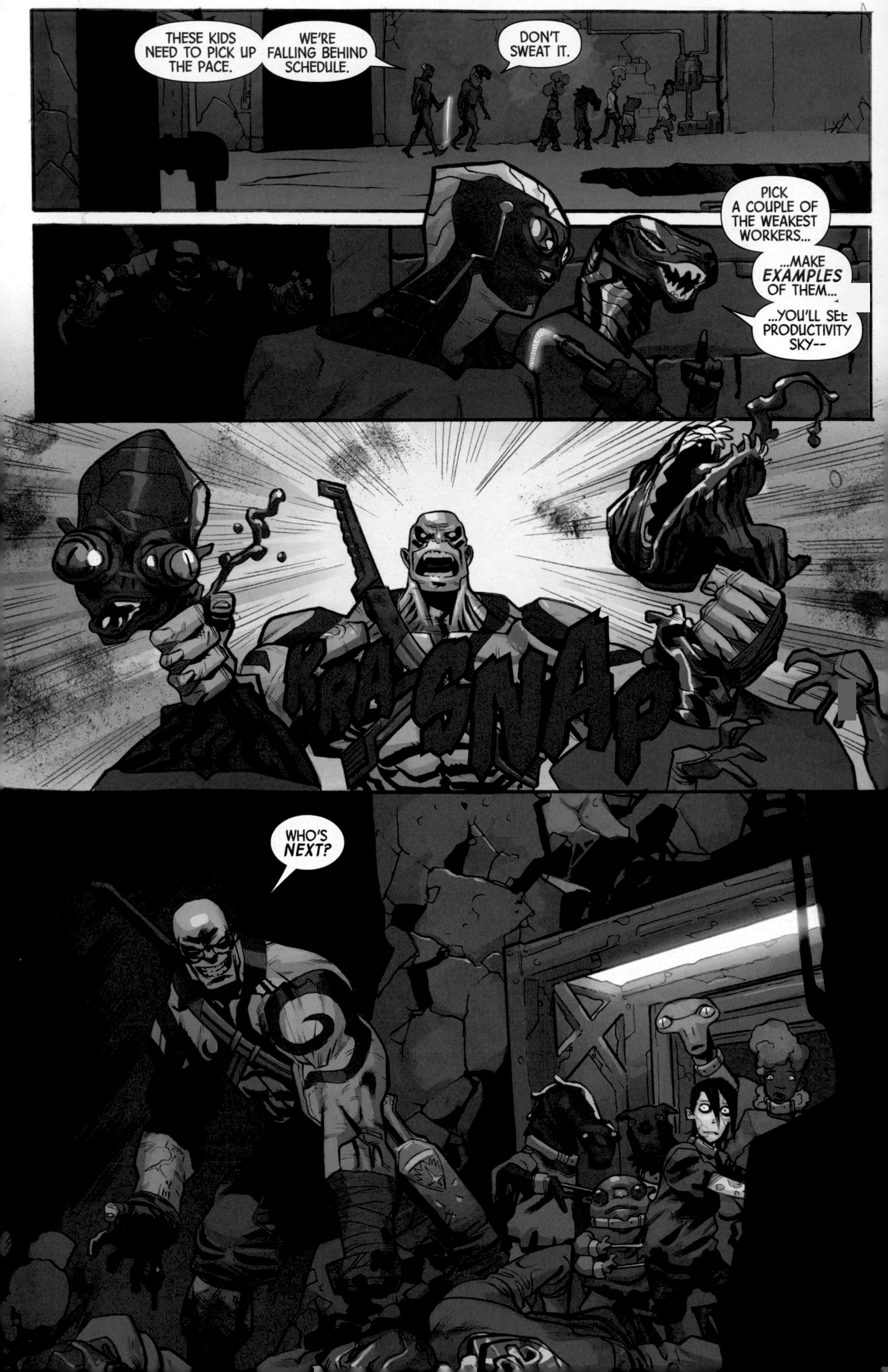
THESE KIDS NEED TO PICK UP THE PACE.
WE'RE FALLING BEHIND SCHEDULE.
DON'T SWEAT IT.
PICK A COUPLE OF THE WEAKEST WORKERS...
...MAKE *EXAMPLES* OF THEM...
...YOU'LL SEE PRODUCTIVITY SKY--
KRA-SNAP
WHO'S *NEXT?*

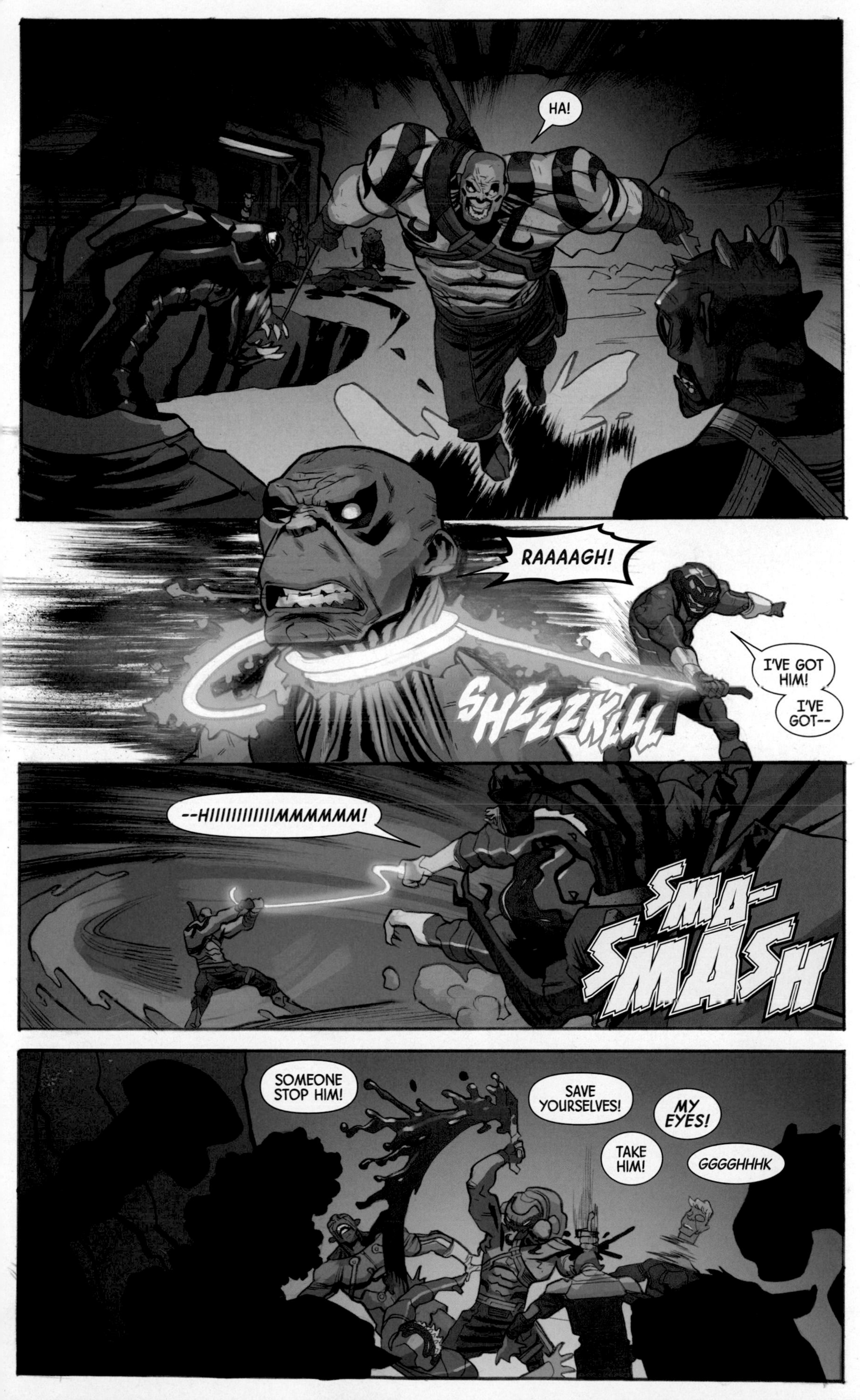
HA!
RAAAAGH!
SHZZZKLLL
I'VE GOT HIM!
I'VE GOT--
--HIIIIIIIIIIIMMMMMM!
SMA-SMASH
SOMEONE STOP HIM!
SAVE YOURSELVES!
MY EYES!
TAKE HIM!
GGGGHHHK

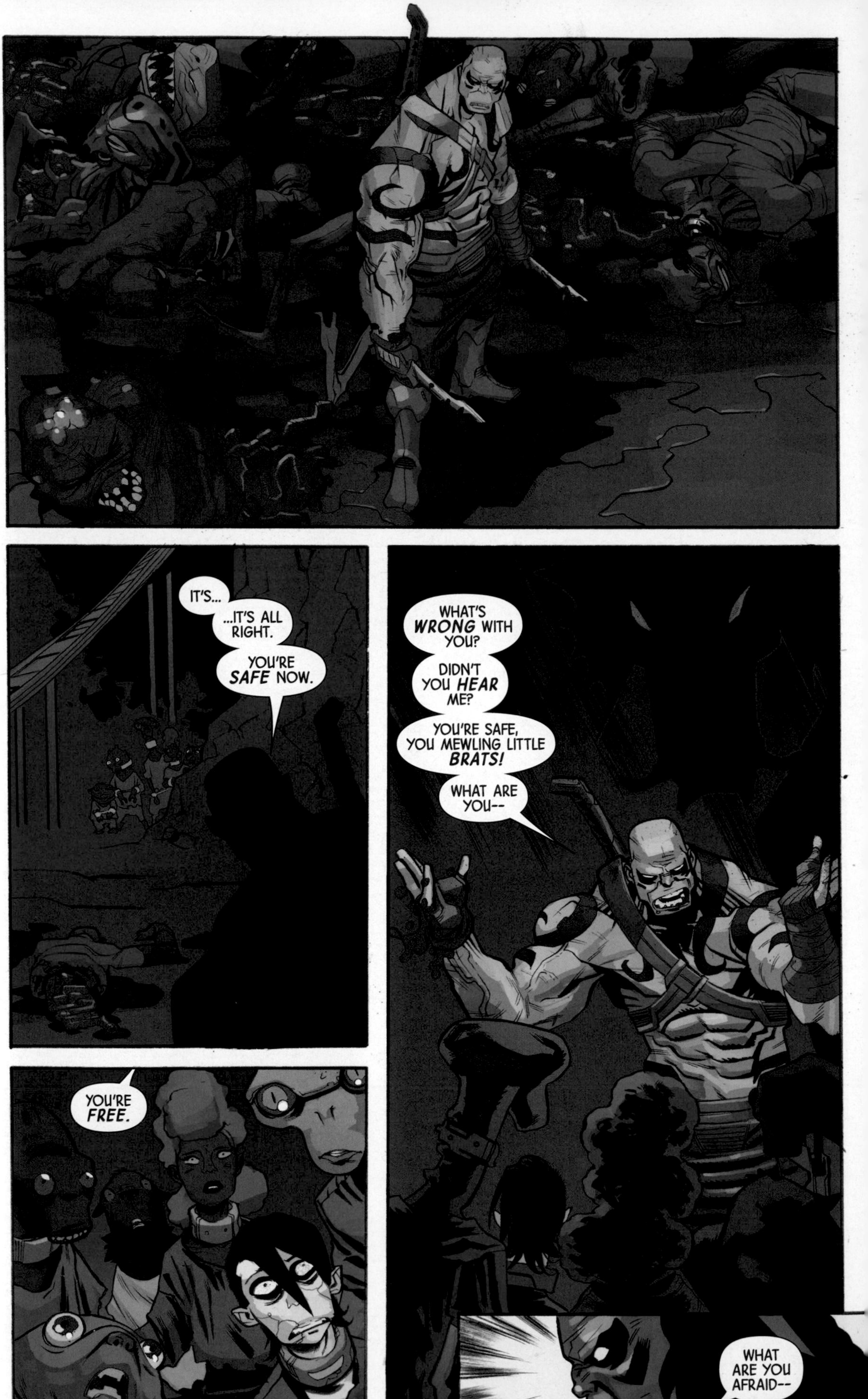
IT'S...
...IT'S ALL RIGHT.
YOU'RE SAFE NOW.
YOU'RE FREE.
WHAT'S WRONG WITH YOU?
DIDN'T YOU HEAR ME?
YOU'RE SAFE, YOU MEWLING LITTLE BRATS!
WHAT ARE YOU--
WHAT ARE YOU AFRAID--

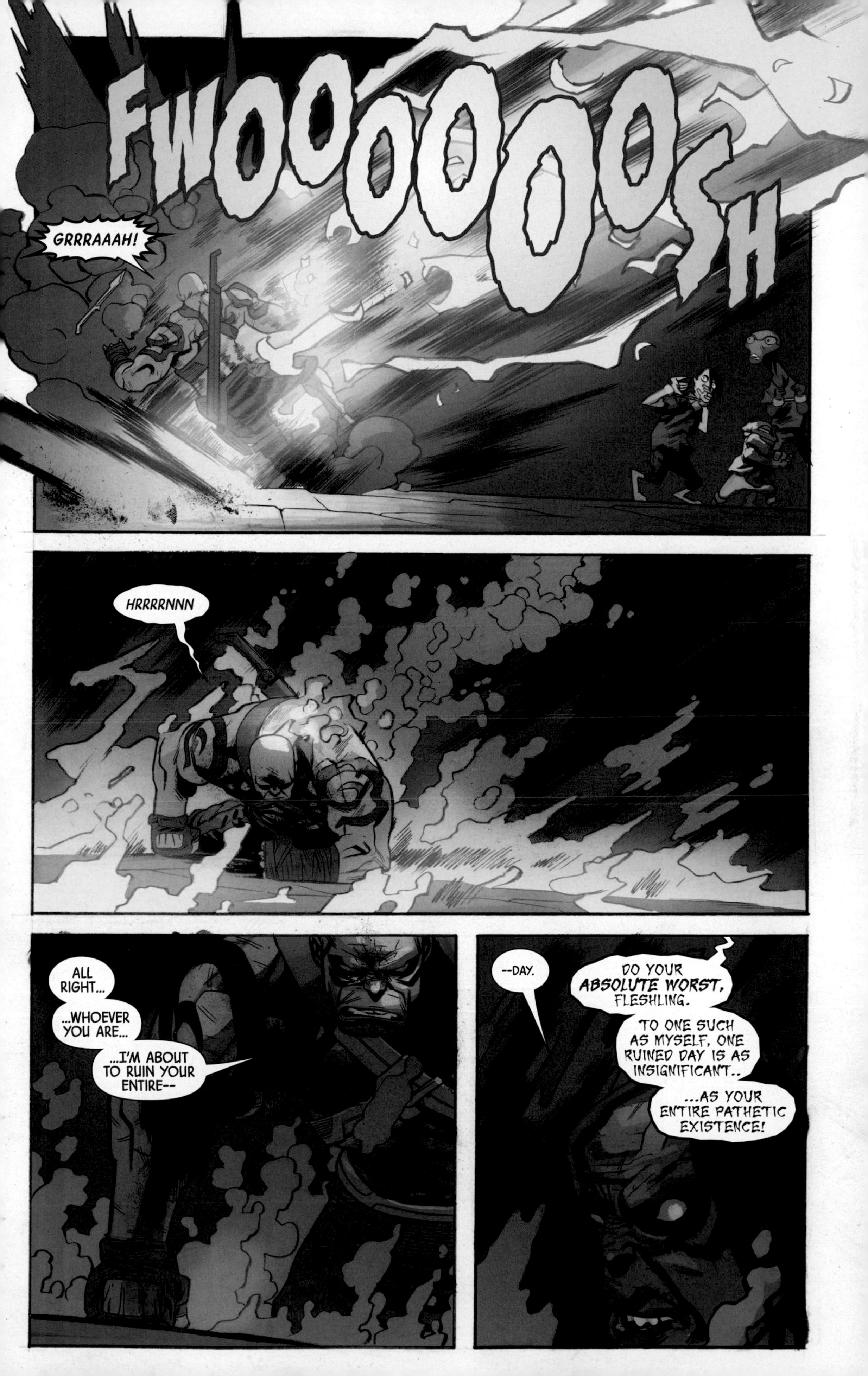
FWOOOOOOOSH
GRRRAAAH!
HRRRRNNN
ALL RIGHT...
...WHOEVER YOU ARE...
...I'M ABOUT TO RUIN YOUR ENTIRE--
--DAY.
DO YOUR ABSOLUTE WORST, FLESHLING.
TO ONE SUCH AS MYSELF, ONE RUINED DAY IS AS INSIGNIFICANT..
...AS YOUR ENTIRE PATHETIC EXISTENCE!

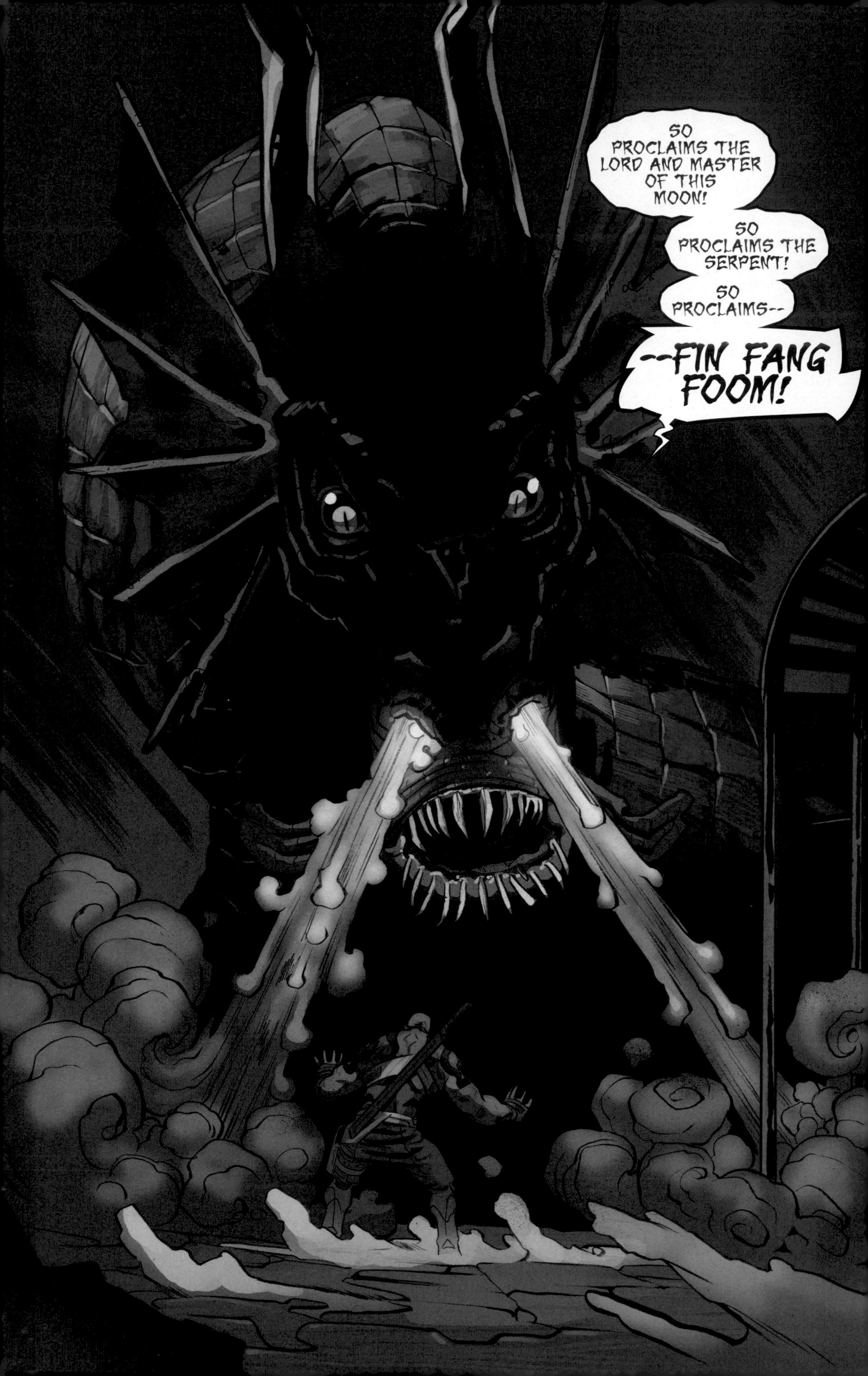
SO PROCLAIMS THE LORD AND MASTER OF THIS MOON!
SO PROCLAIMS THE SERPENT!
SO PROCLAIMS--
--FIN FANG FOOM!

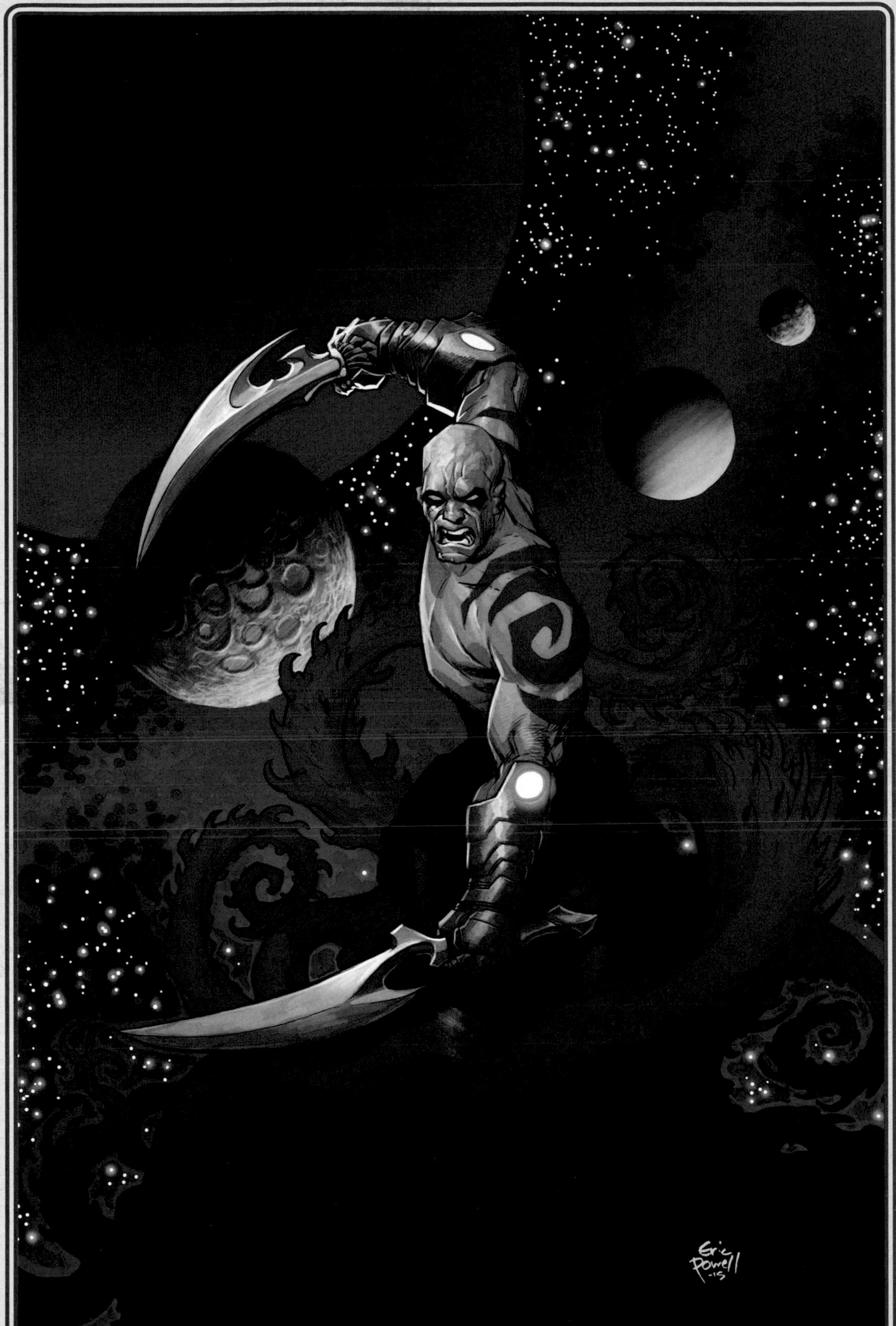
Eric Powell '15

No. 3 VARIANT BY

ERIC POWELL

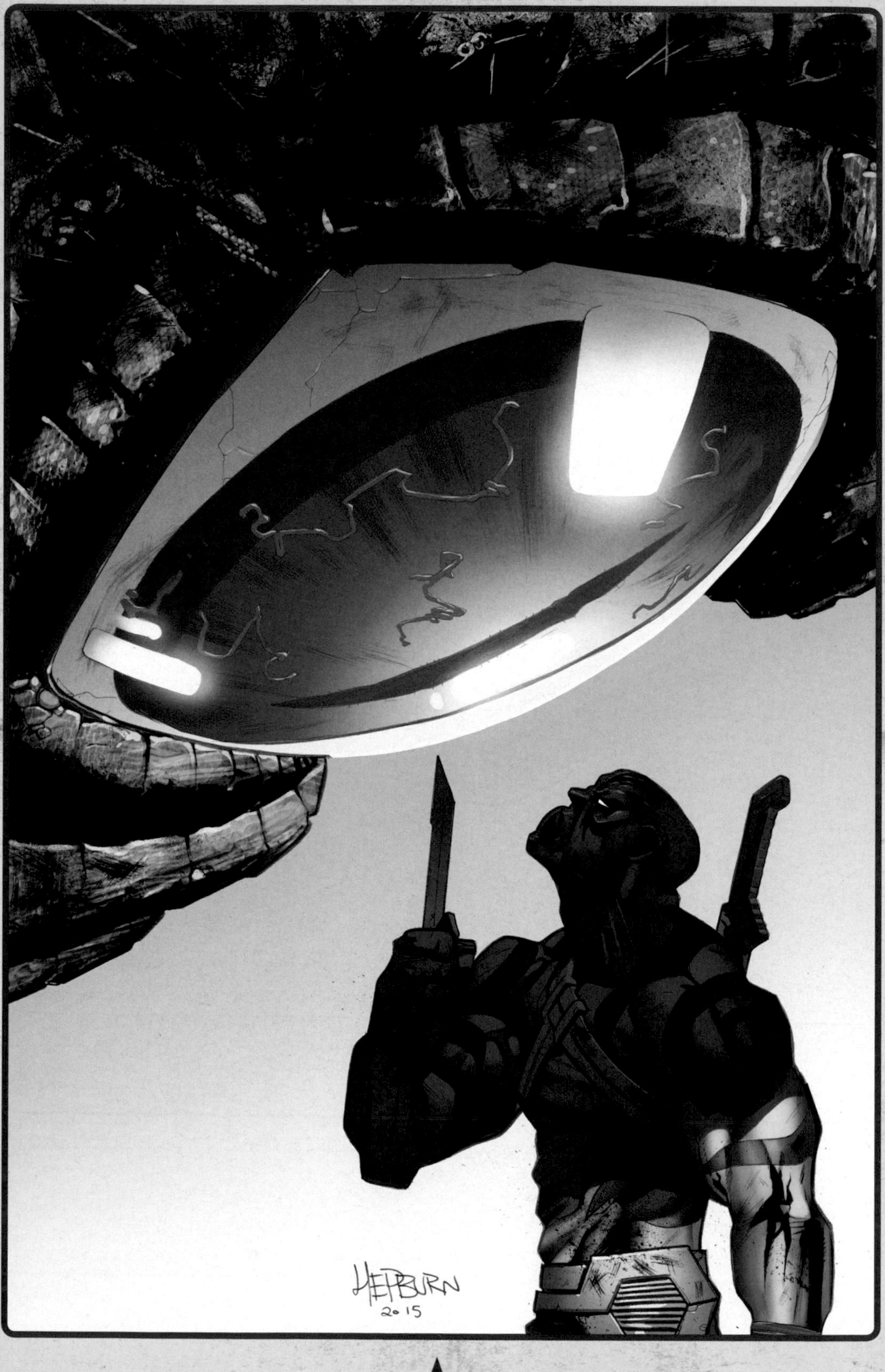
HEPBURN
2015

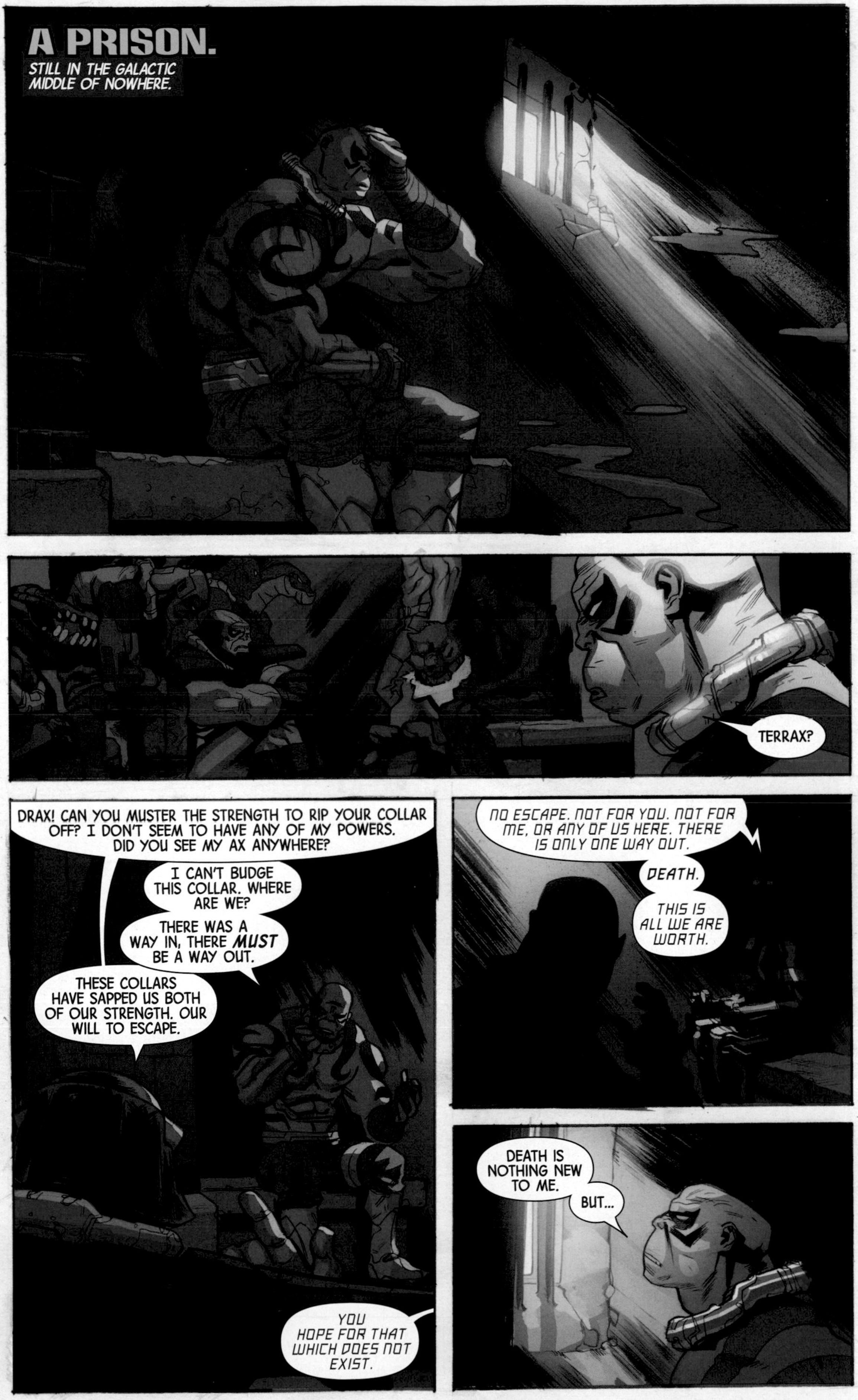
A PRISON.
STILL IN THE GALACTIC MIDDLE OF NOWHERE.
TERRAX?
DRAX! CAN YOU MUSTER THE STRENGTH TO RIP YOUR COLLAR OFF? I DON'T SEEM TO HAVE ANY OF MY POWERS. DID YOU SEE MY AX ANYWHERE?
I CAN'T BUDGE THIS COLLAR. WHERE ARE WE?
THERE WAS A WAY IN, THERE MUST BE A WAY OUT.
THESE COLLARS HAVE SAPPED US BOTH OF OUR STRENGTH. OUR WILL TO ESCAPE.
YOU HOPE FOR THAT WHICH DOES NOT EXIST.
NO ESCAPE. NOT FOR YOU. NOT FOR ME, OR ANY OF US HERE. THERE IS ONLY ONE WAY OUT.
DEATH.
THIS IS ALL WE ARE WORTH.
DEATH IS NOTHING NEW TO ME.
BUT...

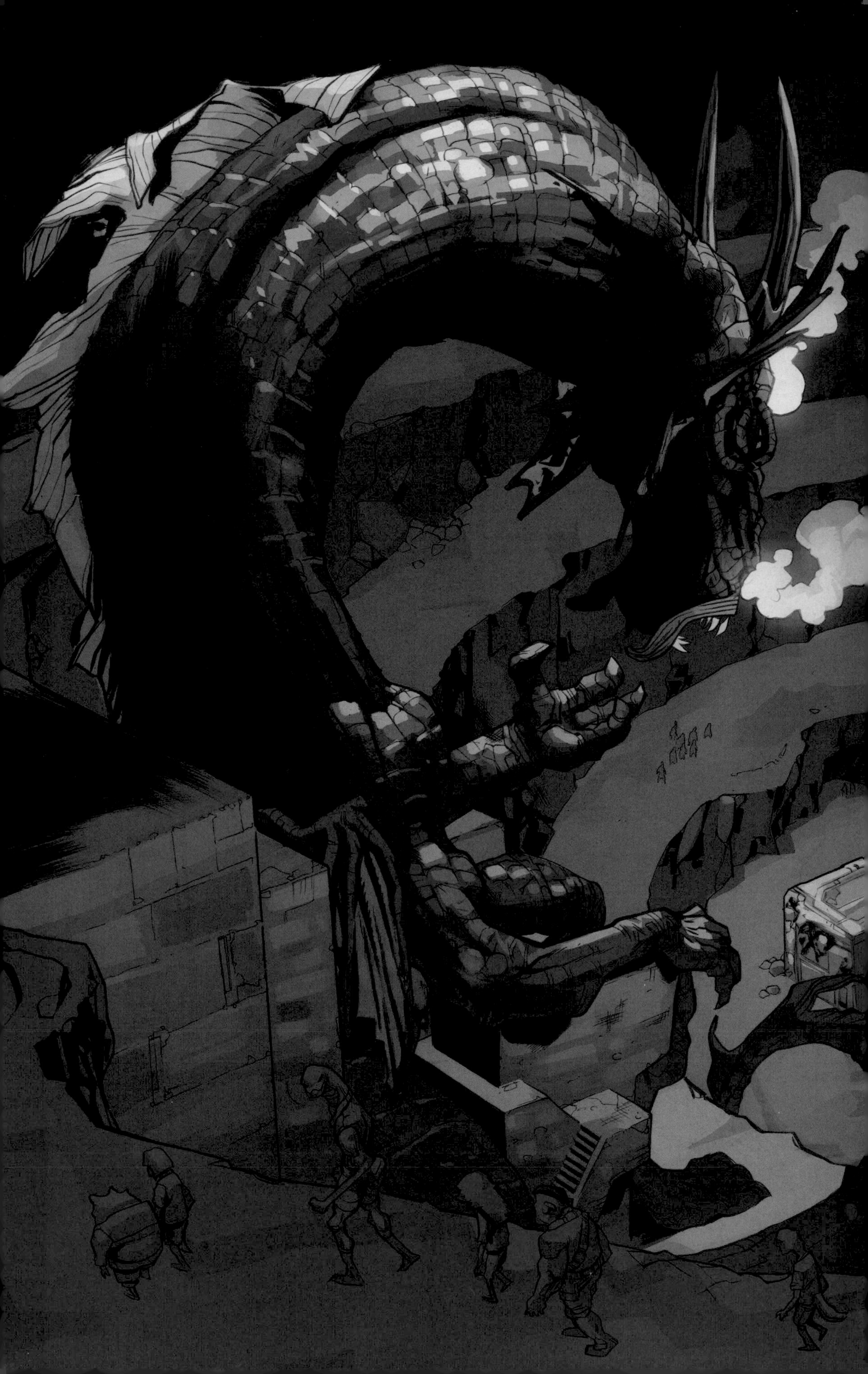

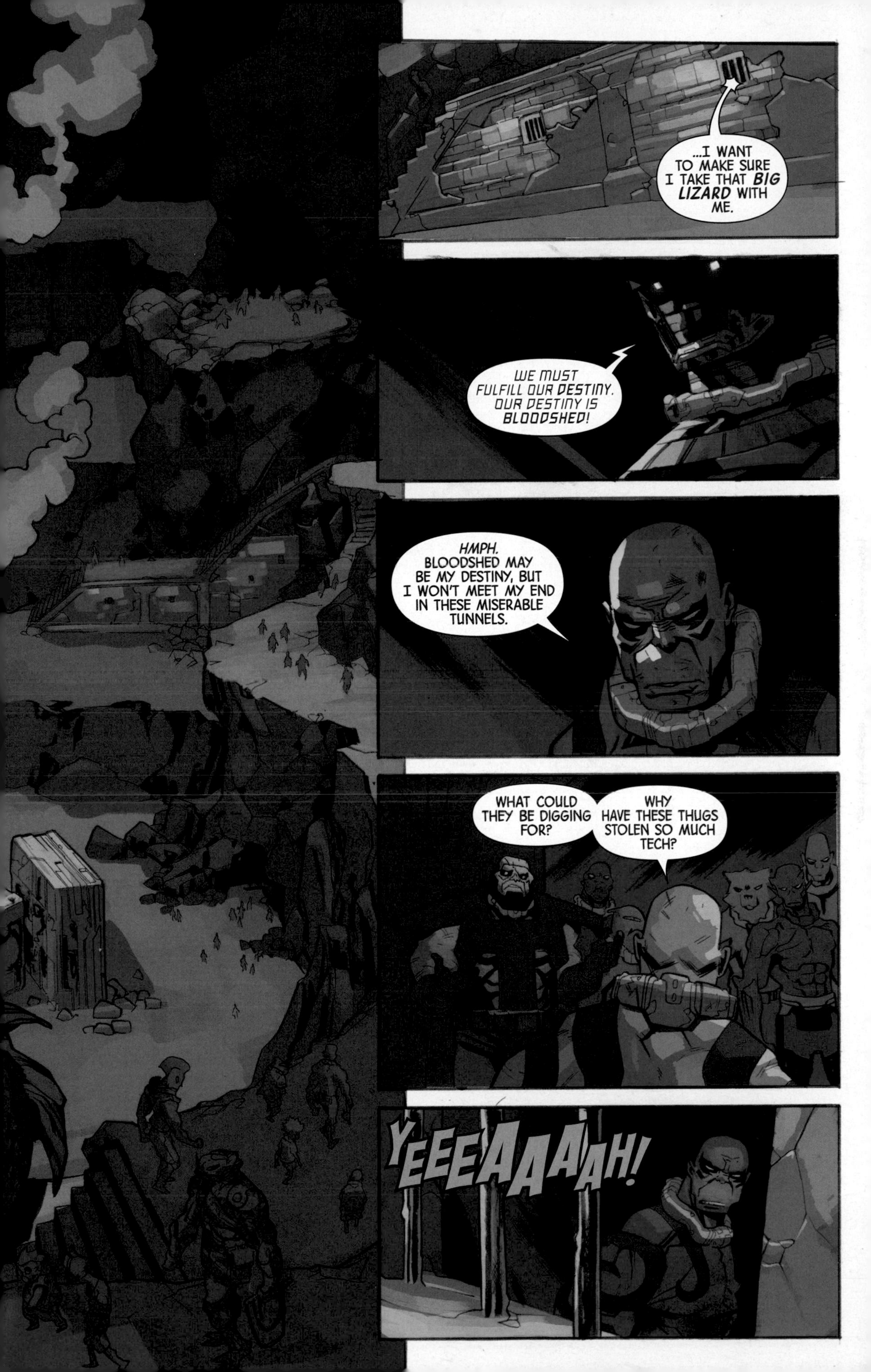
...I WANT TO MAKE SURE I TAKE THAT BIG LIZARD WITH ME.
WE MUST FULFILL OUR DESTINY. OUR DESTINY IS BLOODSHED!
HMPH. BLOODSHED MAY BE MY DESTINY, BUT I WON'T MEET MY END IN THESE MISERABLE TUNNELS.
WHAT COULD THEY BE DIGGING FOR?
WHY HAVE THESE THUGS STOLEN SO MUCH TECH?
YEEEAAAAAH!

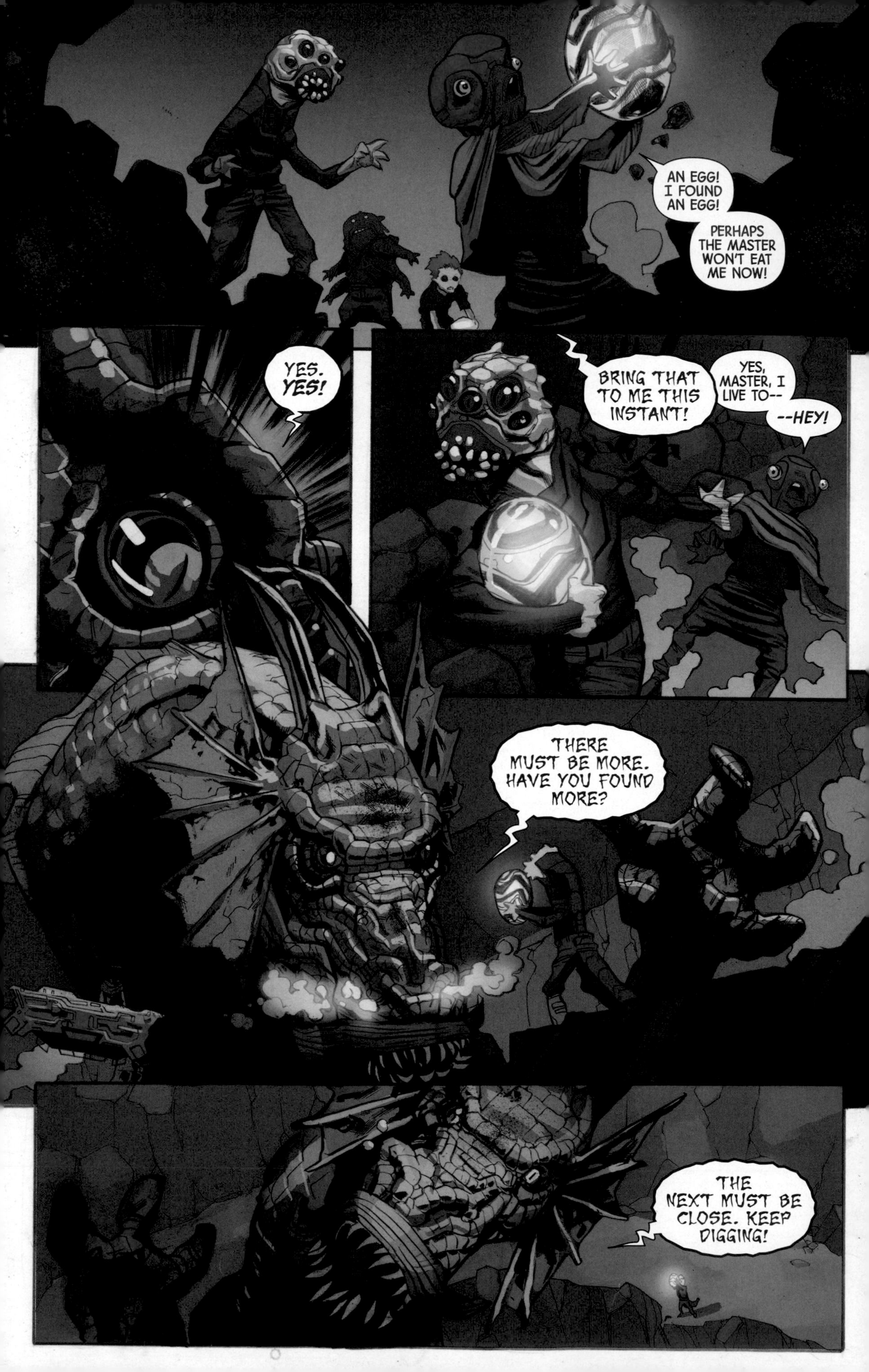
AN EGG! I FOUND AN EGG!
PERHAPS THE MASTER WON'T EAT ME NOW!
YES. YES!
BRING THAT TO ME THIS INSTANT!
YES, MASTER, I LIVE TO--
--HEY!
THERE MUST BE MORE. HAVE YOU FOUND MORE?
THE NEXT MUST BE CLOSE. KEEP DIGGING!

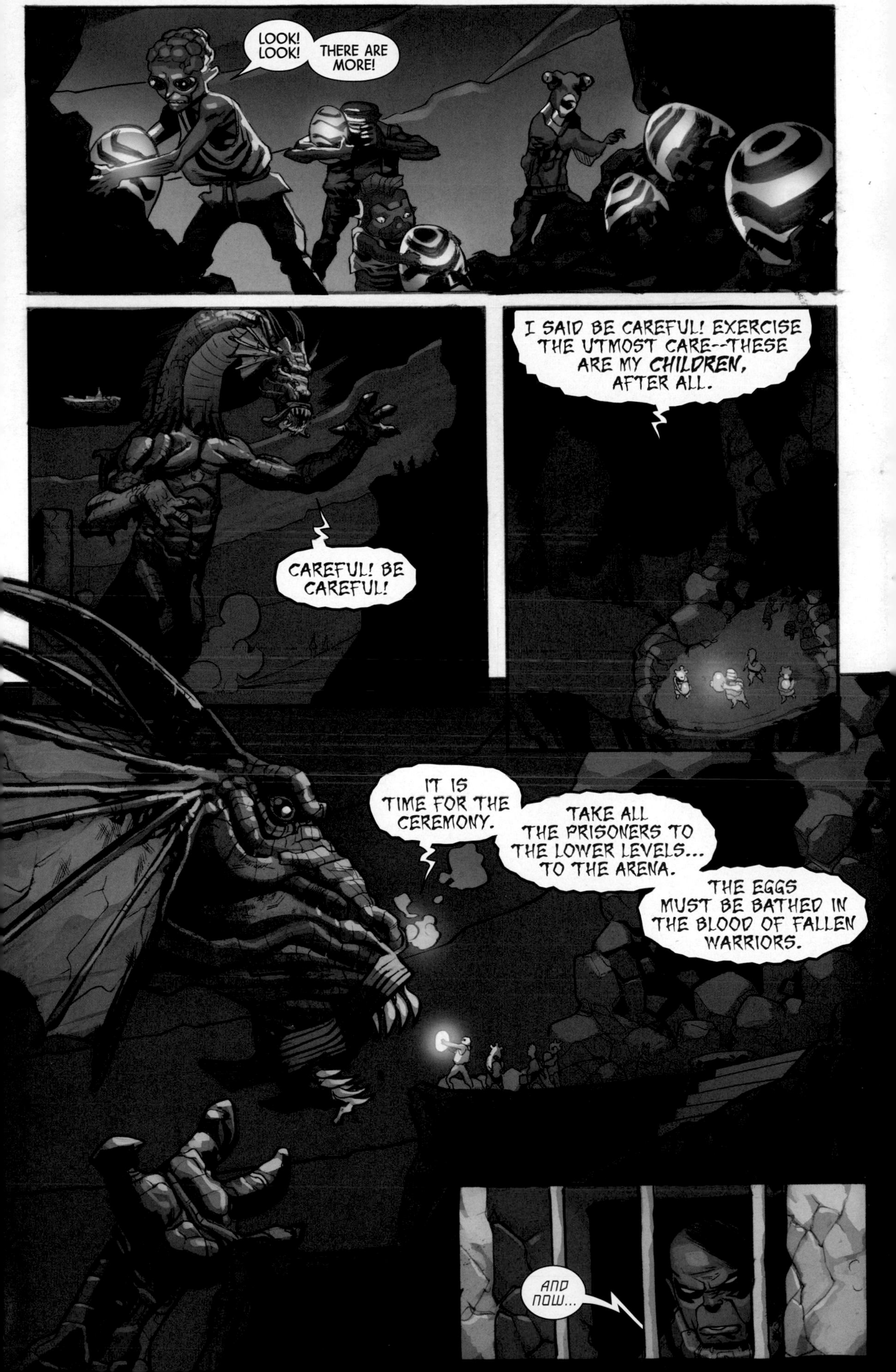
LOOK! LOOK!
THERE ARE MORE!
CAREFUL! BE CAREFUL!
I SAID BE CAREFUL! EXERCISE THE UTMOST CARE--THESE ARE MY CHILDREN, AFTER ALL.
IT IS TIME FOR THE CEREMONY.
TAKE ALL THE PRISONERS TO THE LOWER LEVELS... TO THE ARENA.
THE EGGS MUST BE BATHED IN THE BLOOD OF FALLEN WARRIORS.
AND NOW...

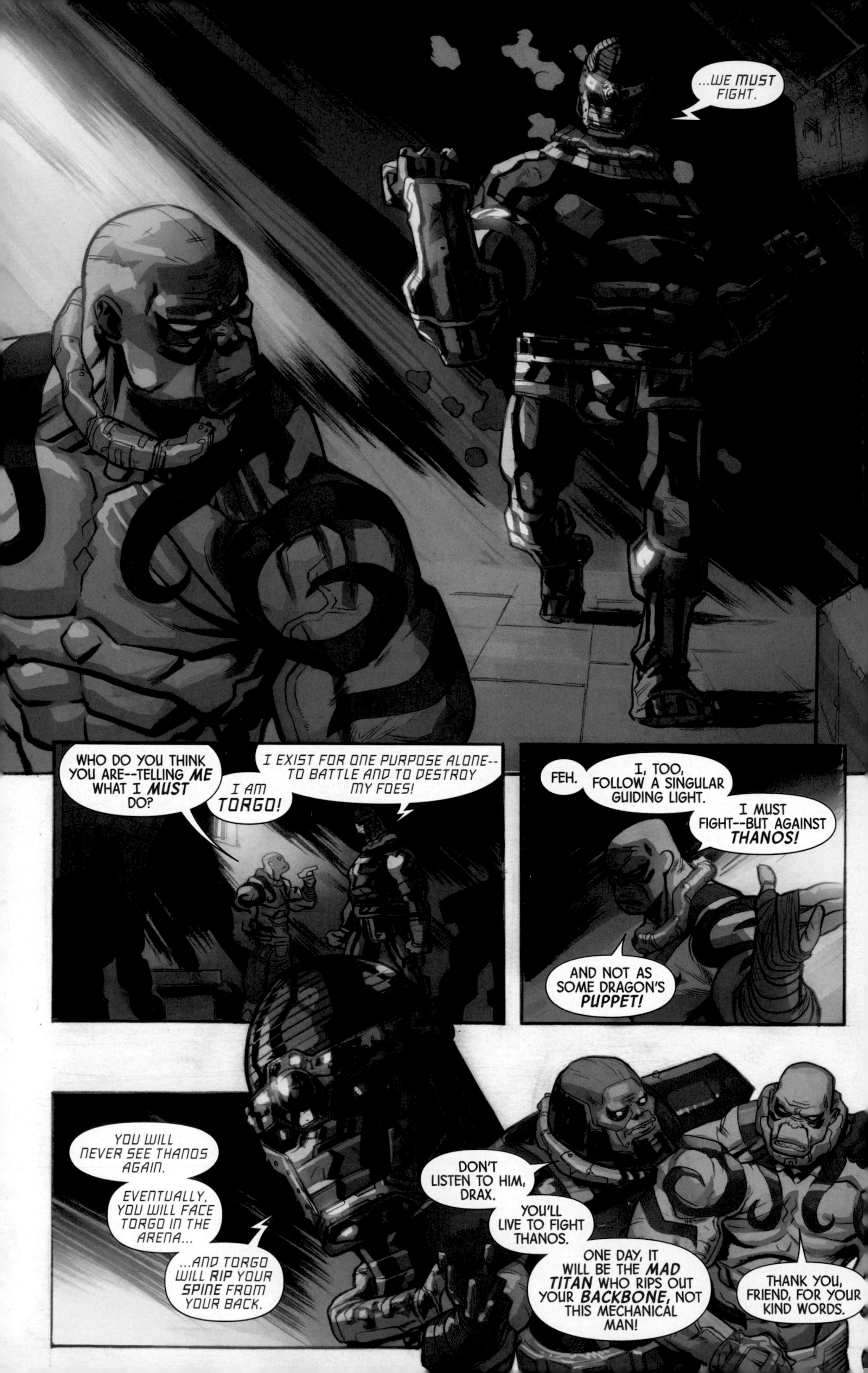
...WE MUST FIGHT.
WHO DO YOU THINK YOU ARE--TELLING ME WHAT I MUST DO?
I AM TORGO!
I EXIST FOR ONE PURPOSE ALONE--TO BATTLE AND TO DESTROY MY FOES!
FEH.
I, TOO, FOLLOW A SINGULAR GUIDING LIGHT.
I MUST FIGHT--BUT AGAINST THANOS!
AND NOT AS SOME DRAGON'S PUPPET!
YOU WILL NEVER SEE THANOS AGAIN.
EVENTUALLY, YOU WILL FACE TORGO IN THE ARENA...
...AND TORGO WILL RIP YOUR SPINE FROM YOUR BACK.
DON'T LISTEN TO HIM, DRAX.
YOU'LL LIVE TO FIGHT THANOS.
ONE DAY, IT WILL BE THE MAD TITAN WHO RIPS OUT YOUR BACKBONE, NOT THIS MECHANICAL MAN!
THANK YOU, FRIEND, FOR YOUR KIND WORDS.

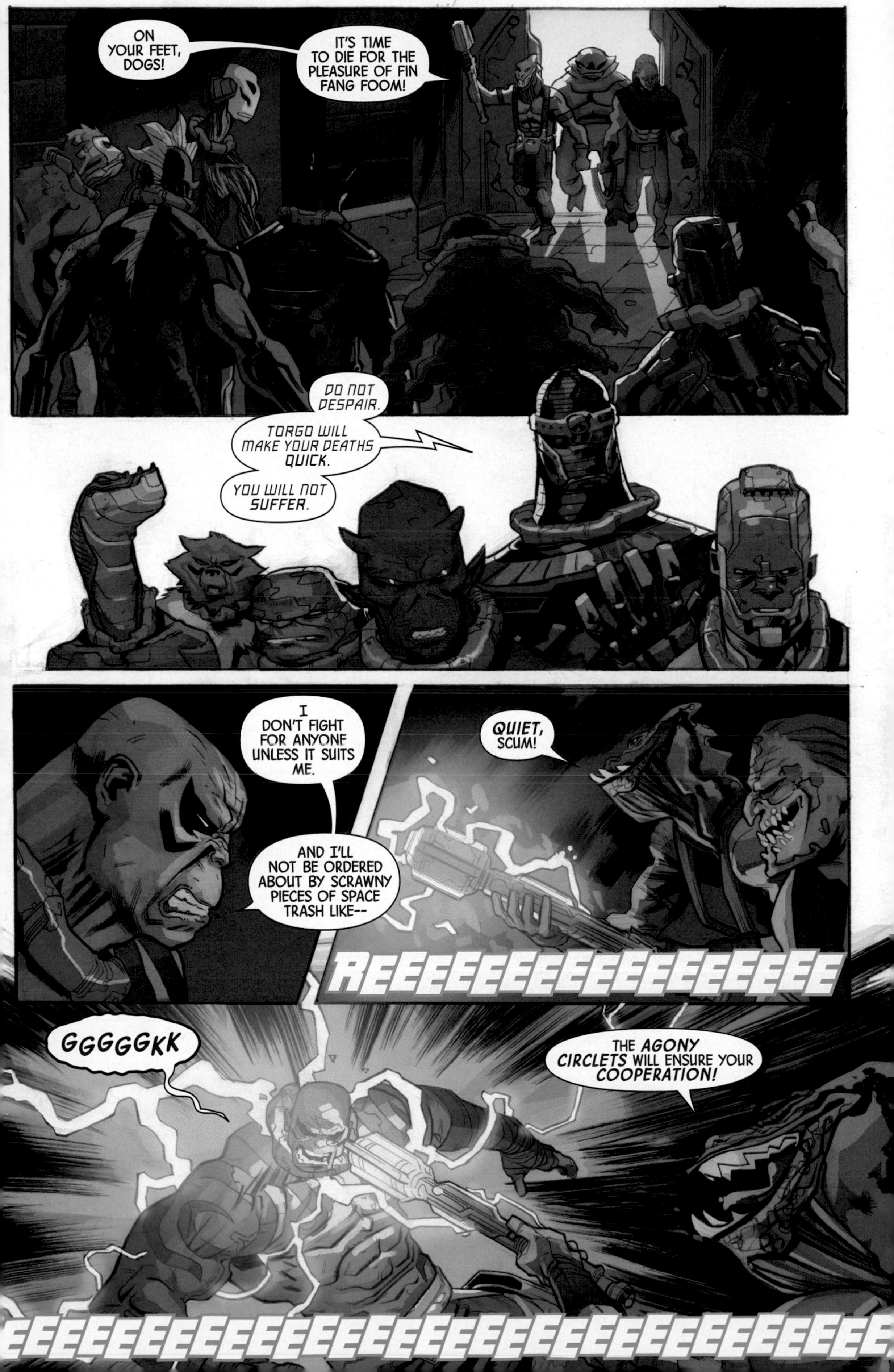

ON YOUR FEET, DOGS!
IT'S TIME TO DIE FOR THE PLEASURE OF FIN FANG FOOM!
DO NOT DESPAIR.
TORGO WILL MAKE YOUR DEATHS QUICK.
YOU WILL NOT SUFFER.
I DON'T FIGHT FOR ANYONE UNLESS IT SUITS ME.
AND I'LL NOT BE ORDERED ABOUT BY SCRAWNY PIECES OF SPACE TRASH LIKE--
QUIET, SCUM!
REEEEEEEEEEEEEEEEE
GGGGGKK
THE AGONY CIRCLETS WILL ENSURE YOUR COOPERATION!
EEEEEEEEEEEEEEEEEEEEEEEEEEEEEEEEEE

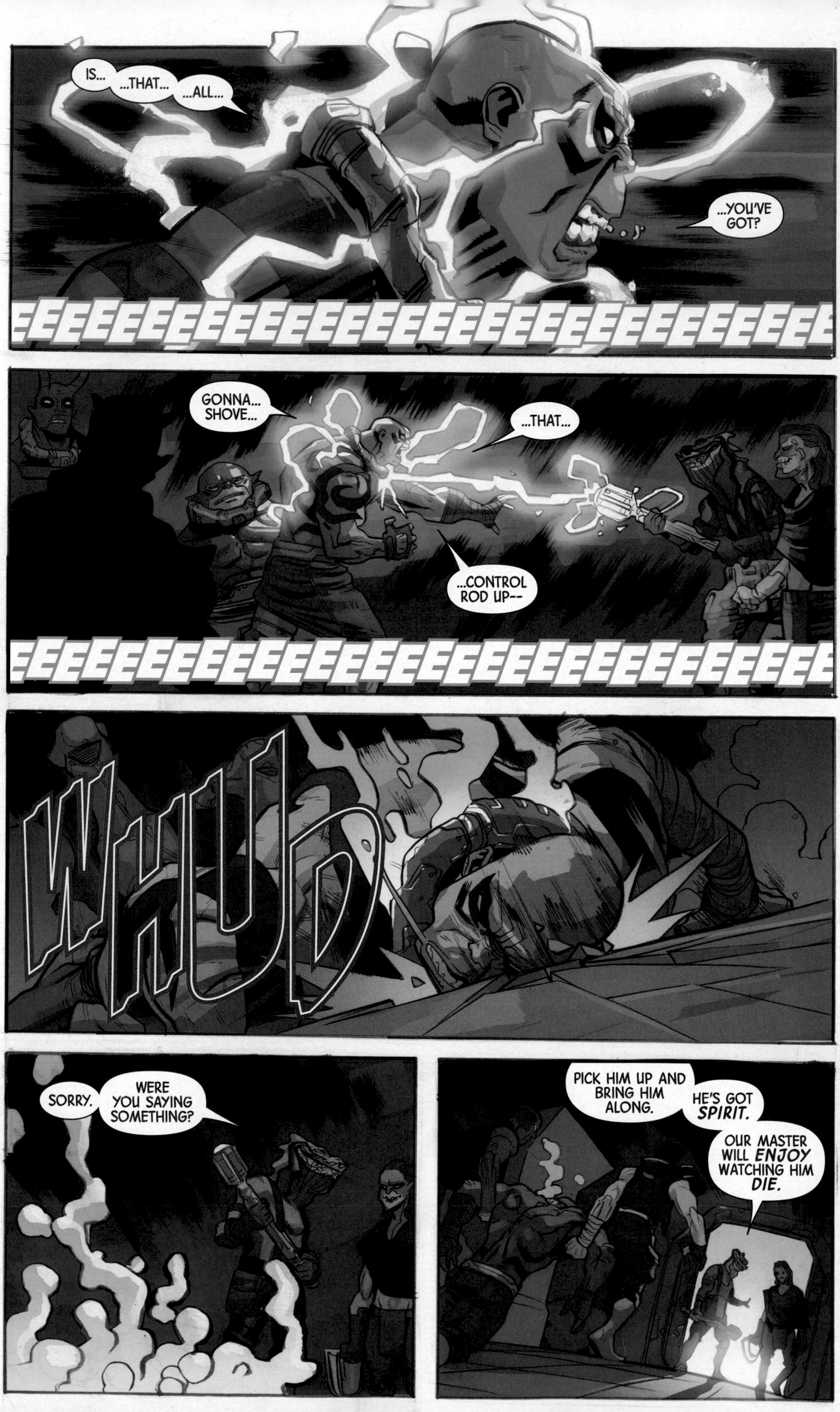
IS...
...THAT...
...ALL...
...YOU'VE GOT?
EEEEEEEEEEEEEEEEEEEEEEEEEEEEEEEEEEEEEEE
GONNA... SHOVE...
...THAT...
...CONTROL ROD UP--
EEEEEEEEEEEEEEEEEEEEEEEEEEEEEEEEEEEEEEE
WHUD
SORRY.
WERE YOU SAYING SOMETHING?
PICK HIM UP AND BRING HIM ALONG.
HE'S GOT SPIRIT.
OUR MASTER WILL ENJOY WATCHING HIM DIE.

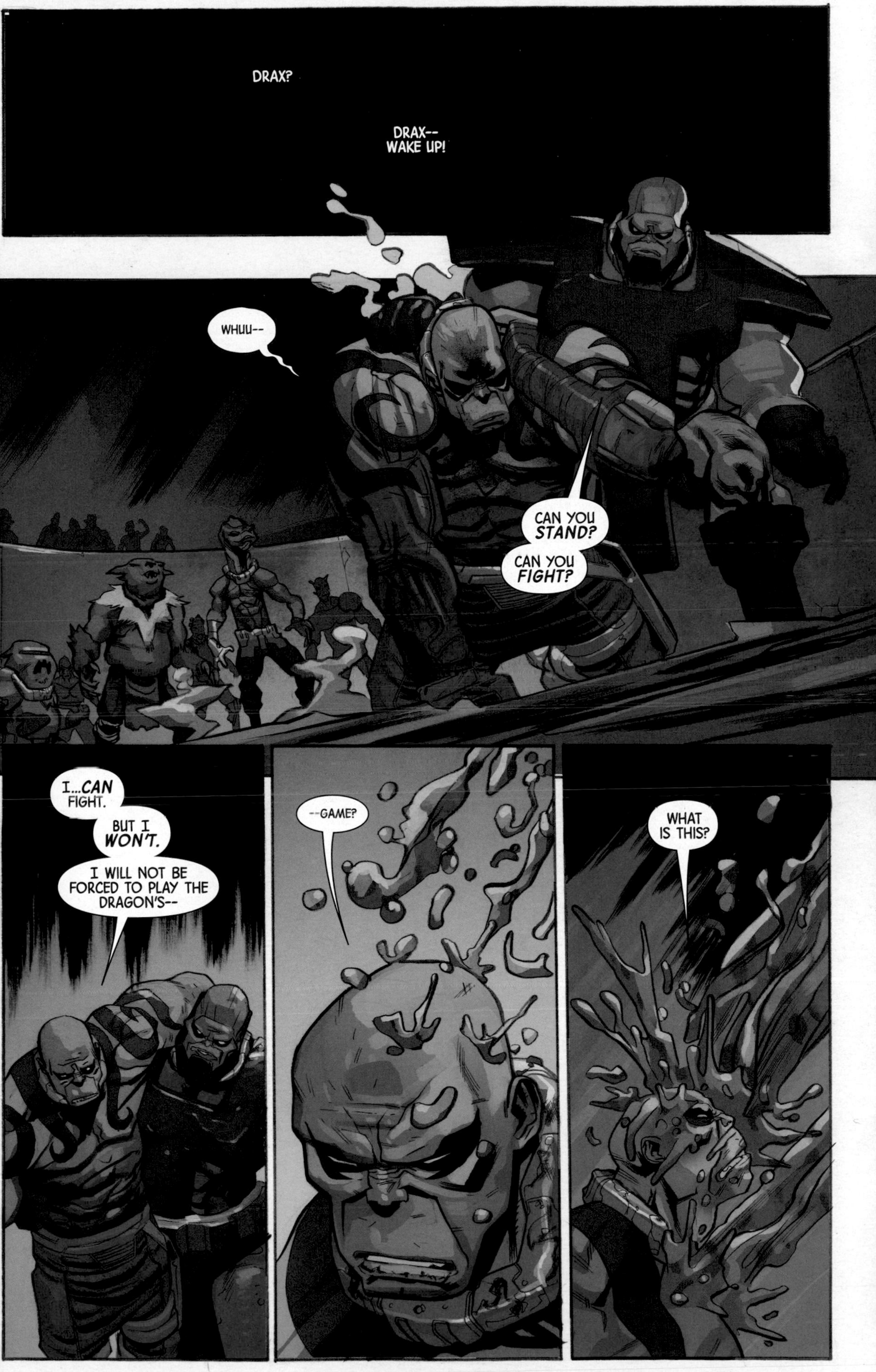
DRAX?
DRAX--
WAKE UP!
WHUU--
CAN YOU *STAND?*
CAN YOU *FIGHT?*
I...*CAN* FIGHT.
BUT I *WON'T.*
I WILL NOT BE FORCED TO PLAY THE DRAGON'S--
--GAME?
WHAT IS THIS?

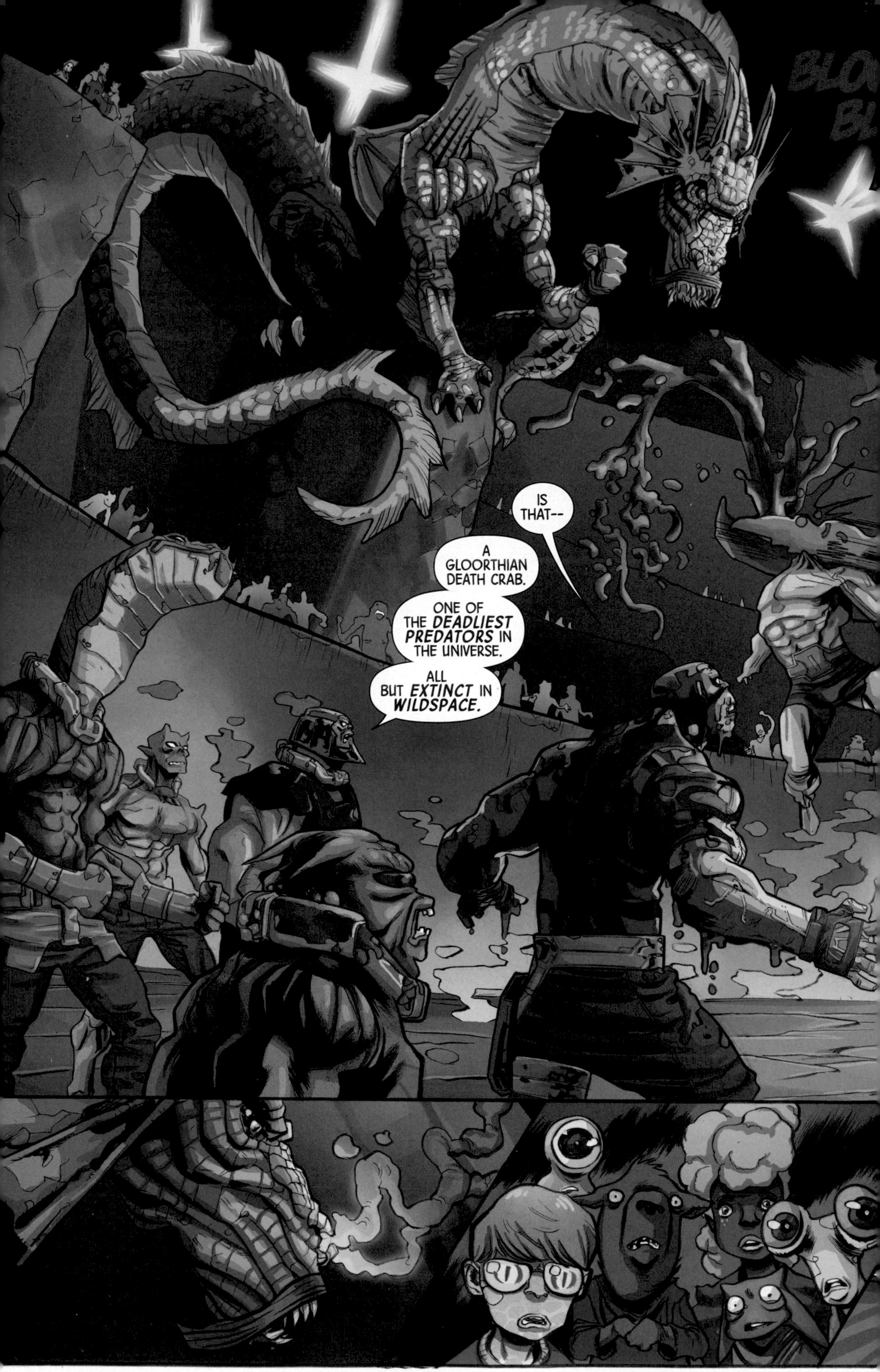
IS THAT--
A GLOORTHIAN DEATH CRAB.
ONE OF THE *DEADLIEST PREDATORS* IN THE UNIVERSE.
ALL BUT *EXTINCT* IN *WILDSPACE.*

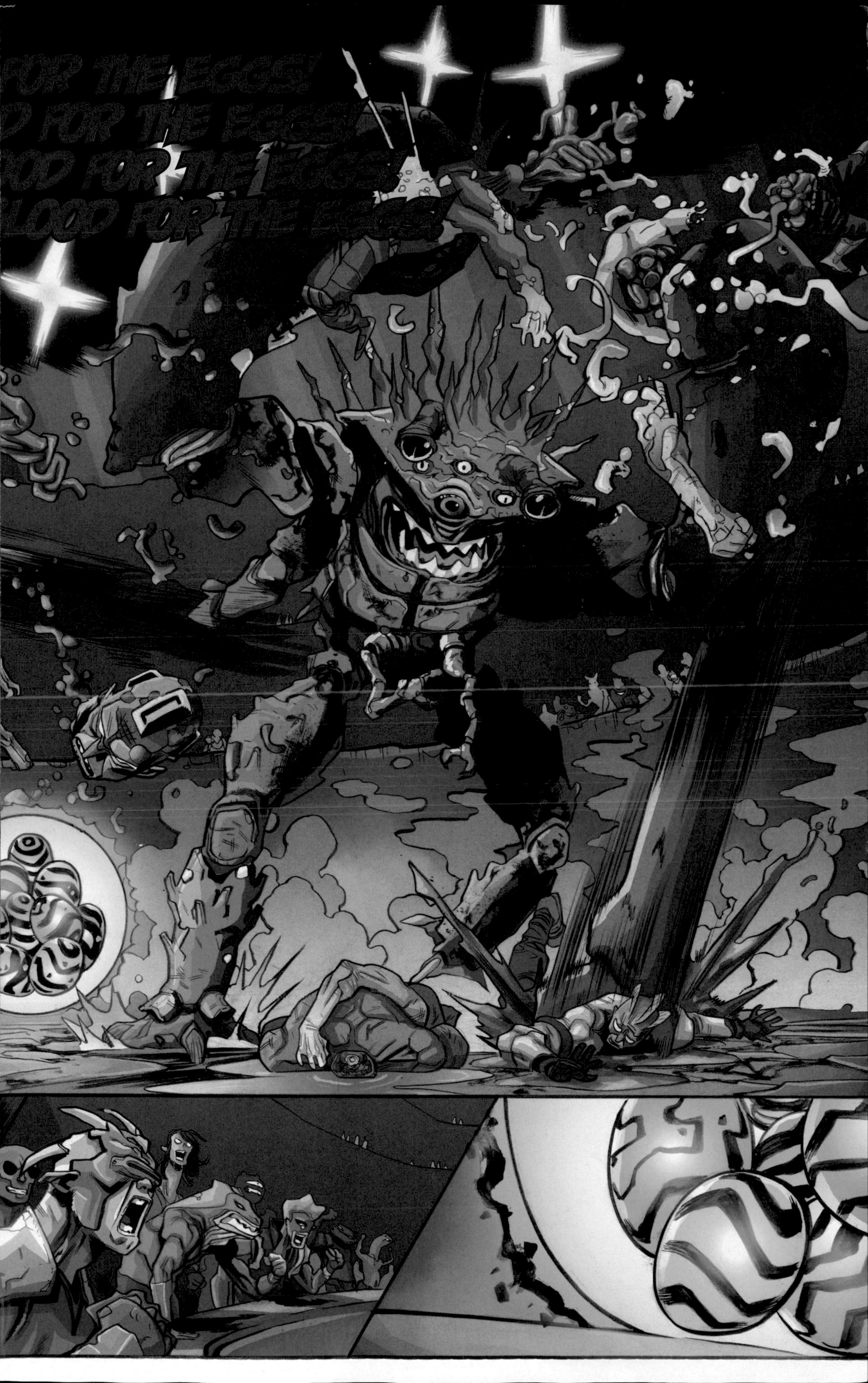
FOR THE EGGS!
D FOR THE EGGS!
OOD FOR THE EGGS!
LOOD FOR THE EGGS!

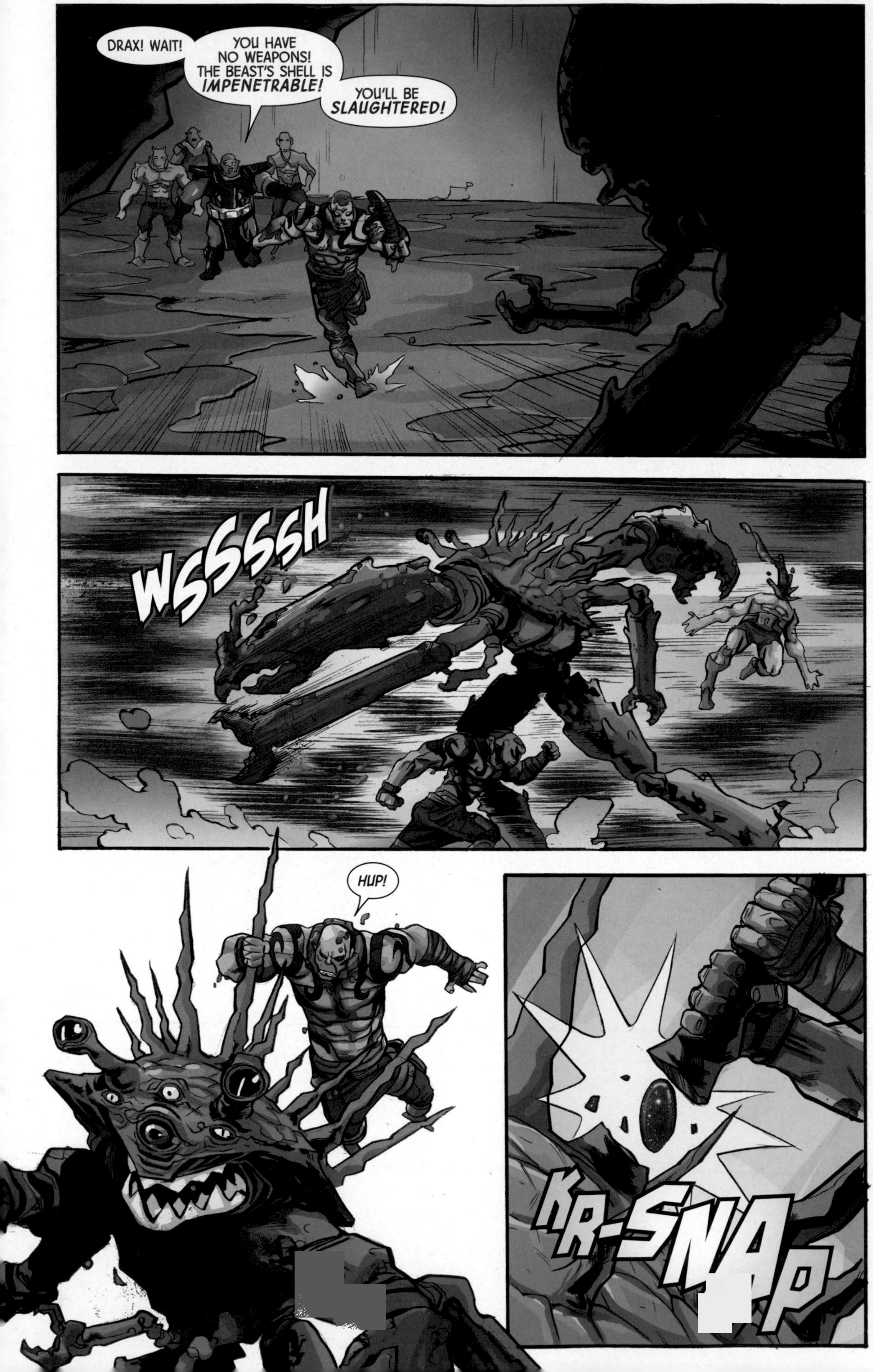
DRAX! WAIT!
YOU HAVE NO WEAPONS! THE BEAST'S SHELL IS IMPENETRABLE!
YOU'LL BE SLAUGHTERED!
WSSSSH
HUP!
KR-SNAP

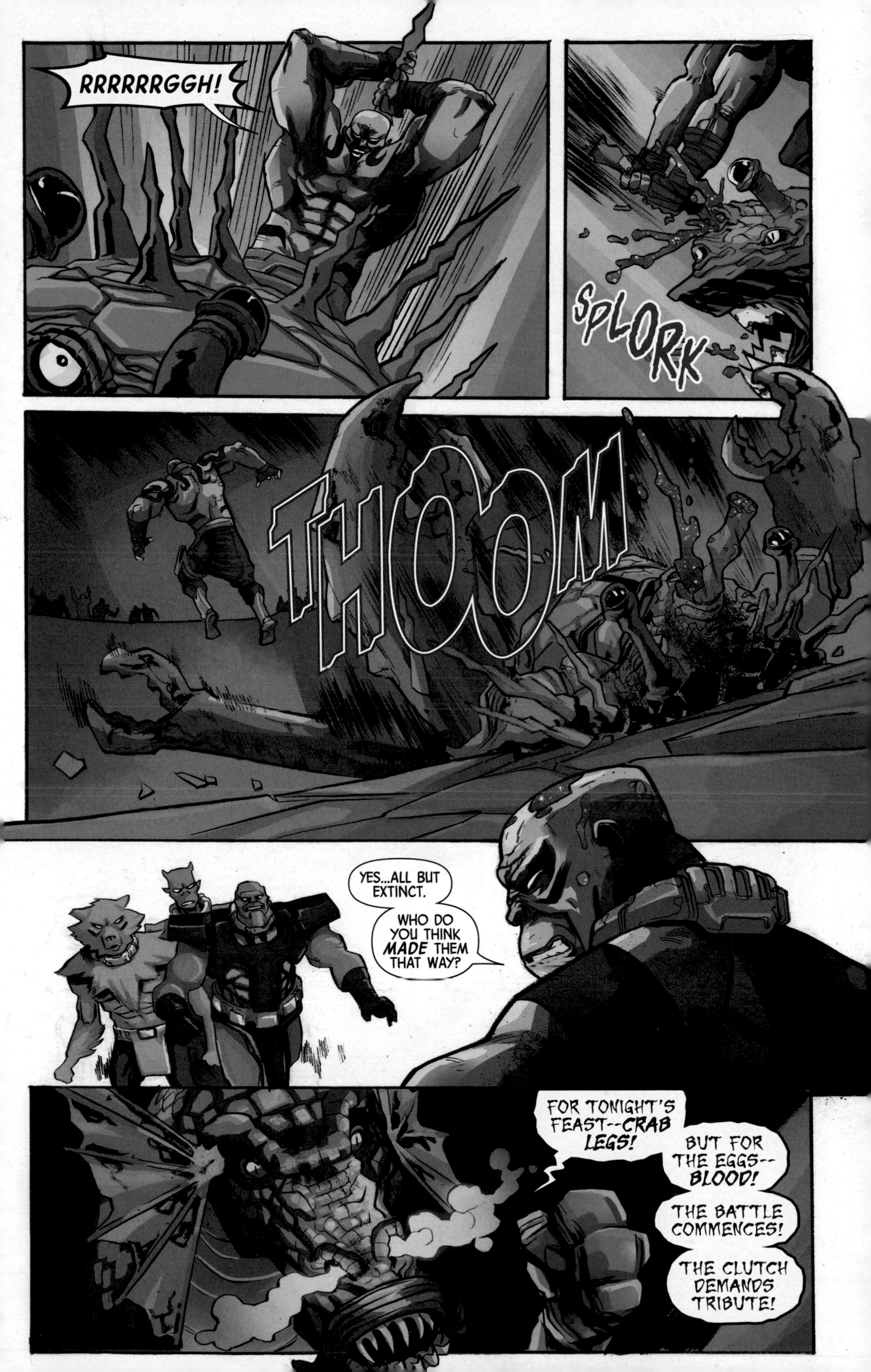
RRRRRRGGH!
SPLORK
THOOM
YES...ALL BUT EXTINCT.
WHO DO YOU THINK MADE THEM THAT WAY?
FOR TONIGHT'S FEAST--CRAB LEGS!
BUT FOR THE EGGS--BLOOD!
THE BATTLE COMMENCES!
THE CLUTCH DEMANDS TRIBUTE!

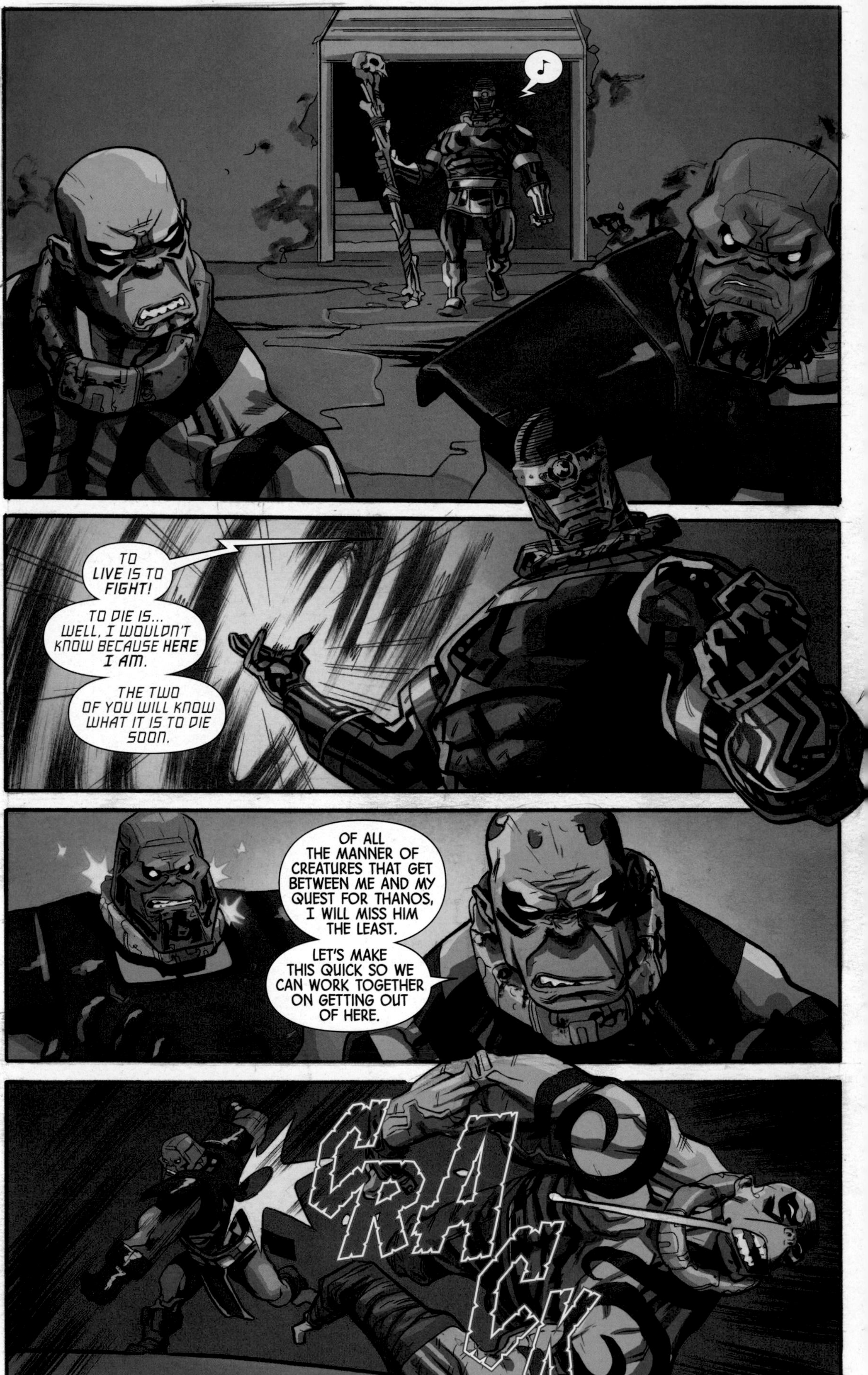
♪
TO LIVE IS TO FIGHT!
TO DIE IS... WELL, I WOULDN'T KNOW BECAUSE HERE I AM.
THE TWO OF YOU WILL KNOW WHAT IT IS TO DIE SOON.
OF ALL THE MANNER OF CREATURES THAT GET BETWEEN ME AND MY QUEST FOR THANOS, I WILL MISS HIM THE LEAST.
LET'S MAKE THIS QUICK SO WE CAN WORK TOGETHER ON GETTING OUT OF HERE.
CRACK

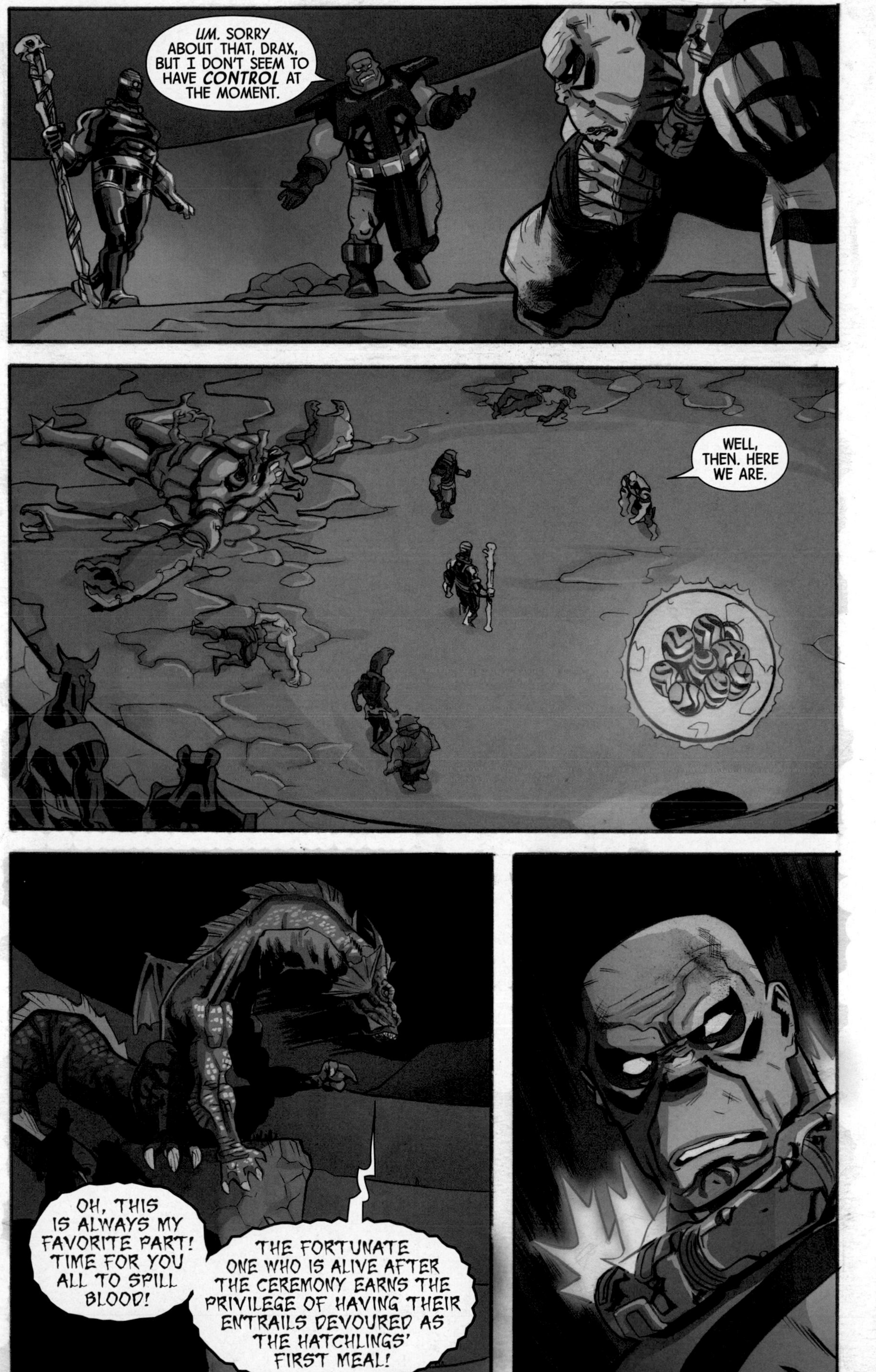
UM. SORRY ABOUT THAT, DRAX, BUT I DON'T SEEM TO HAVE CONTROL AT THE MOMENT.
WELL, THEN. HERE WE ARE.
OH, THIS IS ALWAYS MY FAVORITE PART! TIME FOR YOU ALL TO SPILL BLOOD!
THE FORTUNATE ONE WHO IS ALIVE AFTER THE CEREMONY EARNS THE PRIVILEGE OF HAVING THEIR ENTRAILS DEVOURED AS THE HATCHLINGS' FIRST MEAL!

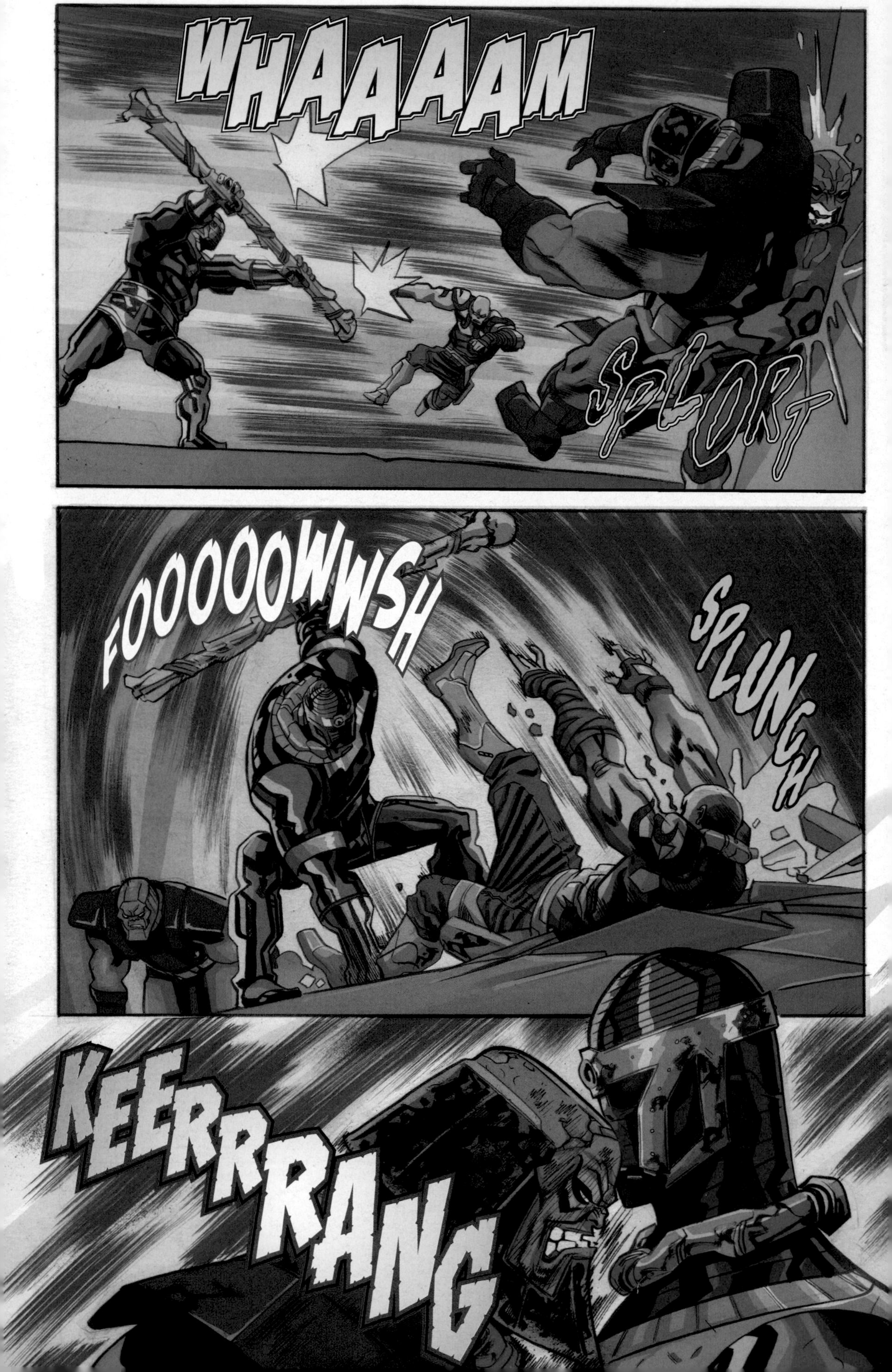
WHAAAAAM
SPLORT
FOOOOOWWSH
SPLUNCH
KEERRRANG

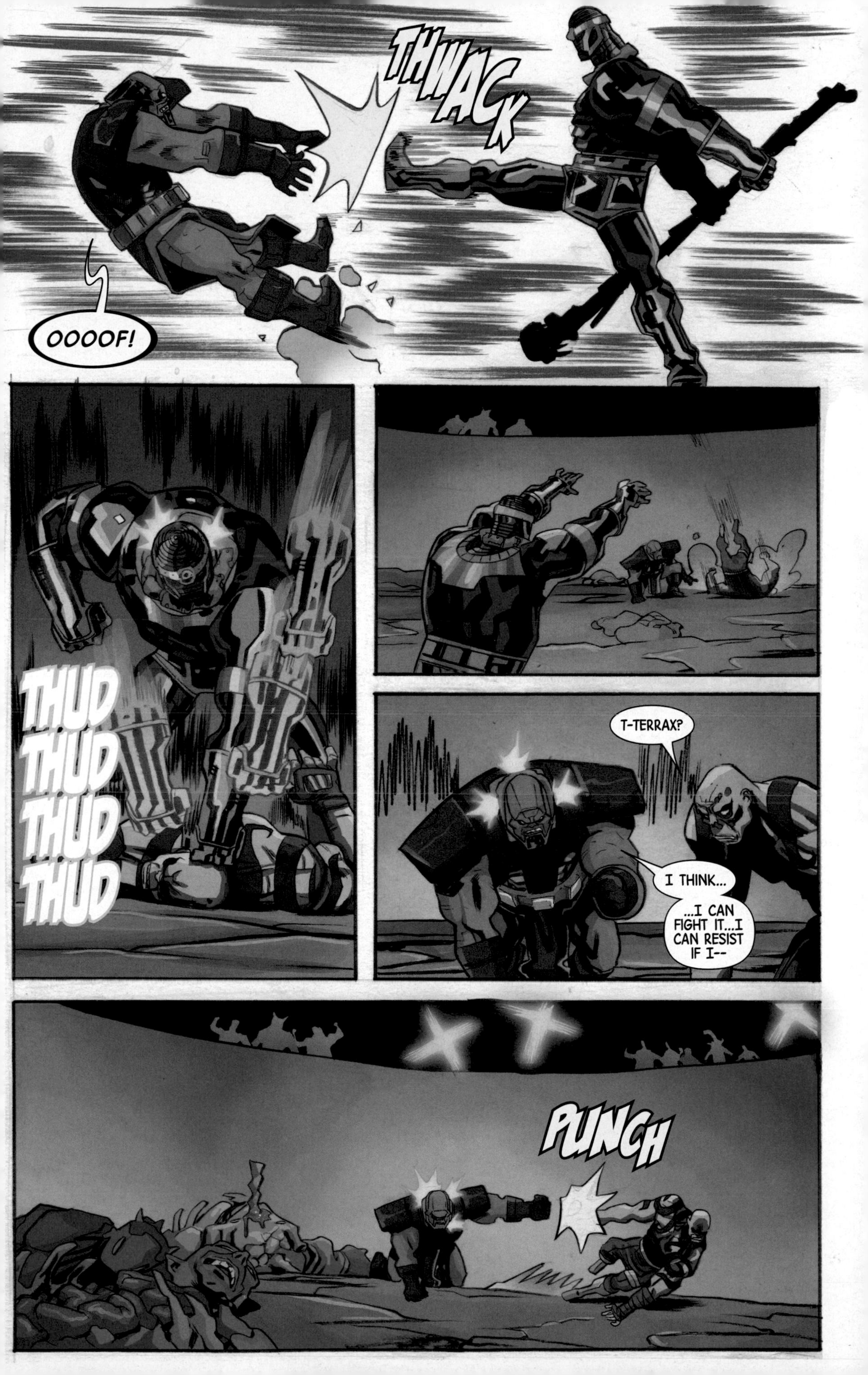
THWACK
OOOOF!
THUD
THUD
THUD
THUD
T-TERRAX?
I THINK...
...I CAN FIGHT IT...I CAN RESIST IF I--
PUNCH

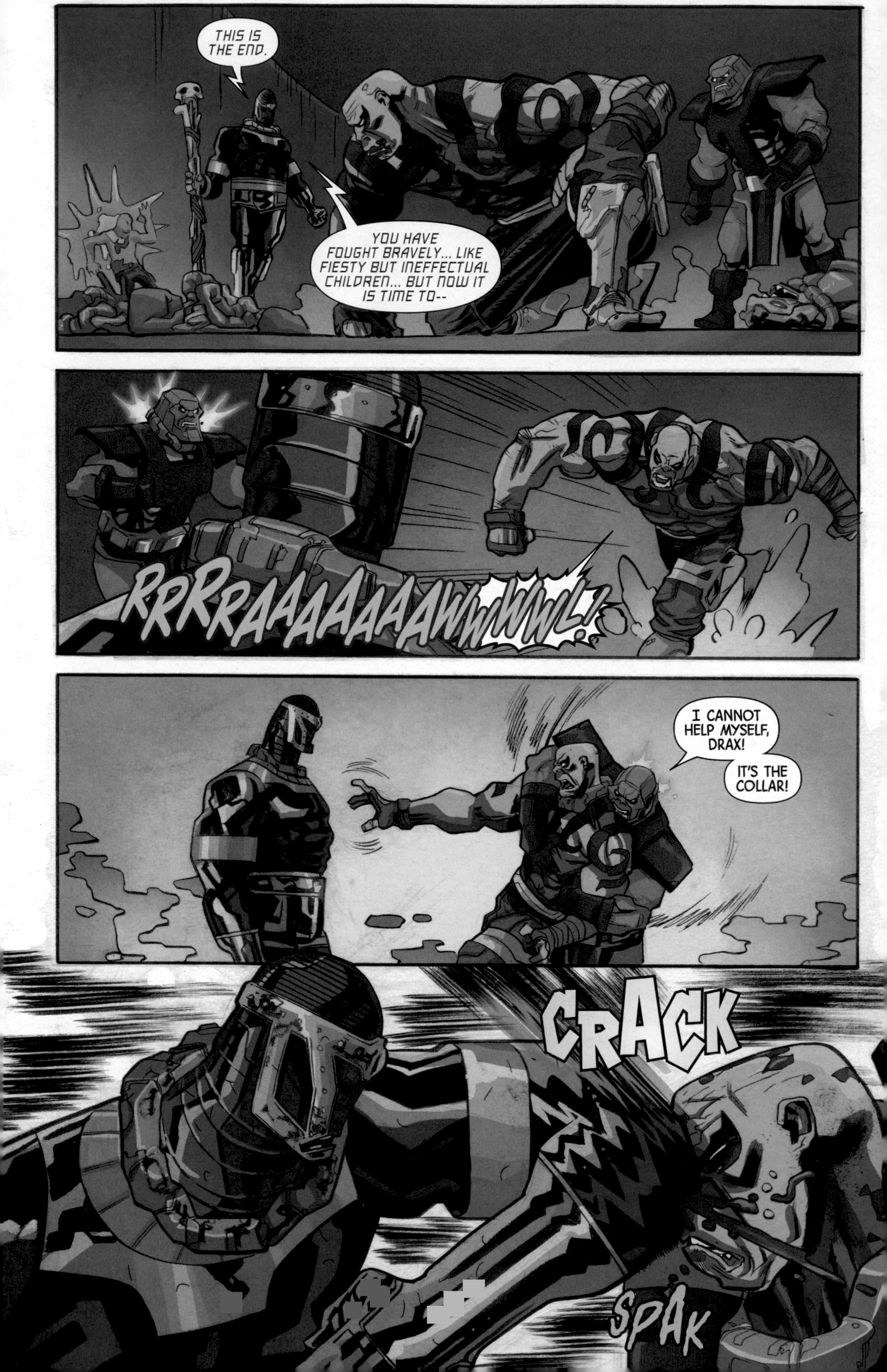
THIS IS THE END.
YOU HAVE FOUGHT BRAVELY... LIKE FIESTY BUT INEFFECTUAL CHILDREN... BUT NOW IT IS TIME TO--
RRRRAAAAAAAAWWWWWL!
I CANNOT HELP MYSELF, DRAX!
IT'S THE COLLAR!
CRACK
SPAK

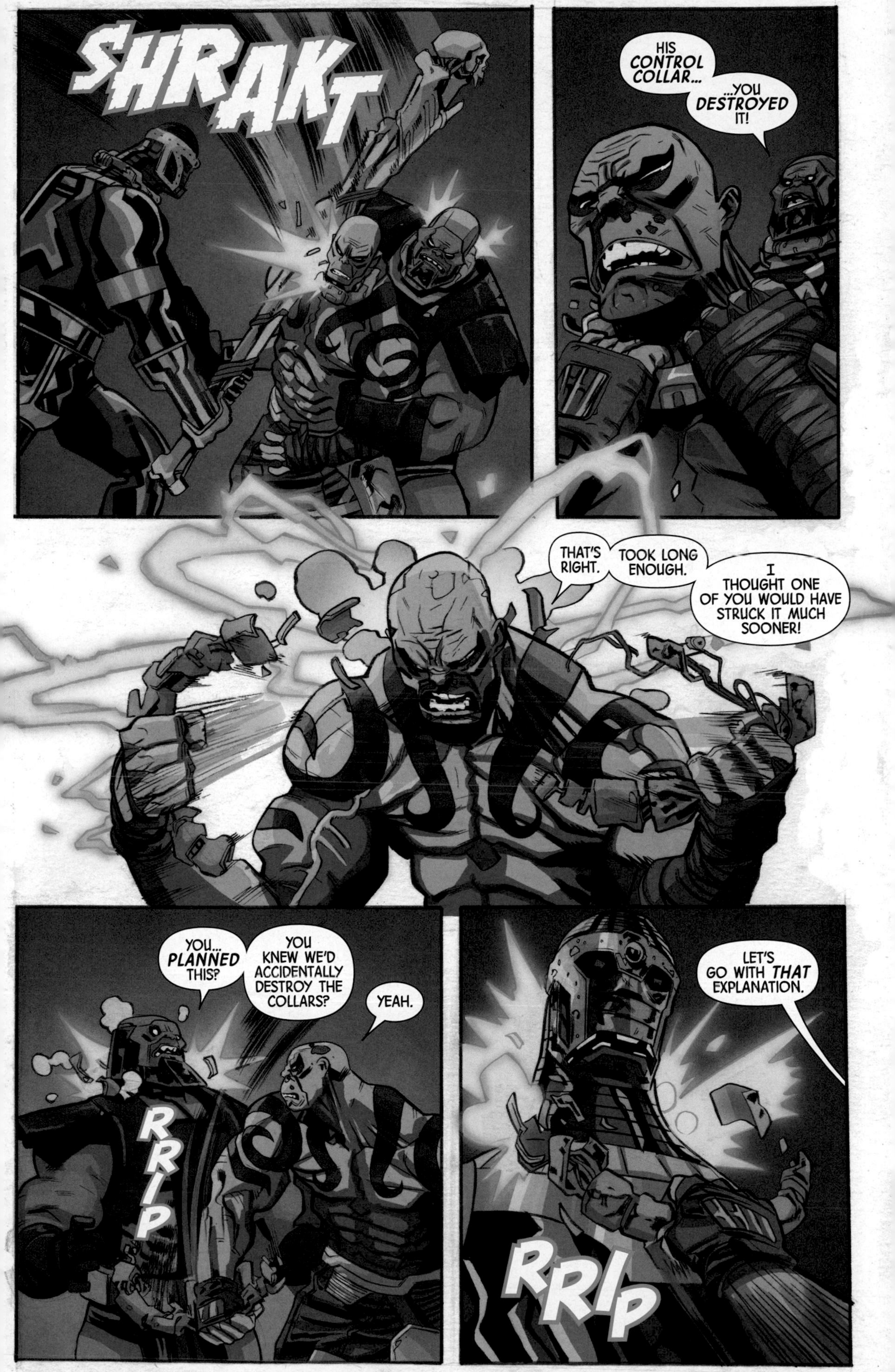
SHRAKT
HIS CONTROL COLLAR...
...YOU DESTROYED IT!
THAT'S RIGHT.
TOOK LONG ENOUGH.
I THOUGHT ONE OF YOU WOULD HAVE STRUCK IT MUCH SOONER!
YOU... PLANNED THIS?
YOU KNEW WE'D ACCIDENTALLY DESTROY THE COLLARS?
YEAH.
RRIP
LET'S GO WITH THAT EXPLANATION.
RRIP

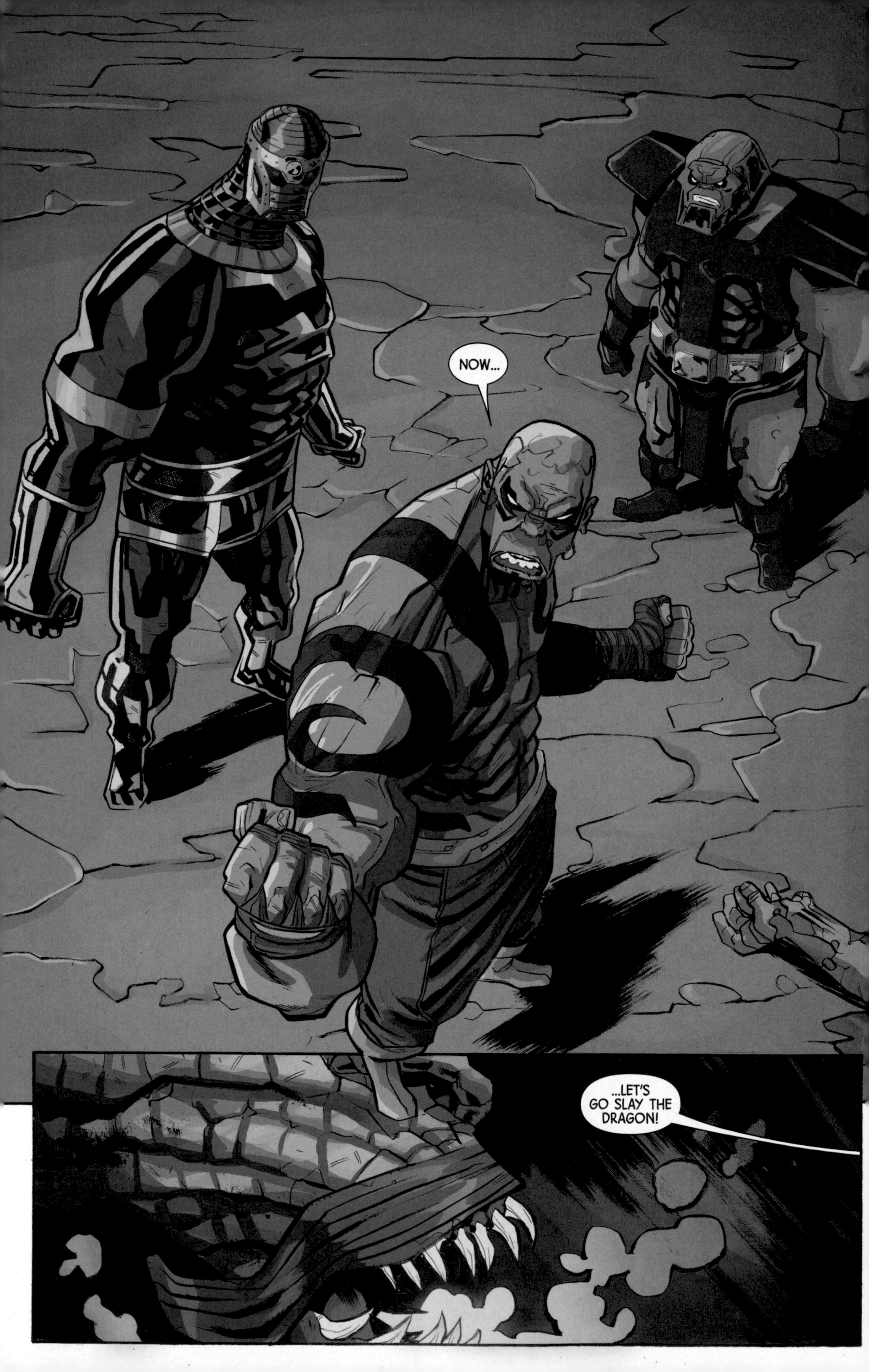
NOW...
...LET'S GO SLAY THE DRAGON!

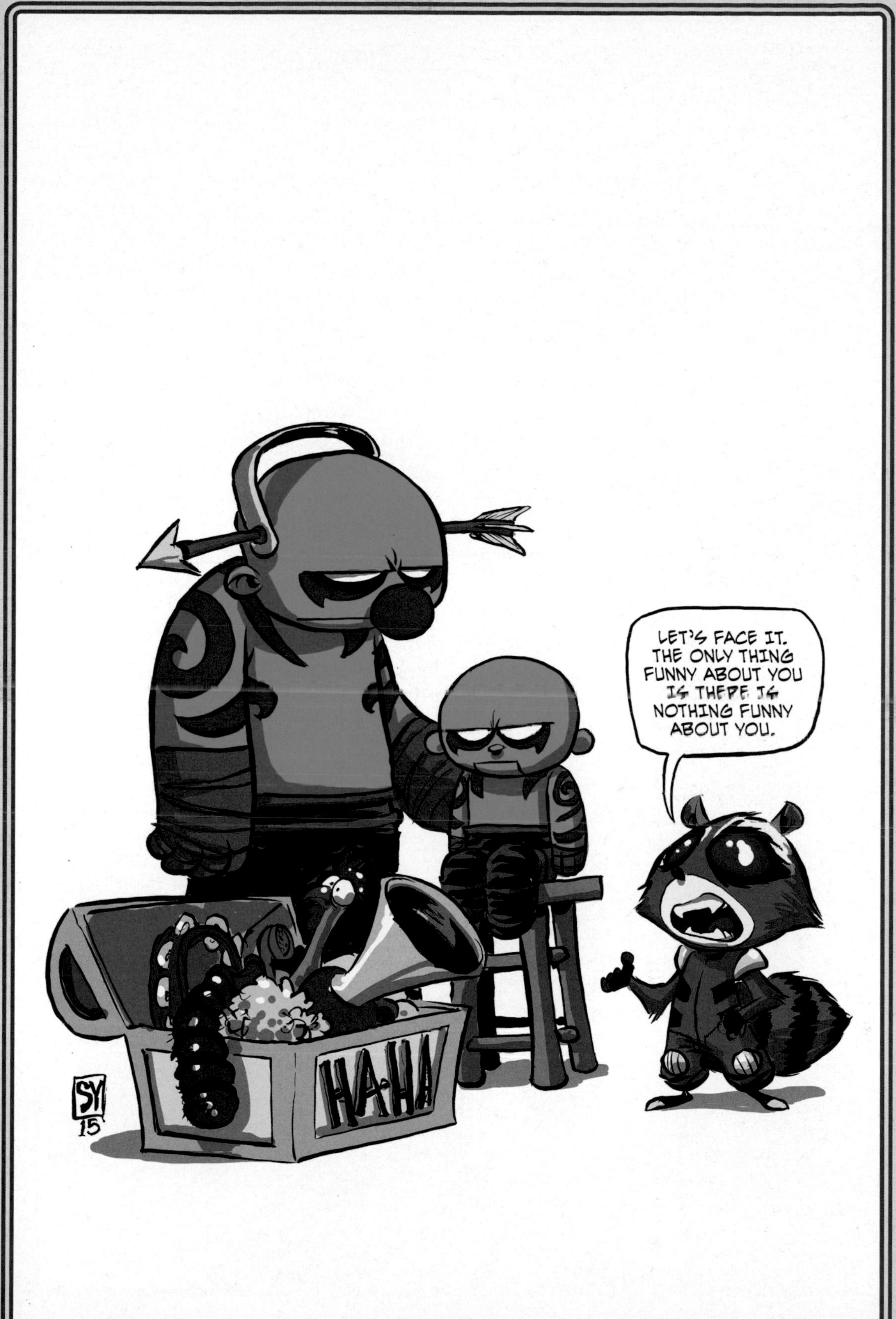
LET'S FACE IT. THE ONLY THING FUNNY ABOUT YOU IS THERE IS NOTHING FUNNY ABOUT YOU.
HA-HA
SY 15

No. 1 VARIANT BY

SKOTTIE YOUNG

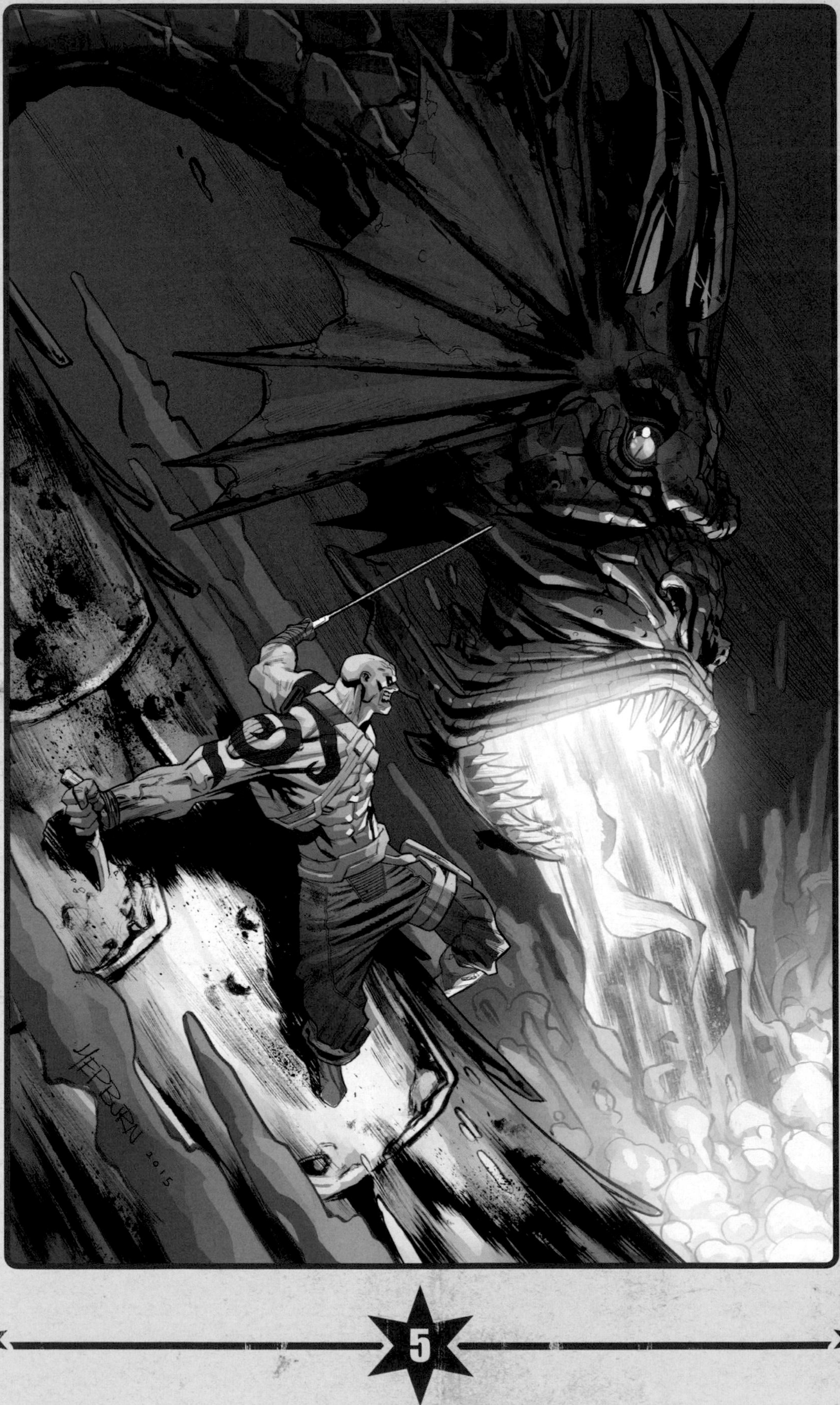
HEPBURN
2015

5

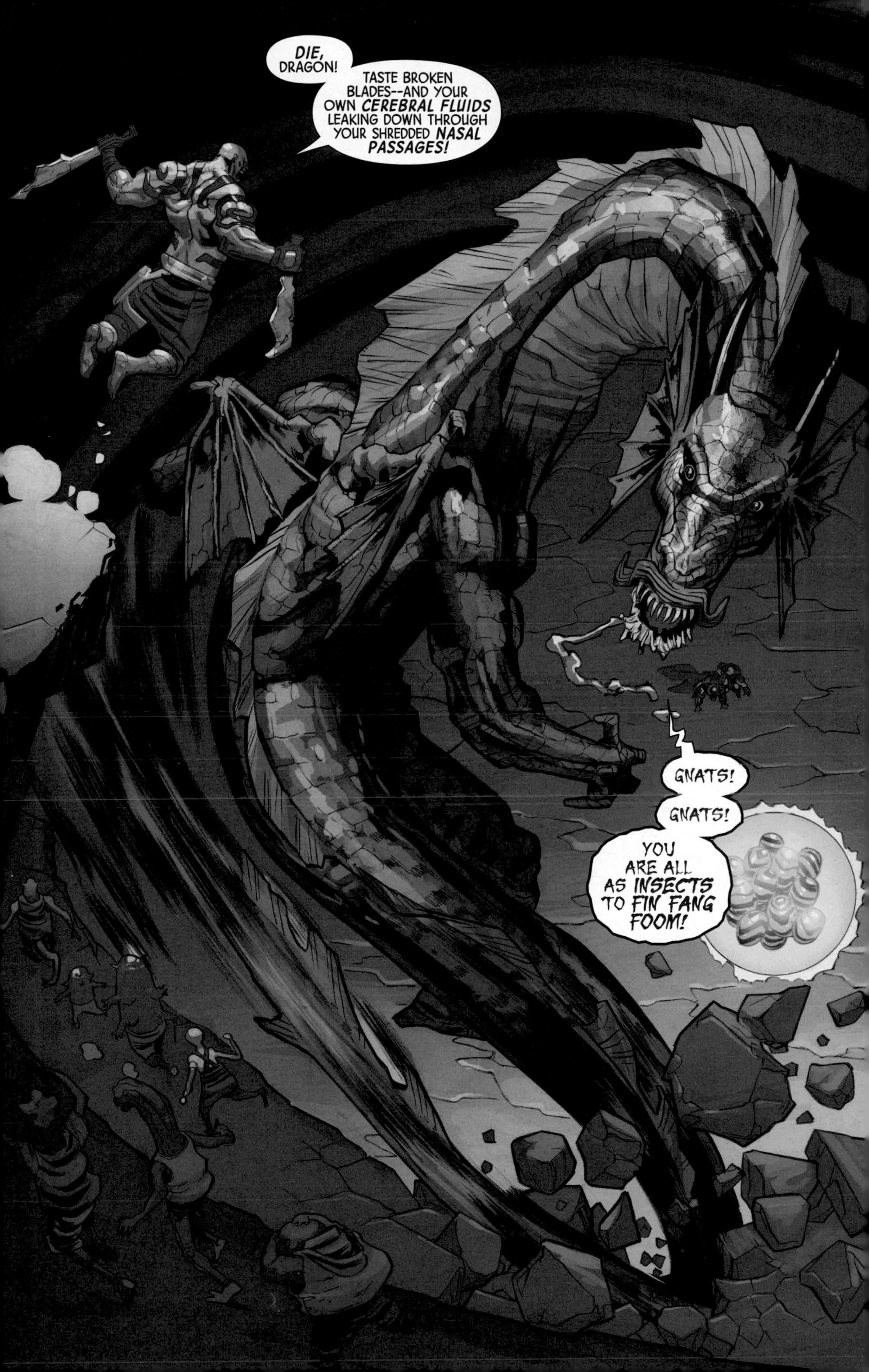
DIE, DRAGON!
TASTE BROKEN BLADES--AND YOUR OWN CEREBRAL FLUIDS LEAKING DOWN THROUGH YOUR SHREDDED NASAL PASSAGES!
GNATS!
GNATS!
YOU ARE ALL AS INSECTS TO FIN FANG FOOM!

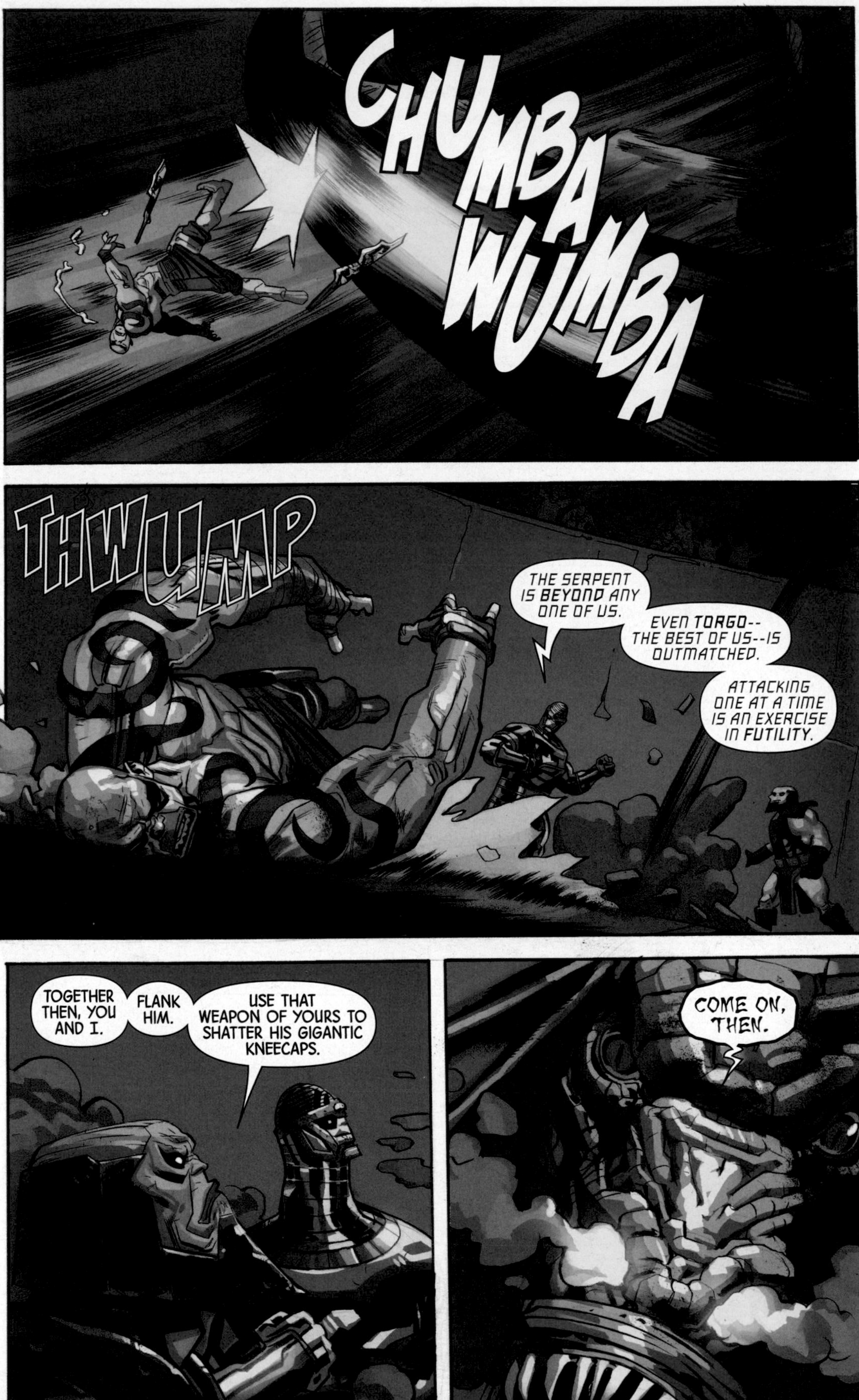
CHUMBA WUMBA
THWUMP
THE SERPENT IS BEYOND ANY ONE OF US.
EVEN TORGO-- THE BEST OF US--IS OUTMATCHED.
ATTACKING ONE AT A TIME IS AN EXERCISE IN FUTILITY.
TOGETHER THEN, YOU AND I.
FLANK HIM.
USE THAT WEAPON OF YOURS TO SHATTER HIS GIGANTIC KNEECAPS.
COME ON, THEN.

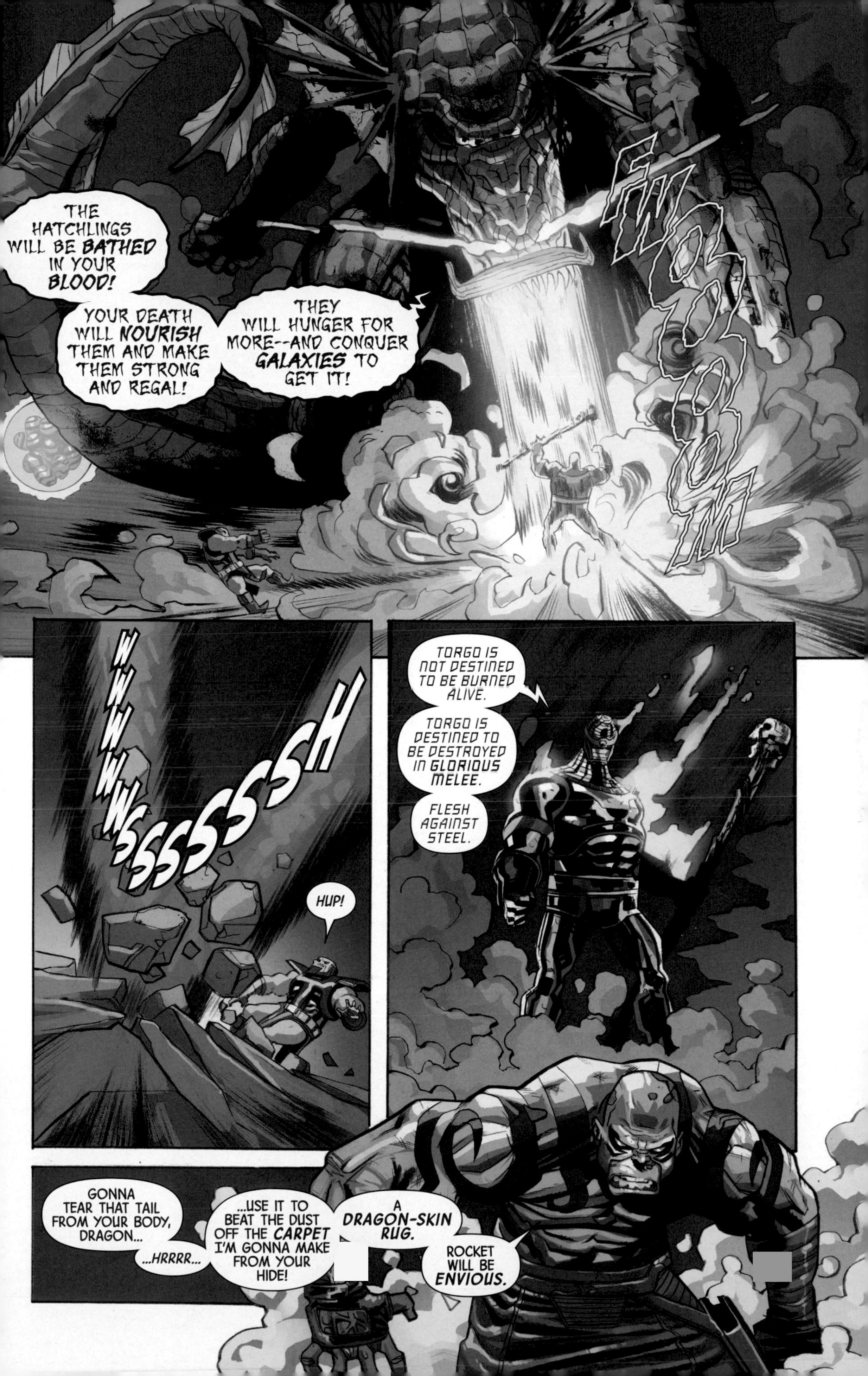
THE HATCHLINGS WILL BE BATHED IN YOUR BLOOD!
YOUR DEATH WILL NOURISH THEM AND MAKE THEM STRONG AND REGAL!
THEY WILL HUNGER FOR MORE--AND CONQUER GALAXIES TO GET IT!
FWOOOOOOM
WWWWWSSSSSSH
HUP!
TORGO IS NOT DESTINED TO BE BURNED ALIVE.
TORGO IS DESTINED TO BE DESTROYED IN GLORIOUS MELEE.
FLESH AGAINST STEEL.
GONNA TEAR THAT TAIL FROM YOUR BODY, DRAGON...
...HRRRR...
...USE IT TO BEAT THE DUST OFF THE CARPET I'M GONNA MAKE FROM YOUR HIDE!
A DRAGON-SKIN RUG.
ROCKET WILL BE ENVIOUS.

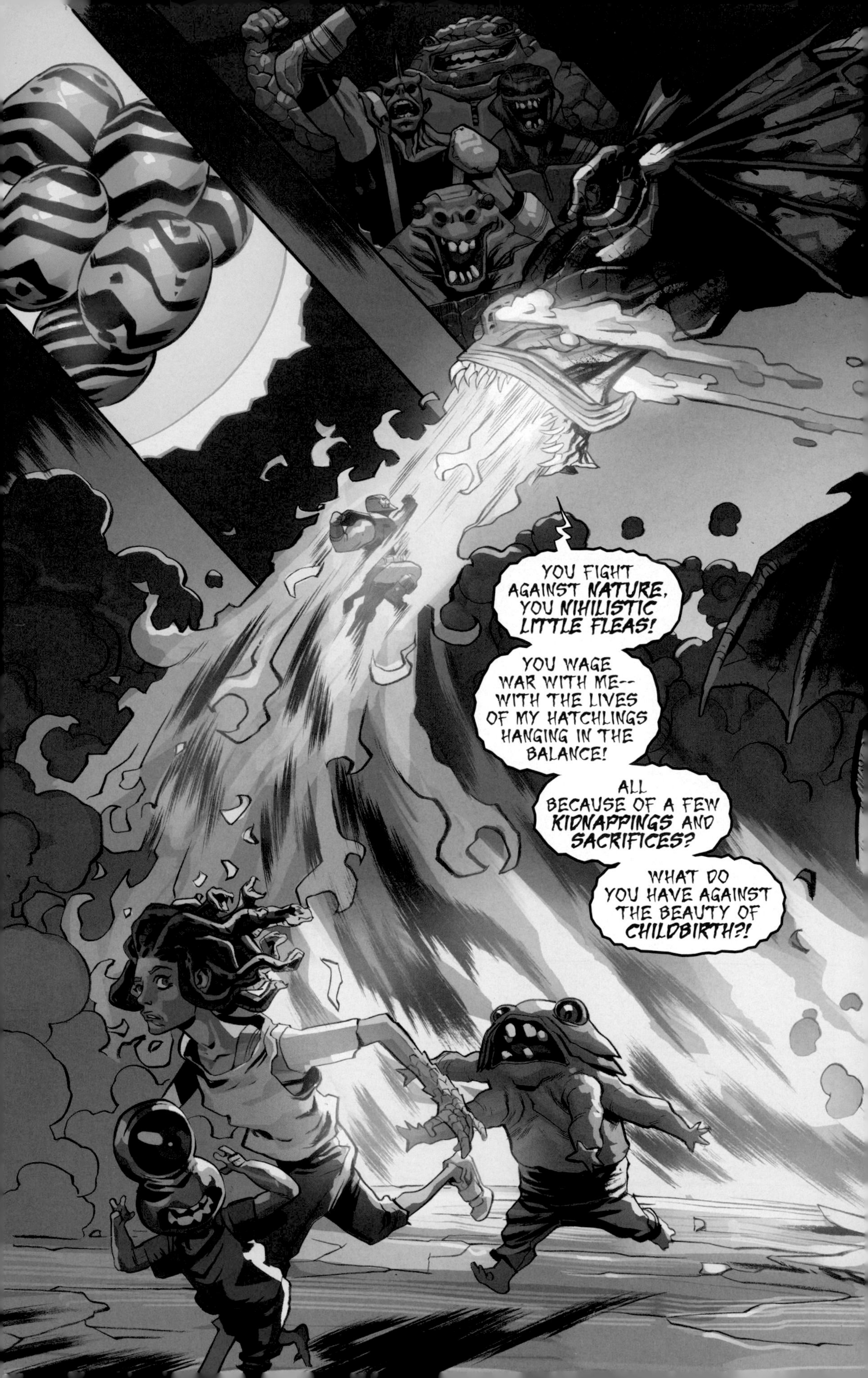
YOU FIGHT AGAINST NATURE, YOU NIHILISTIC LITTLE FLEAS!
YOU WAGE WAR WITH ME-- WITH THE LIVES OF MY HATCHLINGS HANGING IN THE BALANCE!
ALL BECAUSE OF A FEW KIDNAPPINGS AND SACRIFICES?
WHAT DO YOU HAVE AGAINST THE BEAUTY OF CHILDBIRTH?!

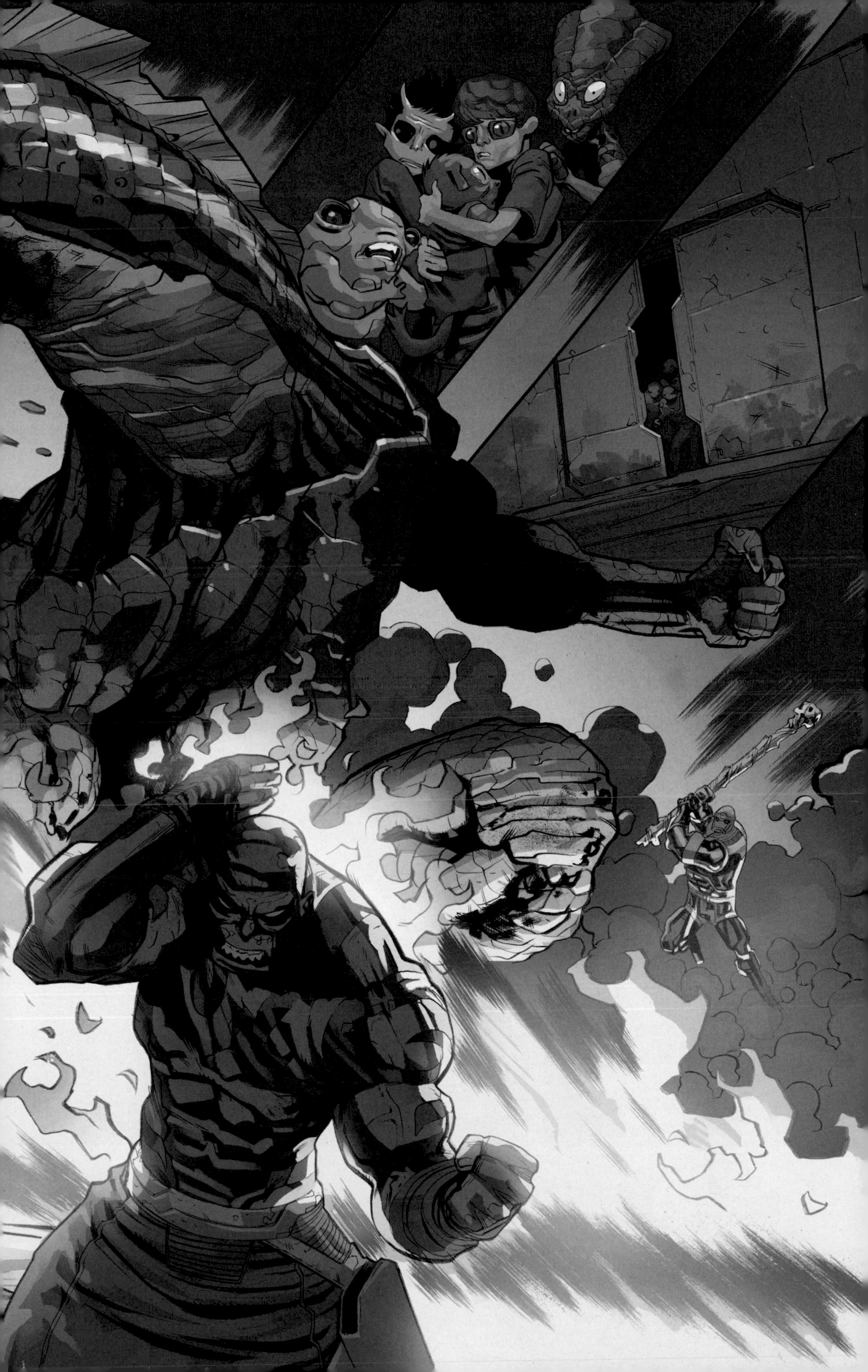

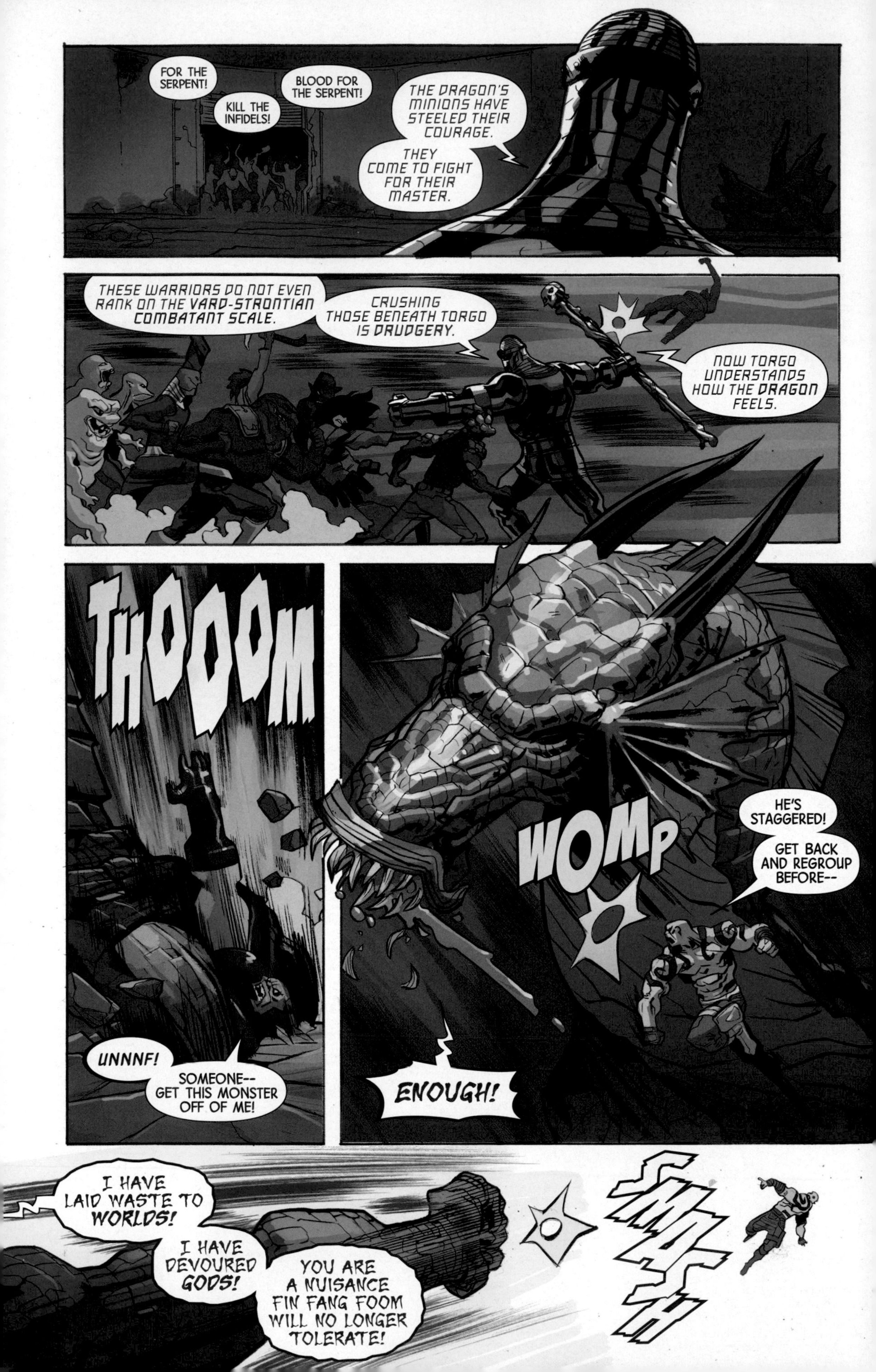
FOR THE SERPENT!
KILL THE INFIDELS!
BLOOD FOR THE SERPENT!
THE DRAGON'S MINIONS HAVE STEELED THEIR COURAGE.
THEY COME TO FIGHT FOR THEIR MASTER.
THESE WARRIORS DO NOT EVEN RANK ON THE VARD-STRONTIAN COMBATANT SCALE.
CRUSHING THOSE BENEATH TORGO IS DRUDGERY.
NOW TORGO UNDERSTANDS HOW THE DRAGON FEELS.
THOOOM
UNNNF!
SOMEONE-- GET THIS MONSTER OFF OF ME!
WOMP
HE'S STAGGERED!
GET BACK AND REGROUP BEFORE--
ENOUGH!
I HAVE LAID WASTE TO WORLDS!
I HAVE DEVOURED GODS!
YOU ARE A NUISANCE FIN FANG FOOM WILL NO LONGER TOLERATE!
SMASH

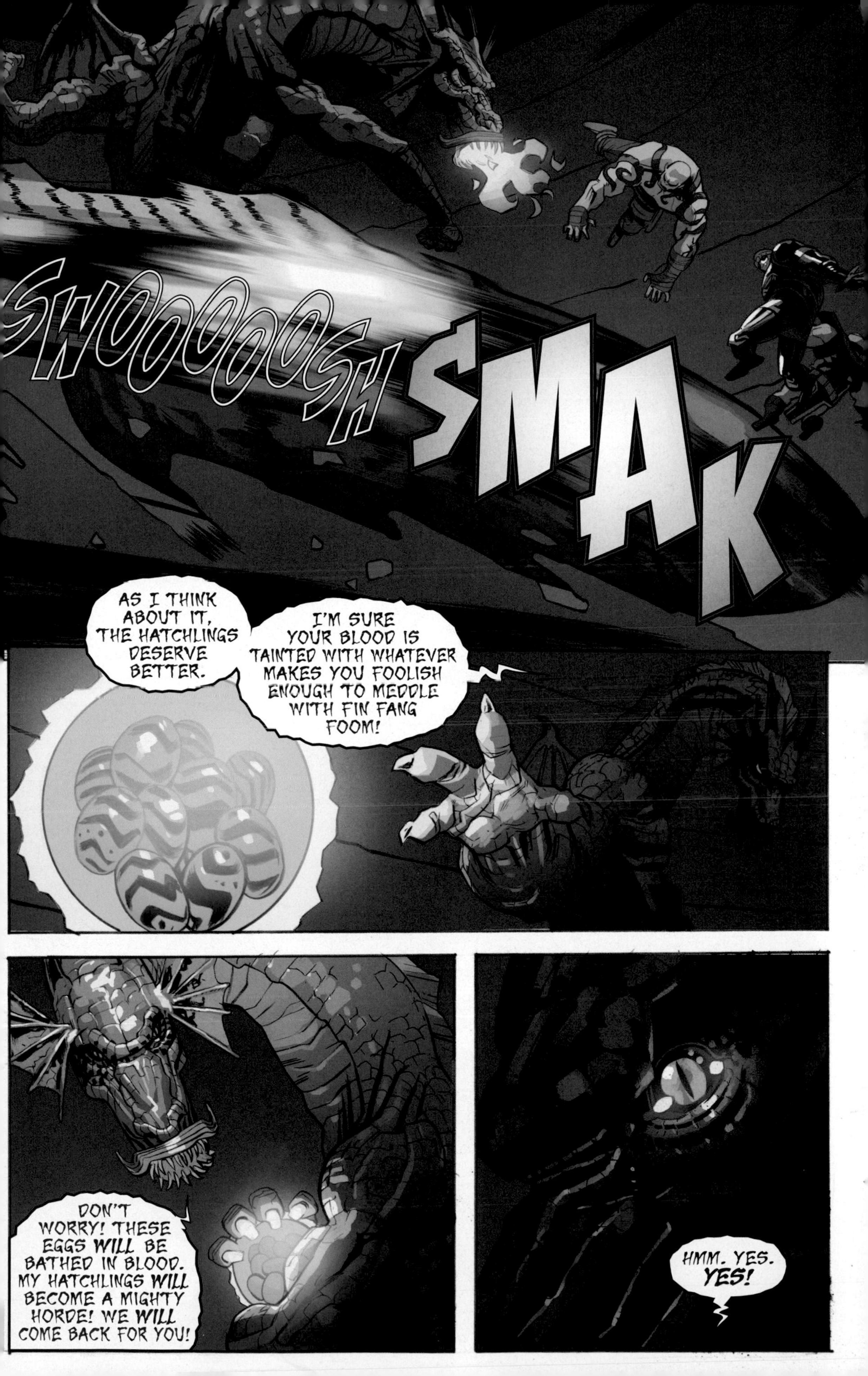
SWOOOOOOSH
SMAK
AS I THINK ABOUT IT, THE HATCHLINGS DESERVE BETTER.
I'M SURE YOUR BLOOD IS TAINTED WITH WHATEVER MAKES YOU FOOLISH ENOUGH TO MEDDLE WITH FIN FANG FOOM!
DON'T WORRY! THESE EGGS WILL BE BATHED IN BLOOD. MY HATCHLINGS WILL BECOME A MIGHTY HORDE! WE WILL COME BACK FOR YOU!
HMM. YES. YES!

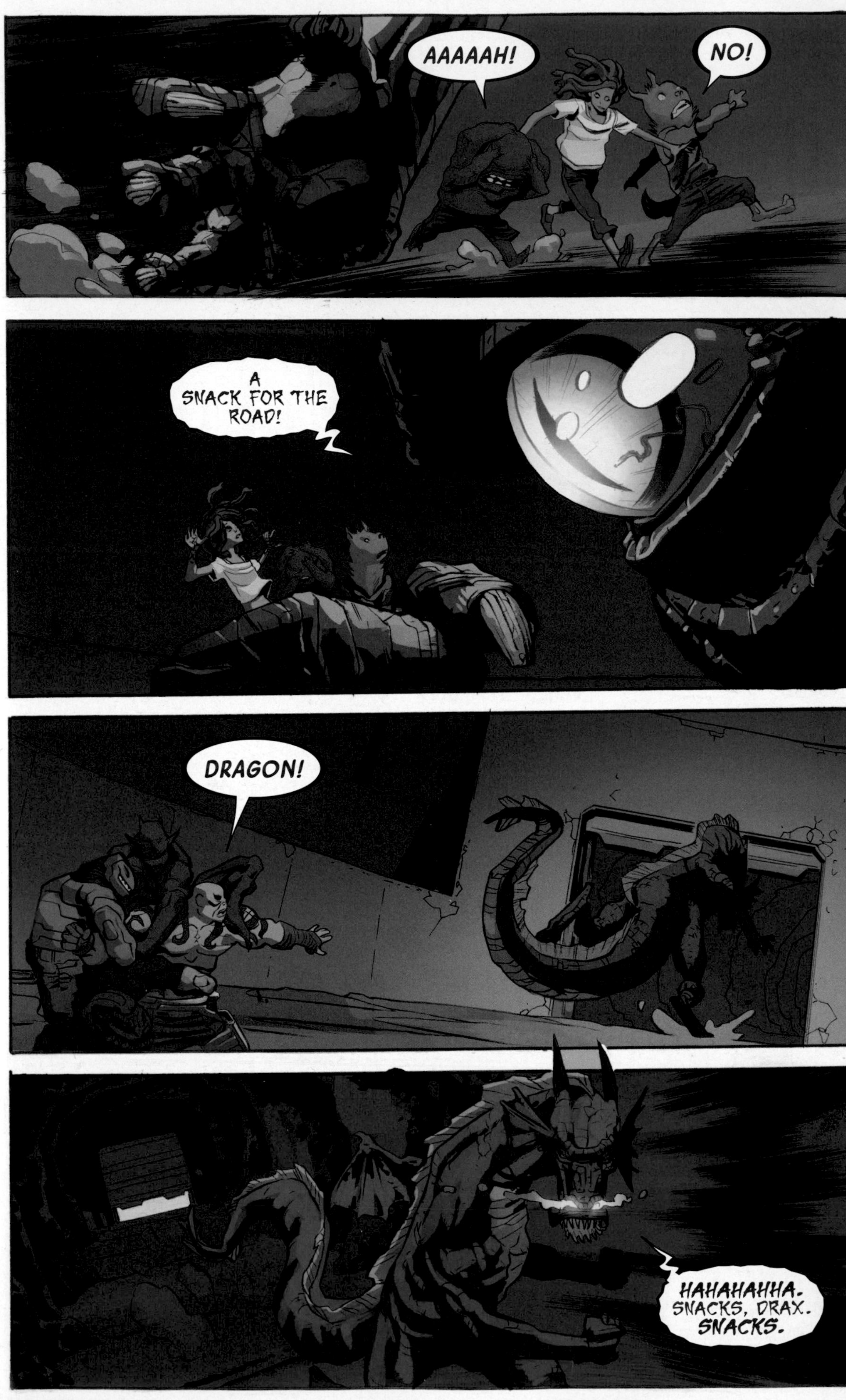
AAAAAH!
NO!
A SNACK FOR THE ROAD!
DRAGON!
HAHAHAHHA. SNACKS, DRAX. SNACKS.

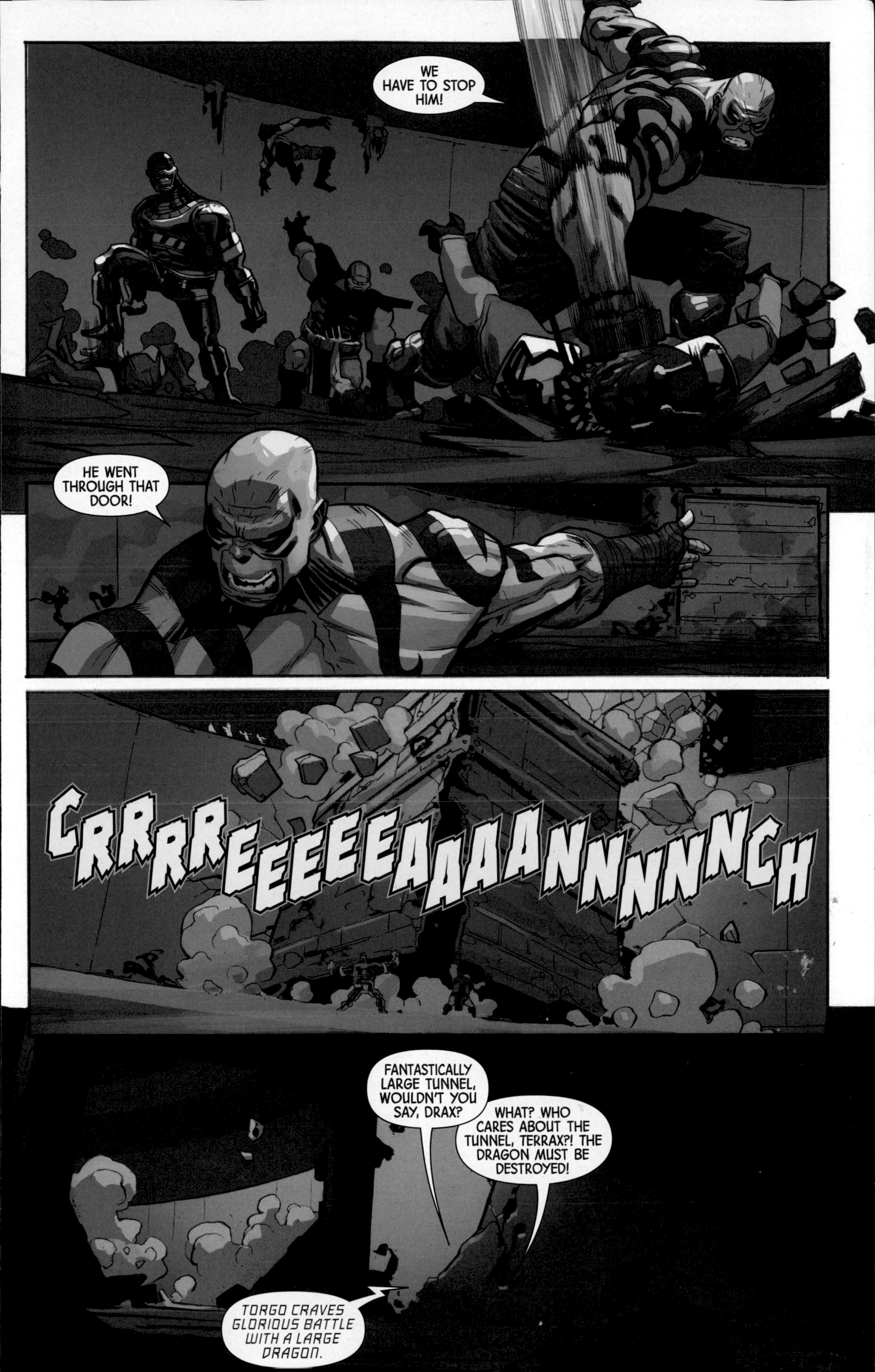
WE HAVE TO STOP HIM!
HE WENT THROUGH THAT DOOR!
CRRRREEEEEAAAANNNNNCH
FANTASTICALLY LARGE TUNNEL, WOULDN'T YOU SAY, DRAX?
WHAT? WHO CARES ABOUT THE TUNNEL, TERRAX?! THE DRAGON MUST BE DESTROYED!
TORGO CRAVES GLORIOUS BATTLE WITH A LARGE DRAGON.

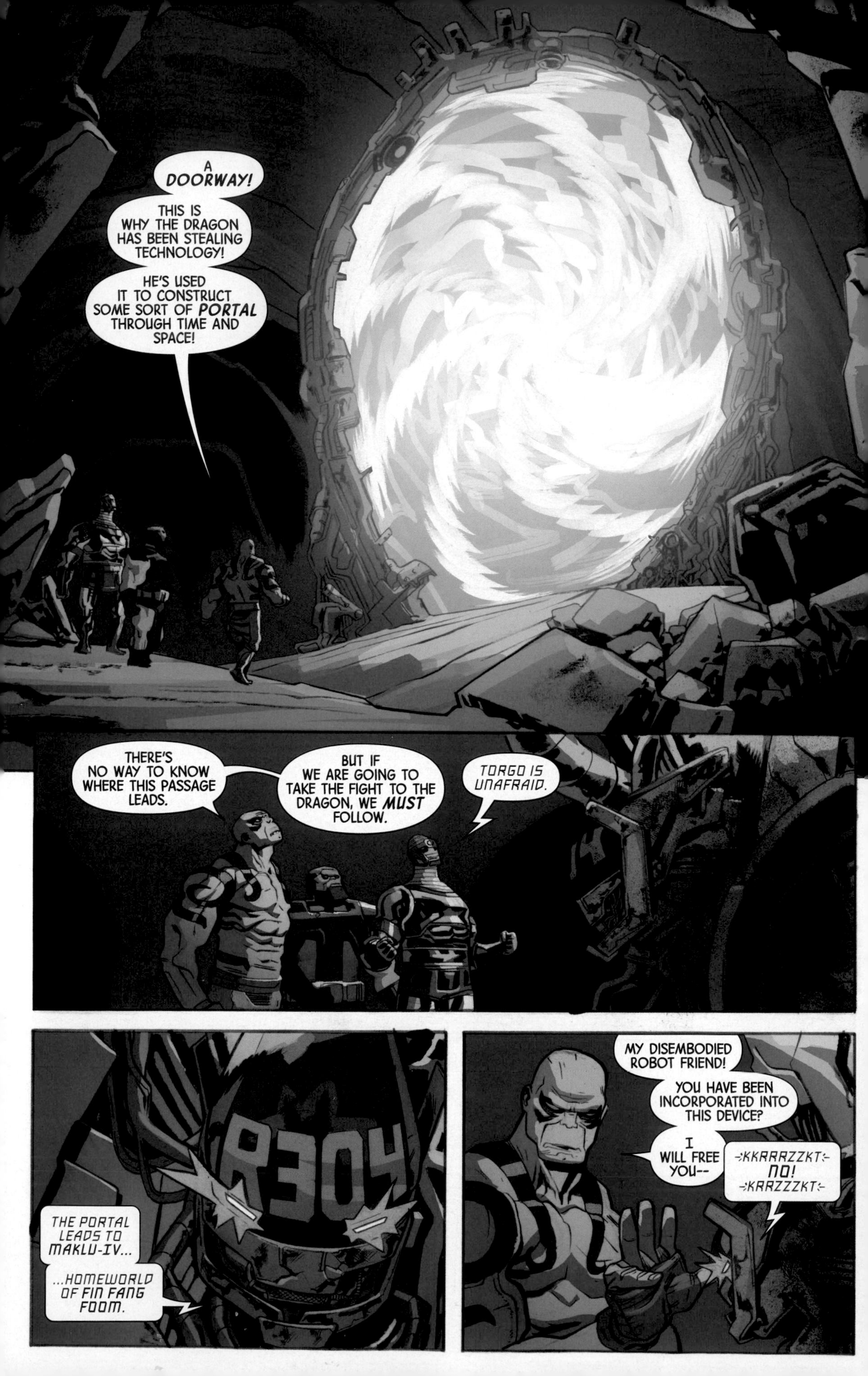
A DOORWAY!
THIS IS WHY THE DRAGON HAS BEEN STEALING TECHNOLOGY!
HE'S USED IT TO CONSTRUCT SOME SORT OF PORTAL THROUGH TIME AND SPACE!
THERE'S NO WAY TO KNOW WHERE THIS PASSAGE LEADS.
BUT IF WE ARE GOING TO TAKE THE FIGHT TO THE DRAGON, WE MUST FOLLOW.
TORGO IS UNAFRAID.
THE PORTAL LEADS TO MAKLU-IV...
...HOMEWORLD OF FIN FANG FOOM.
MY DISEMBODIED ROBOT FRIEND!
YOU HAVE BEEN INCORPORATED INTO THIS DEVICE?
I WILL FREE YOU--
-KKRRRZZKT- NO! -KRRZZZKT-

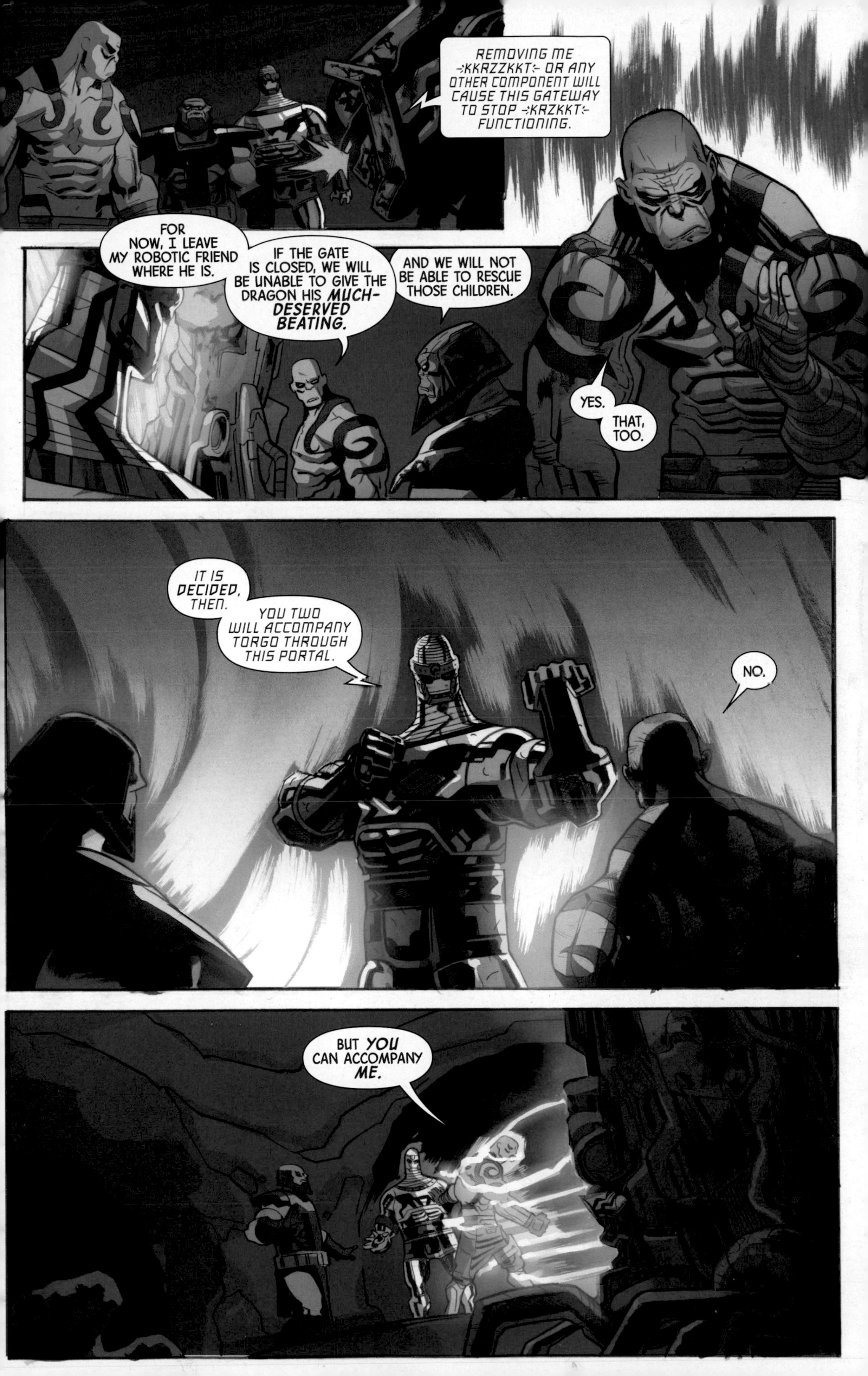
REMOVING ME →KKRZZKKT← OR ANY OTHER COMPONENT WILL CAUSE THIS GATEWAY TO STOP →KRZKKT← FUNCTIONING.
FOR NOW, I LEAVE MY ROBOTIC FRIEND WHERE HE IS.
IF THE GATE IS CLOSED, WE WILL BE UNABLE TO GIVE THE DRAGON HIS MUCH-DESERVED BEATING.
AND WE WILL NOT BE ABLE TO RESCUE THOSE CHILDREN.
YES.
THAT, TOO.
IT IS DECIDED, THEN.
YOU TWO WILL ACCOMPANY TORGO THROUGH THIS PORTAL.
NO.
BUT YOU CAN ACCOMPANY ME.

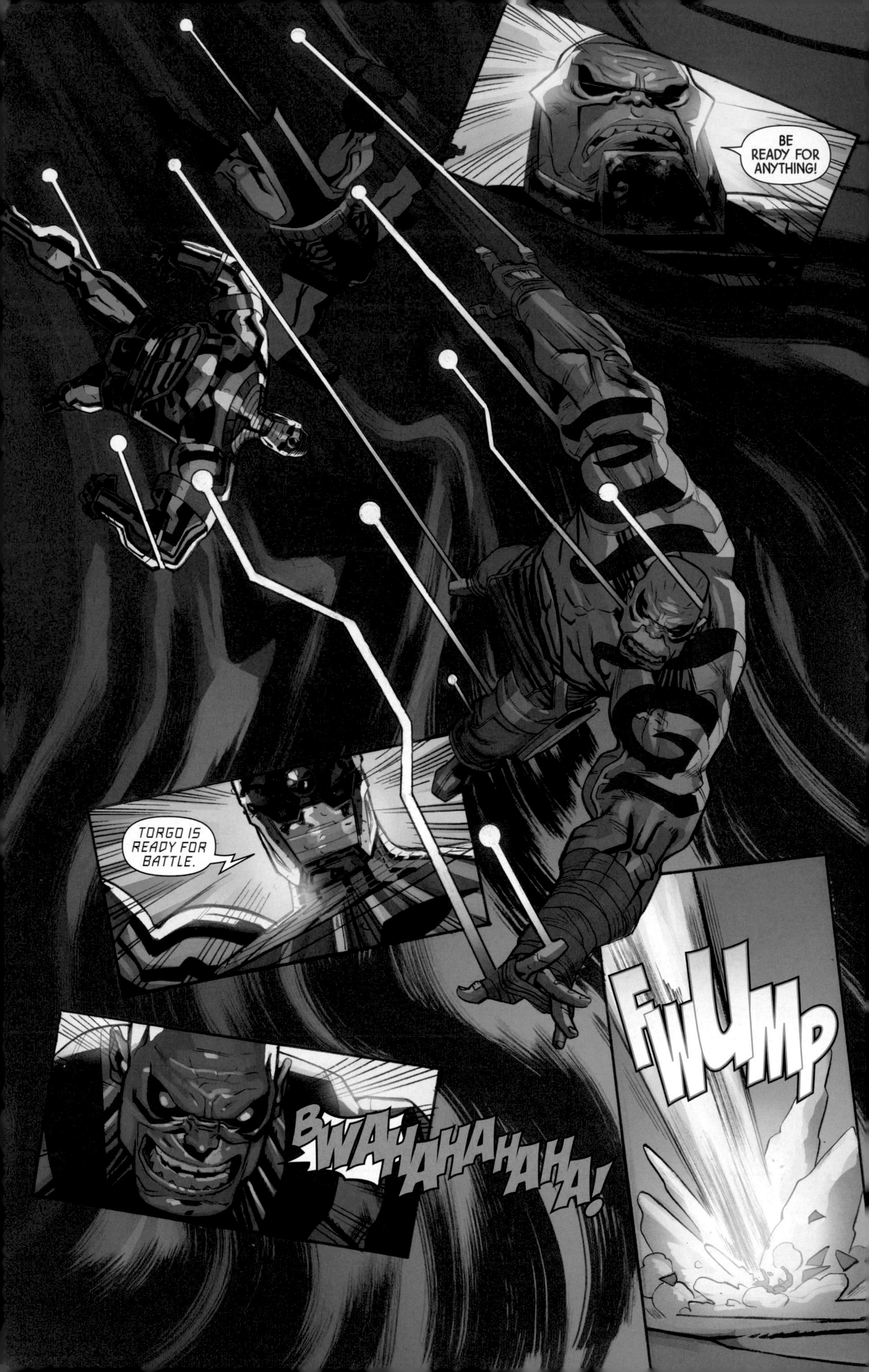
BE READY FOR ANYTHING!
TORGO IS READY FOR BATTLE.
FWUMP
BWAHAHAHAHAHA!

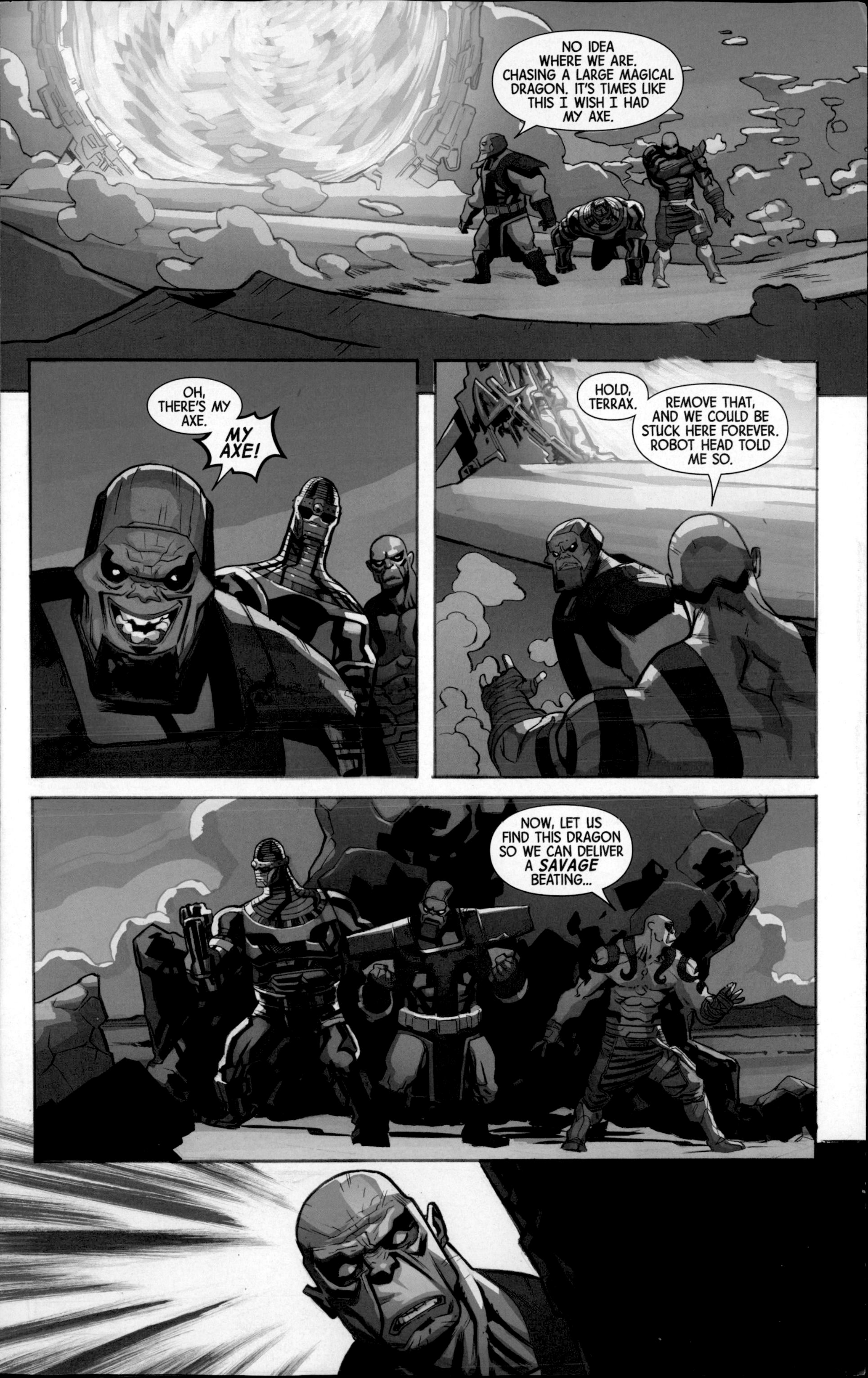
NO IDEA WHERE WE ARE. CHASING A LARGE MAGICAL DRAGON. IT'S TIMES LIKE THIS I WISH I HAD MY AXE.
OH, THERE'S MY AXE.
MY AXE!
HOLD, TERRAX.
REMOVE THAT, AND WE COULD BE STUCK HERE FOREVER. ROBOT HEAD TOLD ME SO.
NOW, LET US FIND THIS DRAGON SO WE CAN DELIVER A SAVAGE BEATING...

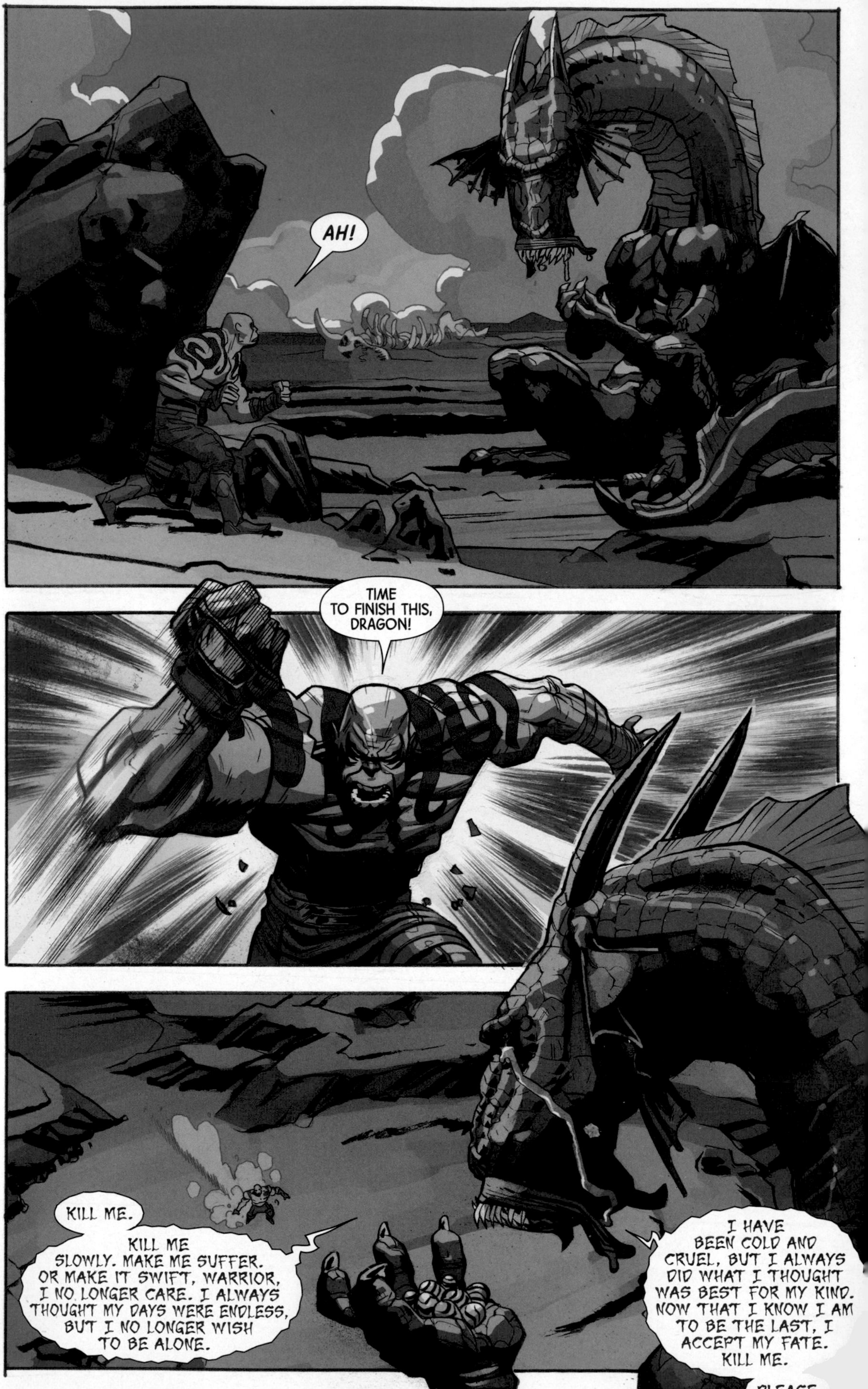
AH!
TIME TO FINISH THIS, DRAGON!
KILL ME.
KILL ME SLOWLY. MAKE ME SUFFER. OR MAKE IT SWIFT, WARRIOR, I NO LONGER CARE. I ALWAYS THOUGHT MY DAYS WERE ENDLESS, BUT I NO LONGER WISH TO BE ALONE.
I HAVE BEEN COLD AND CRUEL, BUT I ALWAYS DID WHAT I THOUGHT WAS BEST FOR MY KIND. NOW THAT I KNOW I AM TO BE THE LAST, I ACCEPT MY FATE. KILL ME.
PLEASE.

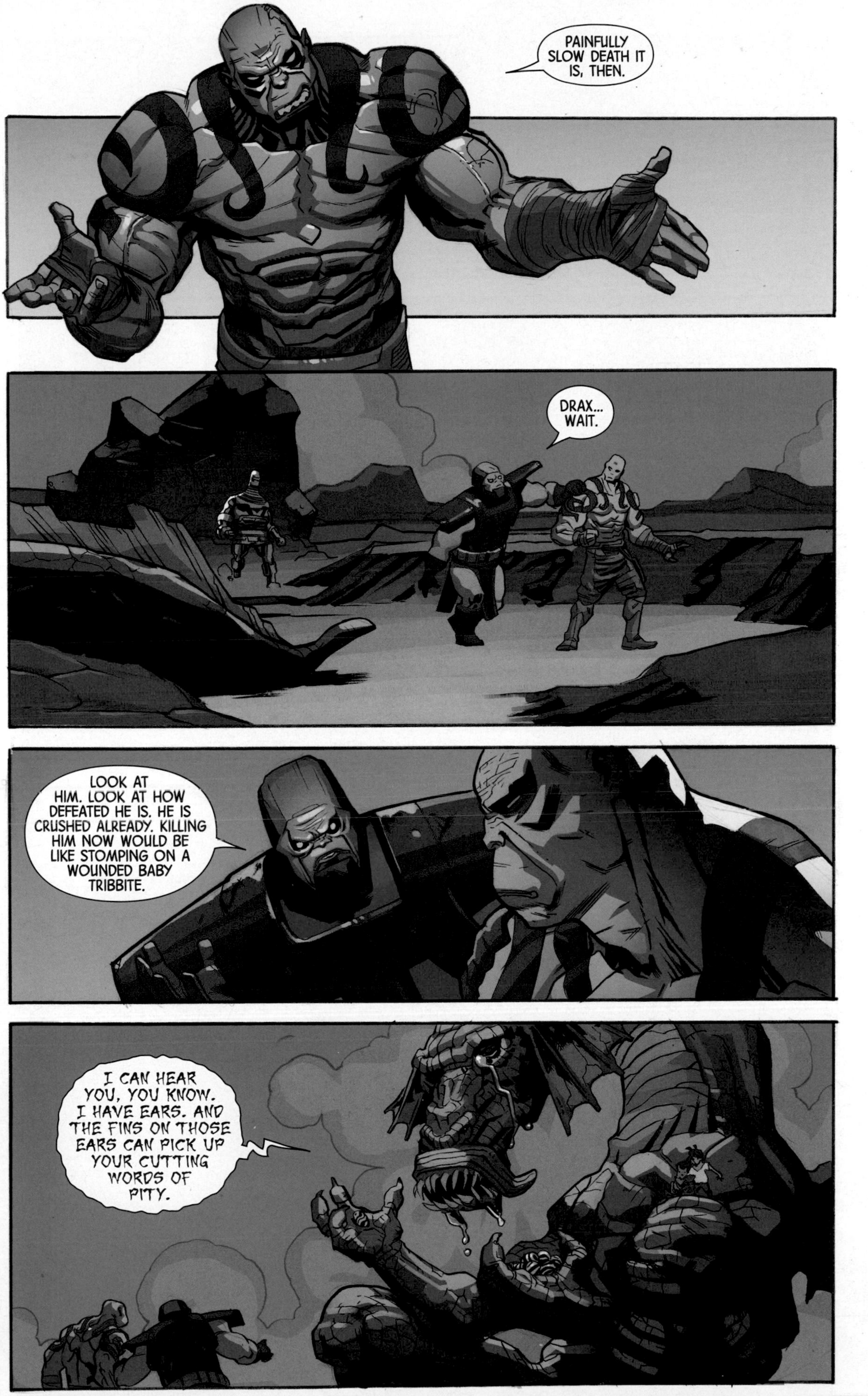
PAINFULLY SLOW DEATH IT IS, THEN.
DRAX... WAIT.
LOOK AT HIM. LOOK AT HOW DEFEATED HE IS. HE IS CRUSHED ALREADY. KILLING HIM NOW WOULD BE LIKE STOMPING ON A WOUNDED BABY TRIBBITE.
I CAN HEAR YOU, YOU KNOW. I HAVE EARS. AND THE FINS ON THOSE EARS CAN PICK UP YOUR CUTTING WORDS OF PITY.

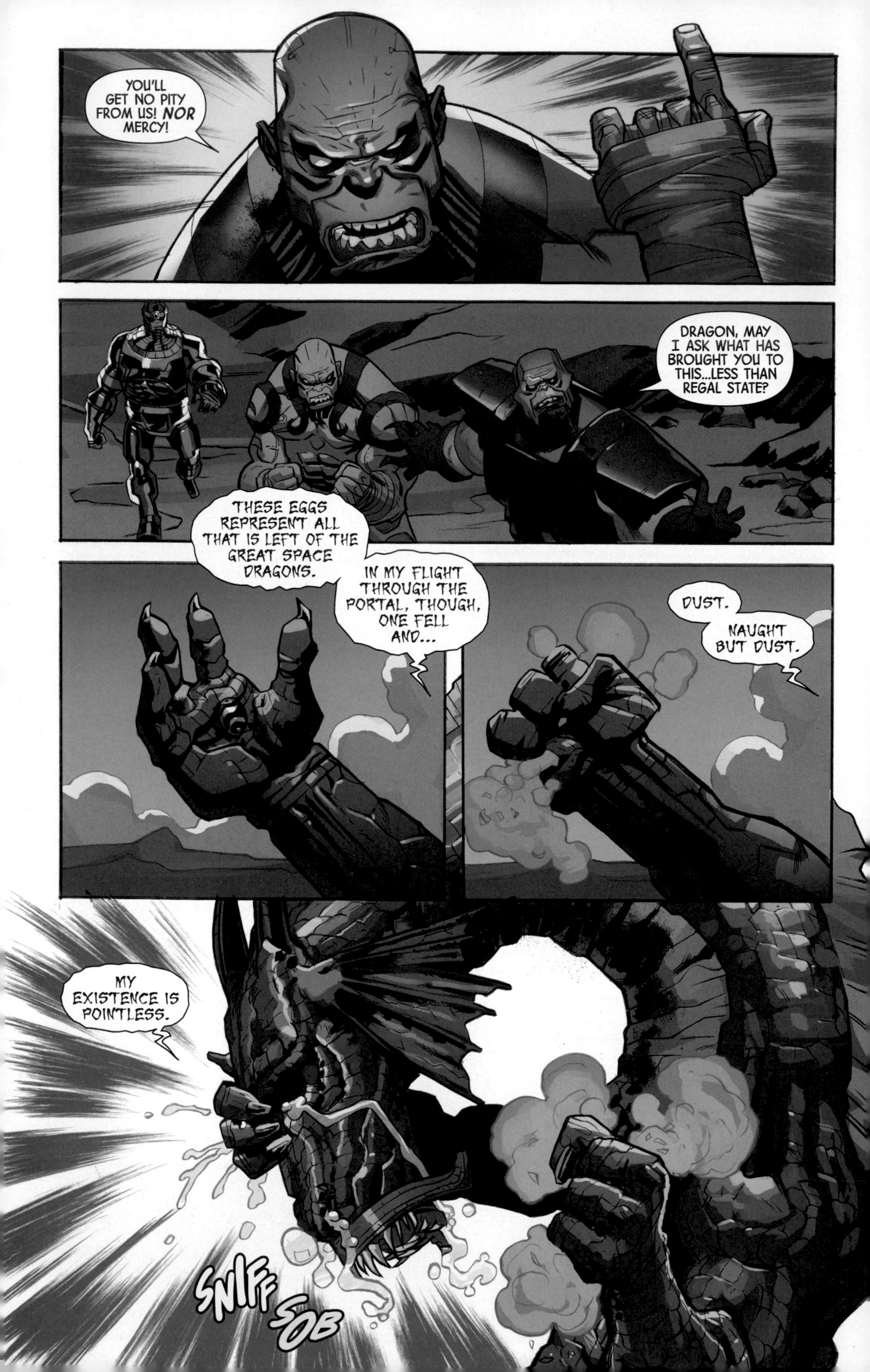
YOU'LL GET NO PITY FROM US! NOR MERCY!
DRAGON, MAY I ASK WHAT HAS BROUGHT YOU TO THIS...LESS THAN REGAL STATE?
THESE EGGS REPRESENT ALL THAT IS LEFT OF THE GREAT SPACE DRAGONS.
IN MY FLIGHT THROUGH THE PORTAL, THOUGH, ONE FELL AND...
DUST.
NAUGHT BUT DUST.
MY EXISTENCE IS POINTLESS.
SNIFF
SOB

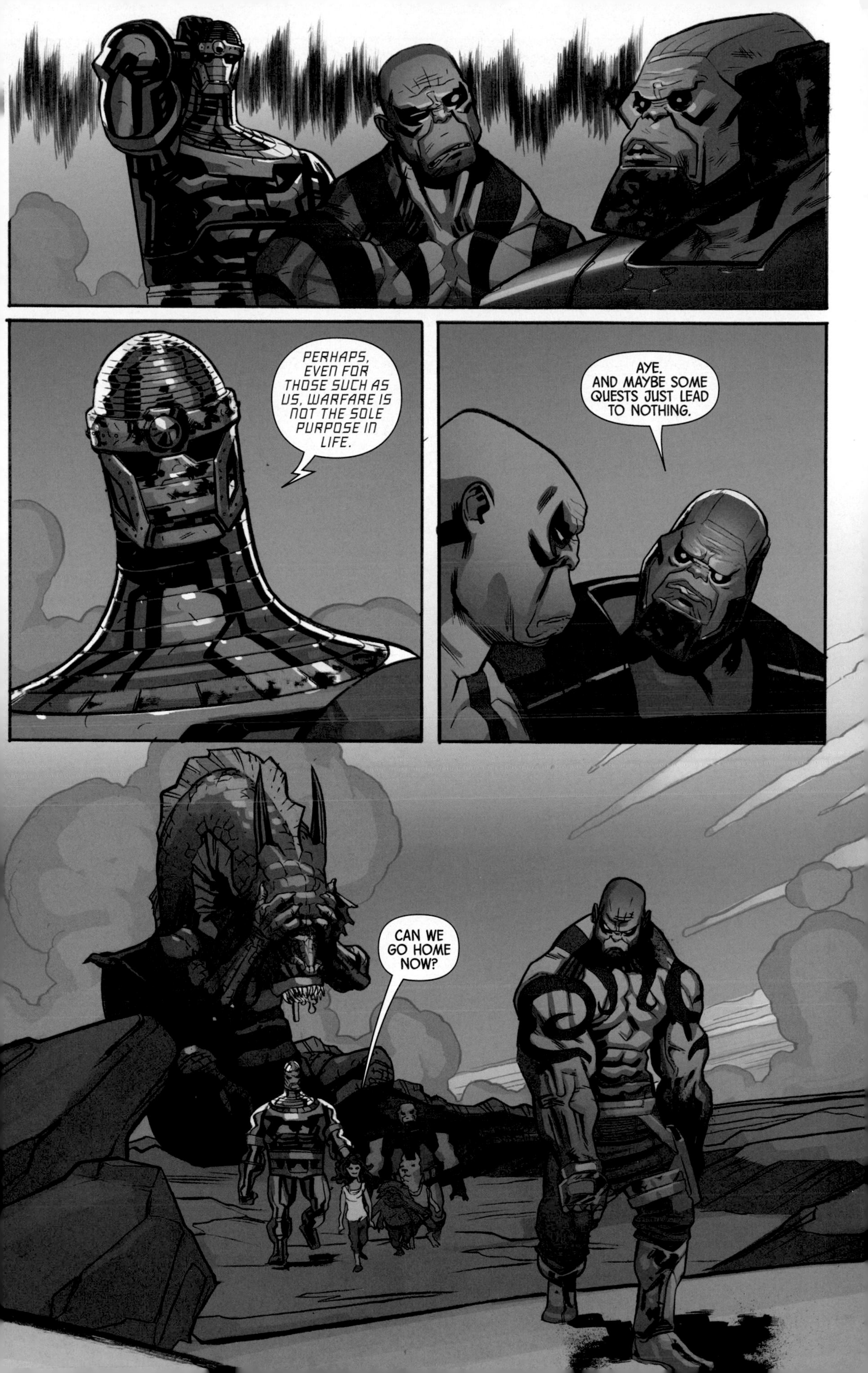
PERHAPS, EVEN FOR THOSE SUCH AS US, WARFARE IS NOT THE SOLE PURPOSE IN LIFE.
AYE. AND MAYBE SOME QUESTS JUST LEAD TO NOTHING.
CAN WE GO HOME NOW?

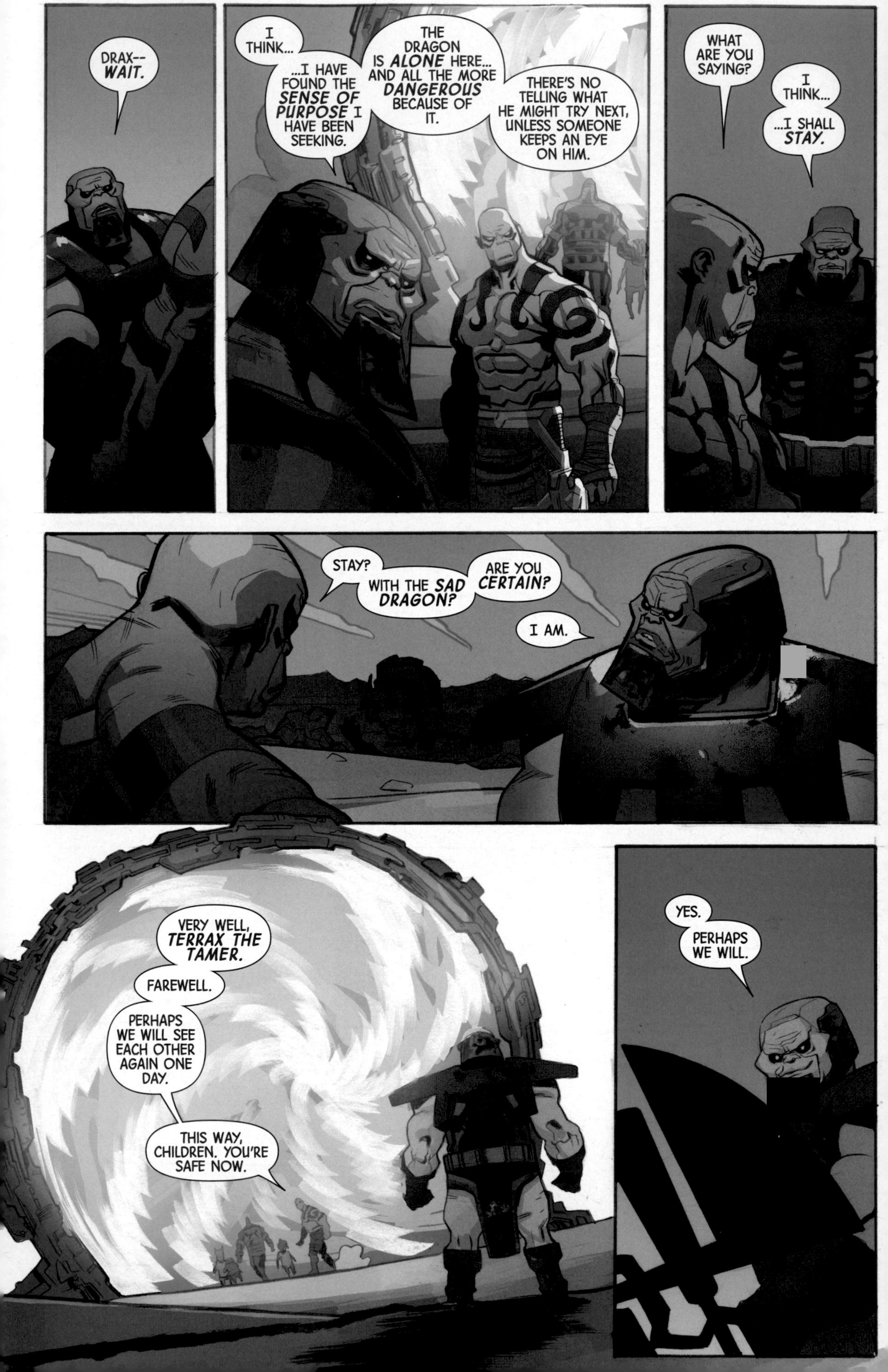
DRAX-- WAIT.
I THINK...
...I HAVE FOUND THE SENSE OF PURPOSE I HAVE BEEN SEEKING.
THE DRAGON IS ALONE HERE... AND ALL THE MORE DANGEROUS BECAUSE OF IT.
THERE'S NO TELLING WHAT HE MIGHT TRY NEXT, UNLESS SOMEONE KEEPS AN EYE ON HIM.
WHAT ARE YOU SAYING?
I THINK...
...I SHALL STAY.
STAY?
WITH THE SAD DRAGON?
ARE YOU CERTAIN?
I AM.
VERY WELL, TERRAX THE TAMER.
FAREWELL.
PERHAPS WE WILL SEE EACH OTHER AGAIN ONE DAY.
THIS WAY, CHILDREN. YOU'RE SAFE NOW.
YES.
PERHAPS WE WILL.

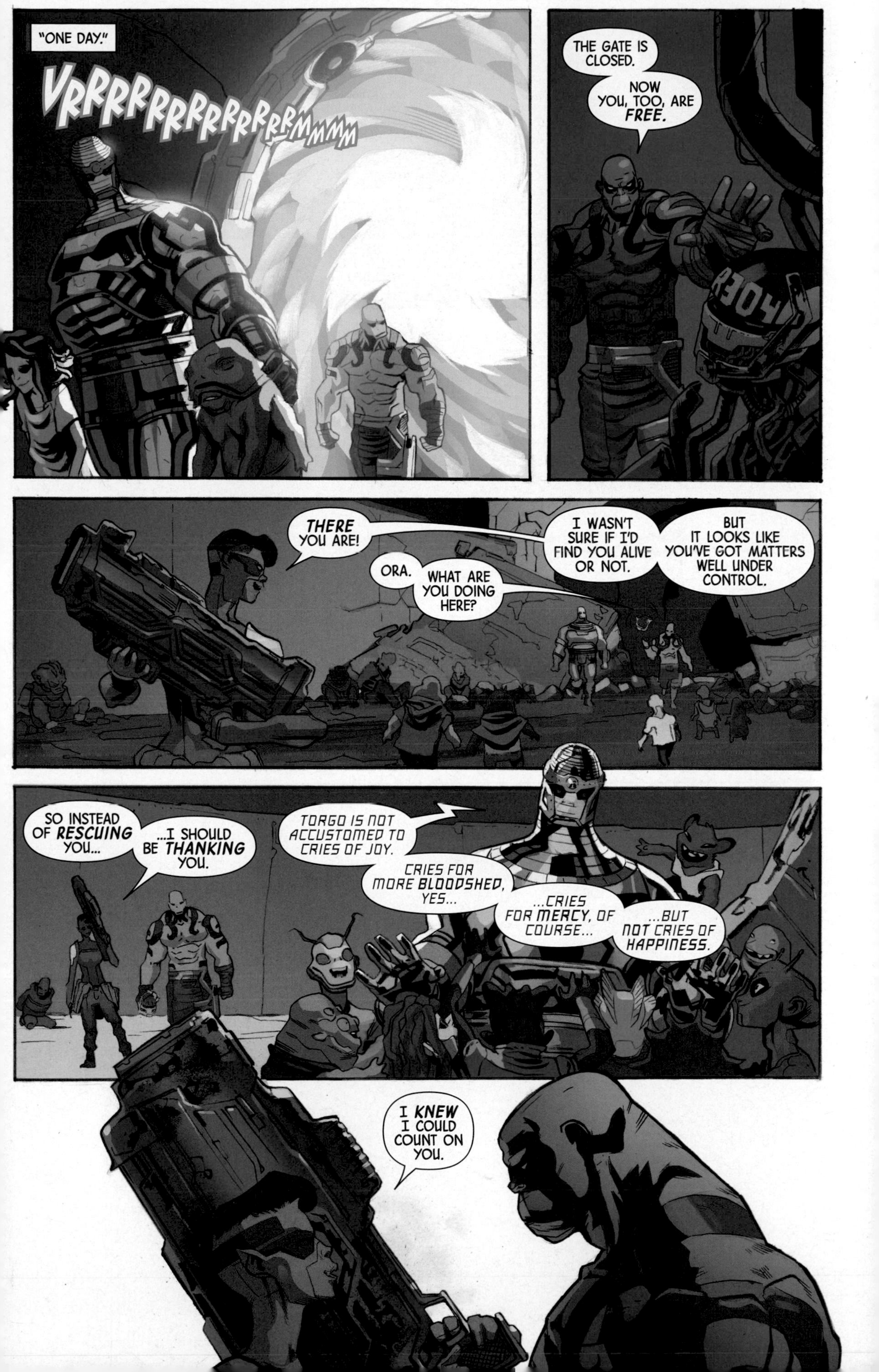
"ONE DAY."
VRRRRRRRRRRRRRMMMM
THE GATE IS CLOSED.
NOW YOU, TOO, ARE FREE.
THERE YOU ARE!
I WASN'T SURE IF I'D FIND YOU ALIVE OR NOT.
BUT IT LOOKS LIKE YOU'VE GOT MATTERS WELL UNDER CONTROL.
ORA.
WHAT ARE YOU DOING HERE?
SO INSTEAD OF RESCUING YOU...
...I SHOULD BE THANKING YOU.
TORGO IS NOT ACCUSTOMED TO CRIES OF JOY.
CRIES FOR MORE BLOODSHED, YES...
...CRIES FOR MERCY, OF COURSE...
...BUT NOT CRIES OF HAPPINESS.
I KNEW I COULD COUNT ON YOU.

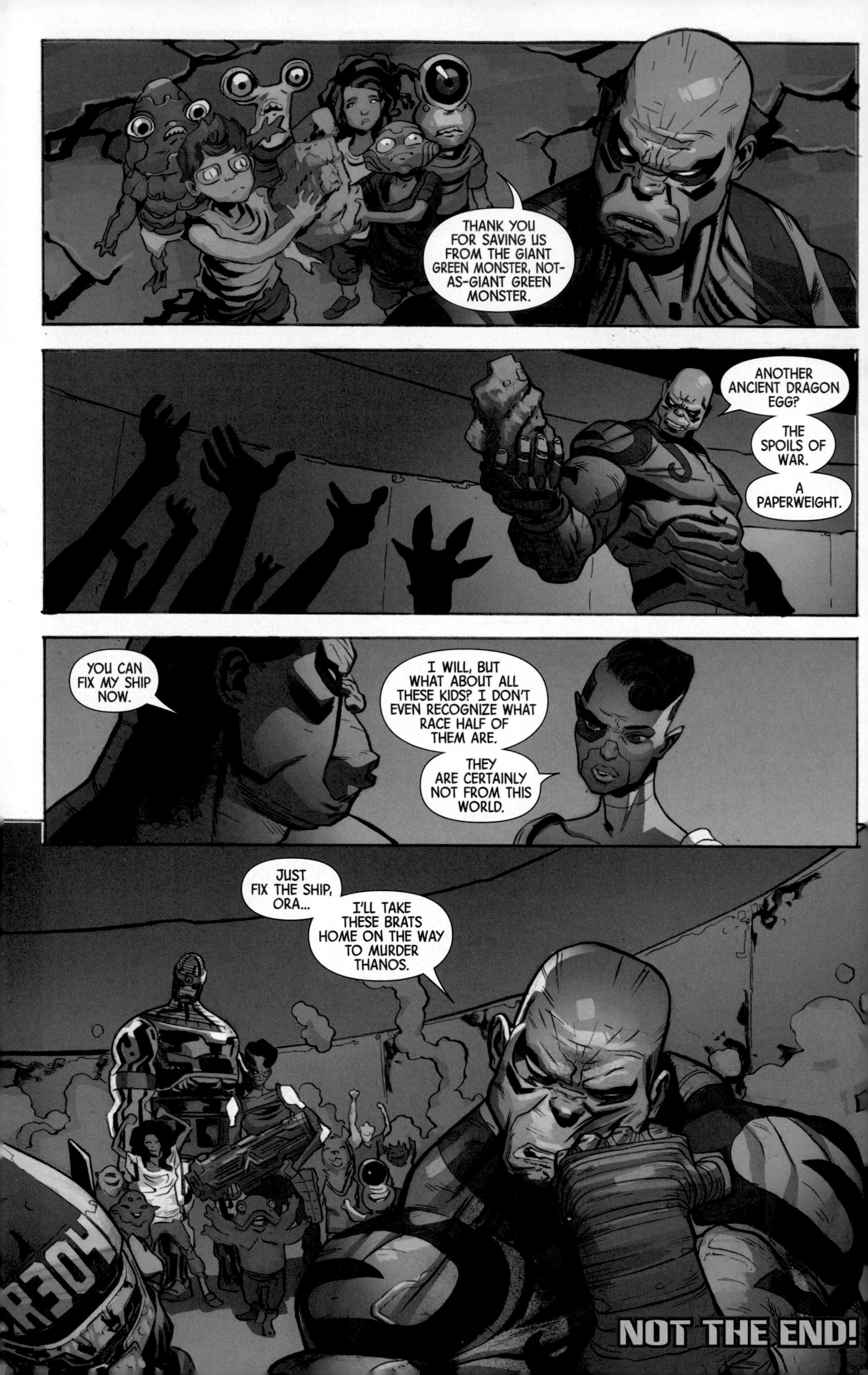
THANK YOU FOR SAVING US FROM THE GIANT GREEN MONSTER, NOT-AS-GIANT GREEN MONSTER.
ANOTHER ANCIENT DRAGON EGG?
THE SPOILS OF WAR.
A PAPERWEIGHT.
YOU CAN FIX MY SHIP NOW.
I WILL, BUT WHAT ABOUT ALL THESE KIDS? I DON'T EVEN RECOGNIZE WHAT RACE HALF OF THEM ARE.
THEY ARE CERTAINLY NOT FROM THIS WORLD.
JUST FIX THE SHIP, ORA...
I'LL TAKE THESE BRATS HOME ON THE WAY TO MURDER THANOS.
NOT THE END!

No. 1 HIP-HOP VARIANT BY
MIKE CHOI

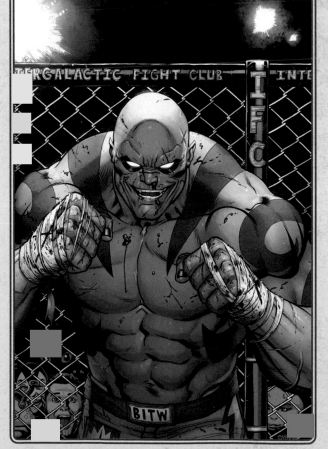

No. 1 VARIANT BY
ED MCGUINNESS &
JASON KEITH

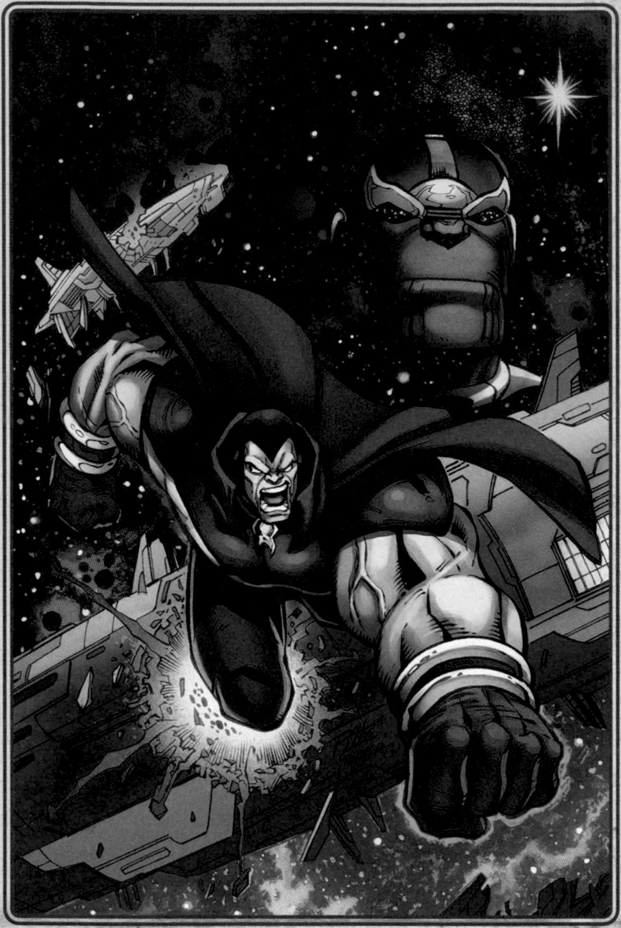

No. 2 MARVEL '92 VARIANT BY

RON LIM, TOM PALMER & RACHELLE ROSENBERG

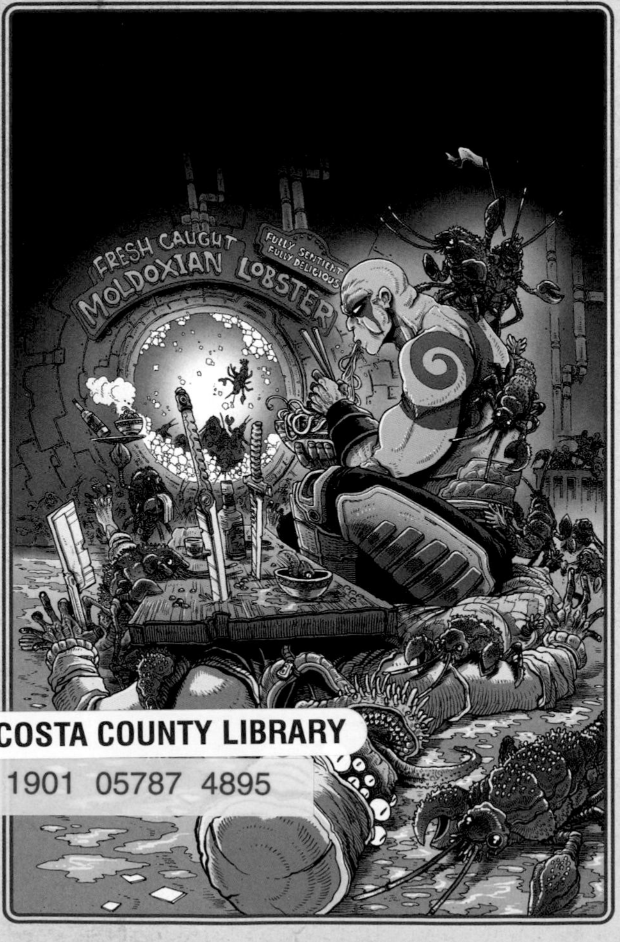
FRESH CAUGHT
MOLDOXIAN LOBSTER
FULLY SENTIENT
FULLY DELICIOUS

No. 2 VARIAN

JAMES STOKOE